Groups in Practice

This practical, user-friendly manual will provide school counselors with the information they need to set up and run twelve different counseling groups. Though the author has test-driven the groups with middle school students, the content is easily adaptable for upper elementary and high school students. Each chapter is devoted to a specific group and includes

- a rationale for the group
- step-by-step breakdowns of each session
- reproducible worksheets and activities
- group-specific evaluation form

Special sections within each chapter provide tips to make implementation easier and address potential problems. Also included are the American School Counselor Association standards that are addressed during the course of the group. Traditional group topics such as Divorce, Grief, and Study Skills join unique groups tailored for students dealing with Asperger Syndrome, Attention Deficit Disorder, Juvenile Diabetes, and Relational Aggression. The author has used her extensive experience to create this invaluable guide which school counselors at all levels of experience will find an essential tool in their group work.

Debra Madaris Efird, MEd, NBCT, has been a school counselor and active member of the American Counseling Association for over 20 years. She currently works for Cabarrus County Schools, CC Griffin Middle School, in Concord, North Carolina.

Groups in Practice

A School Counselor's Collection

Debra Madaris Efird

Routledge
Taylor & Francis Group
LONDON AND NEW YORK

First published 2012
by Routledge

2 Park Square, Milton Park, Abingdon, Oxon OX14 4RN
605 Third Avenue, New York, NY 10017

Routledge is an imprint of the Taylor & Francis Group, an informa business

First issued in hardback 2016

Library of Congress Cataloging in Publication Data
Efird, Debra Madaris.
Groups in practice : a school counselor's collection / Debra Madaris Efird.
p. cm.
Includes bibliographical references and index.
ISBN 978-0-415-50372-3 (pbk. : alk. paper) 1. Group counseling. I. Title.
BF636.7.G76E35 2012
371.4—dc23
2011050770

ISBN: 978-0-415-50372-3 (pbk)
ISBN: 978-1-138-15561-9 (hbk)

Typeset in Caslon and Frutiger
by EvS Communication Networx, Inc.

Contents

Preface

ADD, Asperger Syndrome, Divorce, Grief, Juvenile Diabetes, Latinas, Obesity, Relational Aggression, Self-Esteem, Stress, Study Skills, Underachieving Boys … do these topics fill your days? If so, and you work with children, then you've come to the right place.

Throughout over twenty years of counseling, I have conducted enough groups to earn the title of "Group Guru" among the middle school counselors in my school system. I have always found it to be a most efficient way to reach students, especially when my annual caseload has hit the 500-student mark. After having five articles about my groups published in national magazines (four by the American Counseling Association), I realized I could combine my information and produce a concise book containing everything a counselor needs to know about conducting groups. I have always willingly responded to requests for information from counselors both locally and nationally, and I believe I have something valuable to offer. So, browse through this information and select a couple of groups to pump up your counseling department. Then next year, add more!

Acknowledgments

I would like to thank the students and staff of Cabarrus County Schools and Charlotte-Mecklenburg Schools for the privilege of serving as school counselor for over two decades. I especially appreciate the middle school counselors of Cabarrus County who have been supportive of my group counseling efforts, in particular Catherine Eveland for igniting the spark for my underachieving boys group, Kristen Lavoie for developing a needs assessment which I adapted, and Janet Johnson for emphasizing the importance of group counseling back when I was a neophyte. I would like to acknowledge my daughter, Lydia Efird, M.D., for her critiquing skills. Most of all, I would like to thank my husband, Martin Edward Efird, for his supportive technical expertise during countless rescues from computer difficulties and for his overall patience during the development of this book.

Chapter 1

Off to a Fine Start

Group counseling is a fail-proof way to fire up the fun in your daily work as a counselor. You will find it fulfilling, exasperating, and sometimes astonishing. Let me walk you through it. And if you find anyone out there more dedicated than I am to keeping things simple, let me know.

Using this book will help you develop or enhance your group counseling efforts. To ensure that your group counseling program is grounded in the American School Counselor Association (ASCA) National Standards for Student Competencies, pertinent ones are indicated in each chapter. Including these competencies confirms that your groups rest on a solid foundation and are being provided to meet established needs of students.

A thorough reading of this first chapter is crucial to help you get off the ground and running. Though it is tempting to go straight to the Contents page to see which group topics reach out and grab you, it is wise to spend a few minutes going over background essentials. In this chapter you will learn vital points of soliciting group members, determining the composition of your groups, informing students of group meetings, and setting up group rules. You will discover how to make everything more fun and also manage the occasional problems that come up in groups. You will become familiar with the format of each chapter. At the end of this chapter, you will find forms that you may want to revise or copy for your own use.

There are two basic ways to get started. You can spend time assessing what your population needs or you can just make some general assumptions and go for it: every school can use a divorce group, a grief group, or a stress group. If you like, you could start there and later determine if there are other specific groups you need in your school. For those of you more inclined to use a needs assessment, I have included a sample one that I have found useful.

Though there are some exceptions, I solicit students for most groups through guidance lessons that reach all of the students in my charge. I start at the very beginning of the school year during my introductory guidance lesson. In a five-to-ten minute discussion tacked onto the end of my guidance lesson, I either explain the group sign-up form or the needs assessment form, depending on which route I have chosen for solicitation. I distribute the forms and then collect one from every student. In this way I have been inclusive, offering my services to all.

Some groups necessitate a different solicitation format. Members of the Asperger and Juvenile Diabetes groups are chosen by obtaining from appropriate personnel a list of students with those diagnoses and then sending parent permission letters in advance to determine interest. For my Latina Pride group, I select Latinas who are connected to the English as a Second Language (ESL) class, either by active class membership or by consultation. You could solicit members for this group during the regular guidance lesson method mentioned above, but at many schools you would end up with overwhelming numbers. By limiting membership to those still connected with the ESL program, I believe that I am focusing on students with the greatest need for help with cultural adjustment problems. For membership in the Relational Aggression group, I ask teachers for suggestions on whom to include as well as use my own judgment based on which students are frequently in my office with "girl drama." For the Fitness group, I solicit members by posting signs around the school directing students to the guidance office to pick up more information and parent permission letters. Due to my fear of students being stigmatized for being overweight, I do not find it appropriate to gather these members through my regular guidance lesson format.

After I have completed an almost endless round of guidance lessons to reach the huge numbers in my caseload, I tally the forms to see how many sections of each group I will need. If I use the needs assessment solicitation method, I usually choose to tally only the students who indicate a high number (3 = Very Often) in each topic. If I am really lucky, they will have checked "group counseling" at the bottom of the form. But I include all students who circle a 3 in my initial meetings, regardless of whether or not they noted "group counseling" on their form. Then I choose which groups to start based on the topics that have the most 3's.

If it looks like I am going to have more than four or five groups, I will need to run a few for six weeks and then start the other ones after the first groups are finished. Using the needs assessment form provides you with a lot of information about student needs, which may cause you to feel obligated to run groups back to back all year long. If you are uncomfortable with a schedule that stringent, it is fine to start small. I've run as many as six different groups simultaneously, but I won't try that again. After all, group counseling isn't the only thing a school counselor does! If I have twenty-five students signed up for a particular group, I divide it into three sections. I pay attention to the composition of the groups, too. I try not to end up with only one boy sitting in a group with seven girls. I also have an eye out for rowdies, so I try not to place too many of those types in the same group.

The next step is to write out an individual note for each student, filling in the blank with the student's name and the date and time of the group. Then I place these in homeroom teacher mailboxes the afternoon of the day preceding the meeting. (If you give teachers things too early, they lose them just like the students.) And, of course, I must admit that sometimes I find myself running around crazily to homerooms on the day of the group, dispensing notes to students like I'm handing off the baton in a relay race. Whatever it takes to be ready!

At the first session, I always explain which group is convening. Yes, take nothing for granted. There is always one student who says, "I meant to sign up for the divorce group instead," or, "I thought I signed the line about NOT wanting to be in group." I go over the outline briefly. I explain the schedule in detail to ensure that the students understand how to follow it over the course of six (or however many) weeks. I point out that disruptions may occur (an unscheduled assembly or snowstorm) and that they will be notified via announcements if group must be cancelled or changed. I explain that there will be three ways to help them remember to come to group: (1) looking at the schedule which is now in their hands but later should be taped in their notebooks or locker, (2) listening to announcements, and (3) reading the note their teachers should hand them in homeroom on group days. Yes, that last one is a tall order: completing an individual note for every child in group for a minimum of six whole weeks. But they're worth it.

To provide a level of confidentiality, I identify the groups I am currently running by number when they are announced on the public address system. Group 1 may be the FAIR group, Group 4 may be the Living with JD group, and so on. Group members are told to listen carefully for their group number, which they usually do not have a problem remembering. I also offer students the opportunity to come up with a name for the group if they want, but most of the time they just accept the names I have posted in the Contents of this work.

Be sure to talk about group rules at each introductory session. I ask them to generate a few group rules, and they normally do a fair job. Some points I always make certain are covered: being confidential, taking turns talking (not monopolizing), laughing with (not at) others, and following general school rules. It is wise to emphasize that group membership can be revoked if behavior becomes unmanageable.

I also give students the parent permission form at the first session, though you may choose to hunt them down in advance to distribute them. I like to be able to explain what the group is all about and let them see who else is there before they bother with committing. After all, it is an introductory session that barely moves into the topic. (A few exceptions, as mentioned earlier, are the Asperger and Juvenile Diabetes groups, for which I always send the letter to the parent before meeting with the students.)

A regular annoyance is enticing students to return their signed permission forms promptly. I always ask that they bring them within the next couple of days to my mailbox in the guidance office. The sooner I have all parent signatures in my possession, the sooner I can send out a memo to teachers noting the group schedule excusing the students from class. I do not want to list a student's name on the memo if he has not brought me proof that he can be in the group, but there are invariably a few who insist on returning them late. (Or you may choose to not give teachers a list of students in your groups, relying instead on the individual meeting notes you send each week as sufficient for getting them out of class.) If you can stand a little bribery, you may find that the promise of a small piece of candy or gum (if allowed) works wonders with students. If they return their forms to your box the very next day, they will get the treat at the next meeting. You will need to check your box often and keep accurate records! Sometimes I actually call parents for verbal permission and a promise to send in the form. If you are not in such a hurry to inform your teachers and you can patiently wait until the second meeting, it will reduce your stress over this matter. One thing I am a stickler on, however: if a student shows up for the second meeting and no parent form has been returned, I send him back to class. No form, no group. You may feel heartless, but you have to draw the line somewhere.

Without fail, my last session is somewhat of a review. Sometimes a new activity or topic is combined with it, but you can depend on me doing some sort of summary of the previous sessions. I think this is especially important as a way of reminding my young charges that they were not just "getting out of class" for six weeks! Mainly, I hope the review shows them that deliberate steps have been taken to move them from where they *were* in their thinking, feeling, and behaving to where they are *now*. I want them to assess their own progress (or lack of it) and understand that they must take some responsibility for making changes in their lives. I give them an evaluation form at the end of the last meeting, which helps create closure as well as providing me valuable feedback. I also assure them that they are welcome to see me individually as needed throughout the rest of the year.

I personally believe in conducting groups without expensive supplies. I imagine that most school guidance departments are on tight budgets, so I have not bought costly workbooks or games or other items to complement my groups. You can follow my group plan with little or no measurable cost in supplies. Any guest speakers, of course, are volunteers. I must admit that occasionally I've taken my own money and bought a coffee shop gift card or a small bunch of flowers from the grocery store for outside speakers as a token gesture of gratitude.

You may notice as you browse through this book that sometimes it appears I am suggesting the same activity for various groups. Yes, I am! For example, I suggest the "Things You Can/Cannot Change" worksheet for the Latinas group, the Obesity group, and the Self-Esteem group. However, if you look carefully, you will see that some of the statements have been tailored to fit that particular group. Sentence Completion exercises are used numerous times, but you will find that each set of statements has a totally different focus. If I have found something that works for one group, I am quite fond of tweaking it for another one.

Whenever conducting activities, it is wise to keep in mind that most students prefer something a little more fun than pencil/paper activities. So I have taken many worksheets that could be completed, boring-style, and presented the same information in a more user-friendly way. You will note I frequently have students pull a slip of paper from a basket and respond to it. They find this irresistible and chancy, like opening a fortune cookie. Hand the basket to only one student at a time and have them draw just one slip at a time. Otherwise, they'll spend their time worrying or thinking about how to answer theirs and not listening to the others. There will invariably be one in the group who will have difficulty with the slip drawn. That's fine. You can explain that every question does not apply to everyone and allow that student to draw another. But you may need to put a limit on it—this isn't a shopping trip for just the right fit. After speaking, have them return the slips to you to avoid those being redrawn.

If there is a sheet of information with points to cover, I don't read it to them myself. Instead, I ask them to each take turns reading a sentence. I word things in a simple fashion, so they usually do not stumble. If they do, I gently correct and move on, sometimes reminding them that this is not English class. Sometimes I jazz it up by having them read their statement in a fake accent or while in some weird position like crouched under the table or sitting backwards in their chairs. If there is a questionnaire or other such worksheet, I ordinarily have the group do these together, one by one, instead of individually. After all, this is a *group* setting, and no one is taking grades.

In this book the various groups have been arranged alphabetically by topic. When it comes to actual names of groups, I like to be a little more creative. Examples are "Stuck in the Middle" (for divorce), "ADD + (Plus)", and "Good Grief." First you will see a one-page outline of the group. Next you will find the listing of American School Counselor Association (ASCA) standards, competencies, and indicators that are met through activities in the group. Next you will find a rationale for the group. Then there is a section called "What Makes It Work" which reveals favorable points of conducting that specific group. There is also a section called "Challenges" which will alert you to possible problems, allowing you to troubleshoot in advance.

Next you will see an explanation of each session covering essential information and what supplies you will need. At the end of each session are questions that students should be able to answer after experiencing the group meeting, whether or not you choose to ask them. Last of all, you will find copies of all handouts and worksheets or materials needed for the activities of that session. Following the final session of the group, you will find an evaluation form and references. Any forms, worksheets, or materials in this book can be copied for your own use.

Call me a Scrooge, but I do not have a "party" at the end of my sessions. I try hard to maintain a professional atmosphere in the guidance office and I do not want to lose the faith of teachers and administration. (Well, I actually *do* throw a little party for the Fitness group, but it is after school so that hardly counts.)

Some may wonder about behavior management during group sessions. For most types of groups, misbehavior rarely reaches a level of concern. However, in the ADD and Study Skills groups, you may encounter excessive rowdiness and even disrespect as some of these students have trouble with impulsivity or may have long-ingrained patterns of cutting up to hide learning difficulties. Also, with the Relational Aggression group, sometimes there are feuds brewing on the outside that spill over into the group. I believe in confronting such situations head on. Yes, we counselors are known as "softies" but even we must require a certain amount of order. Everyone is capable of learning respect for you and for each other. Demand it!

Sometimes students will come to group but simply refuse to participate in the activities. We should allow non-participation because group expression is not something to force. The student may be having an especially rough day or merely experiencing one of the mysterious moods that seem to affect all children between the ages of ten to fifteen. Non-participation should not be confused with lack of cooperation.

The uncooperative student could be confronted by the group (with your guidance), or you could choose to deal with the situation privately. If you opt for an individual conference, it can only last for a few seconds outside a cracked door because of student supervision requirements. If the refusal to cooperate borders on disrespect of group members or the leader, then the student should be given a warning. If the behavior persists, write up a back-to-class slip, leaving blank the student name section. Set it nearby so that the student knows you mean business. If the behavior occurs again, put the name on the slip and point to the door. Of course, these rules should have been explained at the first session, so the students know what can happen.

Another behavior-related problem is non-compliance with the makeup work policy. If students do not make up the class work that is missed while in group, the advantages of being in the group are threatened. Parent and teacher rapport suffers majorly. You should remind them that the existence of all groups is in jeopardy when students do not follow through on making up work.

Immediately after this chapter, I have placed sample copies of a needs assessment, group sign-up sheet, parent permission form, memo for teachers affected by the group (using animal names in place of student names—no pun intended), and excuse from class. If information can be condensed to half a sheet of paper, I have provided it twice on the page, ready to make your copying a little easier (and greener).

Though I have given you a step-by-step method of conducting groups, please do not be afraid to venture into your own creativity. As you will see, most groups will run fairly well with only minimal direction from the facilitator. Break a leg!

Needs Assessment

Name: ______________________________ Team: ____________________

Problem areas for me:	Never	Occasionally	Often	Very Often
1. Academics	0	1	2	3
2. ADD symptom management	0	1	2	3
3. Anger management	0	1	2	3
4. Family relationships	0	1	2	3
5. Friend relationships	0	1	2	3
6. Grief issues	0	1	2	3
7. Motivation	0	1	2	3
8. Self-confidence	0	1	2	3
9. Stress	0	1	2	3

I would be interested in help through: __________ individual counseling
__________ group counseling
__________ printed material (handouts)

Needs Assessment

Name: ______________________________ Team: ____________________

Problem areas for me:	Never	Occasionally	Often	Very Often
1. Academics	0	1	2	3
2. ADD symptom management	0	1	2	3
3. Anger management	0	1	2	3
4. Family relationships	0	1	2	3
5. Friend relationships	0	1	2	3
6. Grief issues	0	1	2	3
7. Motivation	0	1	2	3
8. Self-confidence	0	1	2	3
9. Stress	0	1	2	3

I would be interested in help through: __________ individual counseling
__________ group counseling
__________ printed material (handouts)

Name: ______________________________ Team: ____________________

7th GRADE GROUPS—Fall 2011

A support group provides you with a safe place to discuss feelings and problems with peers who have similar concerns. The group is an opportunity to learn new ways of coping with your problems so that you can be more successful in school.

Students who are involved in a group are required to check into class before coming to group. ALL work that is missed is your responsibility to make up.

The groups listed below will meet weekly for six weeks, with a rotating schedule so you only miss each class once. You may sign up for ONLY ONE group.

1. _______ ADD + (Plus)—This group is for students who have been diagnosed with ADD or ADHD and would like to learn more about organization, study skills, and impulse control tips.

2. _______ STUCK IN THE MIDDLE—This group covers issues surrounding separation, divorce and stepfamilies. You learn ways to deal with such topics as custody issues, visitation, and step-parent problems. Even if your parents were never officially married, you are welcome in this group if your parents are experiencing a difficult break-up.

3. _______ GOOD GRIEF—This group provides an opportunity to talk about your feelings about the death of a close family member or friend. Talking helps you get through the painful process of healing.

– –

_____ I do not choose to be in a support group at this time. If I have a problem, I can see the counselor individually.

Student: ______________________________ Team: ____________________

Parent Notification/Permission for Group

Your child has expressed an interest in being part of a support group. The group will meet a total of six times, once a week, on a staggered schedule so that each class is only missed once. Your child will be expected to make up work that is missed. Support groups offer adolescents a chance to meet with peers facing similar issues. Many benefit from learning new ways to cope with a situation or problem.

Please sign below if your child has permission to join the group.

Sincerely,

Debra Efird, Counselor

_______ YES, I want my child to join. _______ NO, I do not want my child to join.

Signature of parent ________________________ Date ____________

Student: ______________________________ Team: ____________________

Parent Notification/Permission for Group

Your child has expressed an interest in being part of a support group. The group will meet a total of six times, once a week, on a staggered schedule so that each class is only missed once. Your child will be expected to make up work that is missed. Support groups offer adolescents a chance to meet with peers facing similar issues. Many benefit from learning new ways to cope with a situation or problem.

Please sign below if your child has permission to join the group.

Sincerely,

Debra Efird, Counselor

_______ YES, I want my child to join. _______ NO, I do not want my child to join.

Signature of parent ________________________ Date ____________

7th Grade Groups—Fall 2011

D. Efird

The following students have signed up to be in support groups. All have returned parent permission forms. Please excuse them from your classes and allow them to make up the work that they miss. Groups are a vital part of the Guidance curriculum and a most effective way to reach numbers of students. Thank you so much for your cooperation.

Group 1	Group 2	Group 3
Armadillo	Iguana	Raccoon
Bear	Jaguar	Snake
Cheetah	Kangaroo	Tiger
Deer	Lion	Vulture
Elephant	Mouse	Walrus
Frog	Owl	Wolf
Gecko	Penguin	Zebra
Hippopotamus	Pig	

	Oct. 15	Oct. 22	Oct. 29	Nov. 5	Nov. 12	Nov. 19
Group 1:	8:45–9:30	1:10–1:55	9:35–10:20	2:10–2:55	10:40–11:25	11:40–12:25
Group 2:	10:40–11:25	8:45–9:30	11:40–12:25	1:10–1:55	9:35–10:20	2:10–2:55
Group 3:	1:10–1:55	9:35–10:20	2:10–2:55	8:45–9:30	11:40–12:25	10:40-11:25

Homeroom Teacher: ___________________________

Please give note to this student: ____

Student: Please give this note to the teacher whose class is affected by your group

meeting on _____________________ at _________________ in the Guidance Office

Conference Room.

Thank you! Debra Efird

Homeroom Teacher: ___________________________

Please give note to this student: ____

Student: Please give this note to the teacher whose class is affected by your group

meeting on _____________________ at _________________ in the Guidance Office

Conference Room.

Thank you! Debra Efird

Chapter 2

ADD + (Plus)[1]

ADD + (Plus) Group Outline

(Please note: I use the more inclusive term, ADD, rather than ADHD.)

I. Introductory Information, Sentence Completion Activity
   A. Outline, Schedule, Parent Permission, and Rules
   B. Sentence Completion Activity
II. Time Management
   A. How Much Time It Takes Activity
   B. Your 24 Hours Activity
   C. Time Management Tips
III. Organization
   A. Explanation of Organization Supplies
   B. Completion of Blank Monthly Calendar
IV. Study Skills, Goal Setting
   A.. Yes, You Can Study
   B. Setting Goals for Grades
V. Impulse Control
   A. Responding Appropriately Scenarios
   B. Appropriate or Annoying Choices Game
VI. Impulse Control, Review
   A. Road Signs Activity
   B. Review of Prior Sessions

1 Parts of this chapter first appeared in *Counseling Today,* September 2005. Reprinted with permission from American Counseling Association.

American School Counselor Association (ASCA) Standards

Academic Development

Standard A: Students will acquire the attitudes, knowledge, and skills that contribute to effective learning in school and across the life span.

A:A1 Improve Academic Self-concept

A:A1.5 Identify attitudes and behaviors which lead to successful learning

A:A2 Acquire Skills for Improving Learning

A:A2.1 Apply time management and task management skills

Standard B: Students will complete school with the academic preparation essential to choose from a wide range of substantial post-secondary options, including college.

A:B2 Plan to Achieve Goals

A:B2.1 Establish challenging academic goals in elementary, middle/jr. high and high school

A:B2.2 Use assessment results in educational planning

Personal/Social Development

Standard A: Students will acquire the knowledge, attitudes, and interpersonal skills to help them understand and respect self and others.

PS:A1 Acquire Self-knowledge

PS:A1.5 Identify and express feelings

PS:A1.6 Distinguish between appropriate and inappropriate behavior

PS:A1.8 Understand the need for self-control and how to practice it

Rationale for ADD + (Plus) Group

Nearly everyone in the field of education is at least slightly familiar with the term "Attention Deficit/Hyperactivity Disorder (ADHD)." It is quite common for students demonstrating excessive inattention, hyperactivity, and impulsiveness to carry this diagnosis. In this work I refer to the disorder as simply Attention Deficit Disorder or ADD (unless I am referencing a source which states otherwise), using it as an "umbrella" term to include students who demonstrate the hyperactive element as well as those who do not.

A recent study by the Mayo Clinic indicates that 7.5% of school-age children may have ADHD (ADDitude, 2011). According to the Centers for Disease Control and Prevention (2010), the *Diagnostic and Statistical Manual of Mental Disorders* (*DSM-IV-TR*) reports that 3%–7% of school-age children are diagnosed with ADHD. This number is considerably lower when compared to the study mentioned earlier. From 2003–2007, the number of parent-reported ADHD occurrence increased 22%. Prevalence is much higher for boys, 13.2 compared to 5.6 for girls. My state, North Carolina, holds the distinction of having the highest parent-reported incidence of ADHD. Parents report ADHD-diagnosed children having more difficulty with peer interaction (21.1% compared to 7.3%). ADD often coexists with learning disabilities. In a study done in 2004, 4% of children were diagnosed with both ADHD and a learning disability (Centers for Disease Control and Prevention, 2010). As many as half the children diagnosed with ADD may also be burdened with an identified learning disability (Witmer, 2011).

Efforts to help ADD students become more successful both academically and socially are definitely in order. Providing a support group can teach them valuable skills while also giving them a place to feel comfortable talking about this disorder among others who understand. My group provides sessions on time management, organization, study skills, and impulse control. To maintain attention, I keep a quick pace and include some lively activities such as cleaning out book bags, allowing them to record themselves as they read, and playing a game. Too many times ADD students are only recognized for their negative qualities. With a little fine-tuning, many of these students are able to bring forward their hidden talents and gifts. Edward M. Hallowell and John J. Ratey wrote, "There is a melody within that cacophony, a symphony yet to be written," in *Driven to Distraction* (1994, p. 262). Offering an ADD support group is one intervention counselors can present to assist in this mission.

What Makes It Work:

1. Most students like being in a group. If being diagnosed with Attention Deficit Disorder (with or without the Hyperactivity) has entitled them to something desirable rather than objectionable, they are interested. They like discovering who else has ADD and will often express surprise upon learning this about some of their peers.
2. Parents are all for it. They like knowing that someone is doing something other than complaining about their ADD children. (I do not require parent permission in advance of my introductory session with these students because—though it is a medical diagnosis—it is more generally perceived as an educational obstacle than a health condition.)
3. Teachers are usually pleased to dismiss these children from their classes for a period.
4. This group requires a physically comfortable environment with a laid-back leader. If a student prefers to lie on the floor, it should be allowed in this setting.

5. This group can be conducted as mixed gender or gender-specific—I have done it both ways multiple times. Though the topics and activities do not change, you may want to consider separating girls and boys if you have enough students. Sometimes the boys' level of rambunctiousness can be disturbing to the girls, who are less apt to exhibit the hyperactivity part of the diagnosis.
6. Some (never all!) of the group members will pick up some study skills and behavioral tips that will truly help them.

Challenges:

1. Well, what do you think? The activity level! Putting together eight students with ADD is not for the faint of heart. It requires big doses of patience and tolerance.
   For squirminess: Give out squishy toys as needed. (Better have enough for all. Try the dollar store.) Or after ten minutes, have a ten-second shakedown where everyone stands up and shakes every part of their body that moves. Promise them another shake in ten more minutes. And another.
   For unadulterated exuberance: First, acknowledge rather than fight the students' enthusiasm. Perhaps all could stand up and do a cheer or a twenty-second mock-dance around the circle. Then have them return to their seats and direct them to the work at hand, commending their excitement and asking them to think about how that liveliness could be channeled into a positive school experience. If, however, the student's behavior goes beyond radiating vibrancy to breaking school rules, then the student should be reminded he is being inappropriate and told to tone it down or leave.
   For interrupting: You must allow more interruption here than in your other groups, but don't lose sight of the fact that your ADD students can practice acceptable classroom behavior even in your relaxed group setting. Have a small beanbag or old stuffed animal that must be in possession to speak. Use a gentle reminder cue, perhaps a tap at your imaginary wristwatch, to indicate it is not his time to talk.
2. Another problem is misbehavior, which may be somewhat elevated in this group compared to others. Emphasize that school rules will be enforced, and then show that you mean what you say. Grit your teeth and toss one out of the session after you've given a couple of warnings. You'll feel miserable, but it is necessary to keep structure and guidelines in effect for the others in the group. Have a positive, encouraging conference with the offending student a day or two later and invite him back into the fold for the next session. Improved behavior is almost guaranteed.
3. Another common problem with ADD groups is that these students tend to be even more forgetful than the general population. Regarding coming to group: try to squelch forgetfulness by having them tape the schedule in their notebooks right then and there at the first session. Yes, I mean bring the tape and pass it around. That will work only for the handful of students who actually have their logs or notebooks with them. Be sure that students know that all they have to do if they lose their schedules is come by your office for replacements. No punishment, no scolding. And you may want to walk the halls a little more on ADD group day to give students a pleasant verbal reminder such as, "I can't wait to see you at 10:30."
4. Most students with ADD like to keep the same routine, and being in a group requires a varied schedule.
5. Teachers may want you to keep pulling these students from their classrooms because they have enjoyed their absences. However, the group must end at some point, and hopefully you are returning them with more coping skills than when you started.

ADD + (Plus) Group Sessions

Session 1 Topic: Introductory Information, Sentence Completion Activity

Session 1 Supplies: For students—Copies of outline, schedule, and parent permission form; For leader—Tape, Copy of ADD Sentence Completion Statements cut into strips, Basket

Session 1 Content:

To begin, explain general group information: outline, schedule, parent permission form, and group rules. Pass around the tape for group members to attach their schedules to their notebooks. All of this preliminary information can take a fairly large portion of time. It may be helpful to inform members in the beginning that you are using the abbreviation ADD (Attention Deficit Disorder) for all session topics rather than making the distinction between it and ADHD (Attention Deficit/Hyperactivity Disorder).

A good introductory topic is the ADD Sentence Completion Statements exercise, which allows for a variety of responses—the expression of facts as well as feelings. Assure group members that there is no specific right or wrong answer. Most students like the element of surprise that comes with drawing the paper slip from the basket. It may work best for you to keep control of the basket, allowing only one student at a time to draw a slip so that they'll give their full attention to who is speaking at the moment. Then if someone wants to volunteer how he'd have answered that one, let him. The more information they are willing to share, the better. An important goal for this first session is for them to become comfortable with expressing their thoughts and feelings about having ADD in front of others in this safe setting.

After you've done one round, they will want to do another and perhaps another if you have time. As you will see, each statement can elicit considerable discussion, and there probably won't be enough time for many rounds. So keep separate the slips that were drawn, and use this activity again to jumpstart another session or as part of the last review session. Feel free to make up some statements yourself and throw them in the hat!

Questions they should be able to answer: What are the topics that will be covered in group? How does the schedule work? What are some of the group rules? When is the parent permission form due? What were some of the feelings and facts expressed in the sentence completion activity? What did you learn about each other in the introductory session?

ADD Sentence Completion Statements

When I first learned I had ADD, I felt ____.

When I hear my mother telling someone that I have ADD, I feel ________________________.

When I want to jump out of my seat, I ____.

When I have worked hard on my homework and still haven't finished, I feel ______________.

When I finish my homework early, I feel ____.

When I tell my friends I have ADD, they ____.

When I am on medication, sometimes I feel ______________________________________.

When I forget my medication, I feel ____.

When the teacher calls on me and I'm not paying attention, I feel ____________________.

When I make a good grade on a test, I feel ______________________________________.

If I make a bad grade on a test, I feel ____.

When someone teases me about having ADD, I ______________________________.

If I blurt out something in class, I feel ______________________________.

I think that having ADD can actually be a good thing because ______________________________.

One thing I'd like to say about taking medications is ______________________________.

When a teacher seems to understand me, I feel ______________________________.

When it takes me longer than most kids to finish a test, I feel ______________________________.

If I get in trouble at school, I feel ______________________________.

The worst thing about having ADD is ______________________________.

When I forget what my homework is, I ______________________________.

When my mind starts to wander during class, I ______________________________.

If I could tell the world one thing about ADD, it would be this: ______________________________.

When I can't find my homework, I feel ______________________________.

Session 2 Topic: Time Management

Session 2 Supplies: For students—Copies of Your 24 Hours, Copies of Time Management Tips; For leader—Copy of How Much Time It Takes (with correct answers at bottom), Copies of those activity topics (one to a page) and answers (cut into large strips)

Session 2 Content:

Begin the session with the How Much Time It Takes activity, a fun guessing game about how many years of their lives they will spend doing certain things. Some of those activities are looking for things they have lost, waiting in line, and doing housework (Fredrikson, 2011). At first it's a little hard for them to get their heads around the idea that this is based on time spent over the course of a lifetime, but eventually they catch on. It really stirs them up! This exercise could be done in paper-and-pencil style, but you especially need to avoid that when working with ADD students. Hold up one topic such as "Looking For Something You've Lost" and place any three of the answer guesses on the table (being certain to include the correct answer). Do the same for the other activity topics, switching up the answer choices each time.

From this activity, they learn the benefits of always putting things in their places instead of spending so much time looking for them—or worse yet—losing them. They learn that they can use their waiting time better if they have something to do (completing homework while at the orthodontist's office). They learn that they can combine activities to obtain the most benefit from each minute (talking to a friend on the phone while doing simple household chores such as sorting laundry or unloading the dishwasher). You may want to suggest that they share this activity with their parents, thus arming the students with something interesting to talk about if parents are questioning what happened in group today.

Next, give them the pie chart worksheet entitled Your 24 Hours. By upper elementary and definitely by middle school they should have encountered these charts in math class and have some idea of how to relate their 24 hours into a circle that must be "fractioned up." (Call it a pizza rather than a pie chart if that seems easier to understand). First, you note that one piece has already been marked and labeled "school." That one is not negotiable. Also, you need to note that "sleep" is a large part of their 24 hours, too, or else they may forget all about it. You may need to show them roughly the size of an "hour" piece. Have them complete the actual chart first, and then the ideal one. Emphasize to them that the ideal one must show time for homework, because many will argue that their ideal time would show them only playing video games and eating. Remind them that if they are truly going to gain something from group, they must be serious about improving their academic situation, which means homework must become a priority. It's also helpful to instill in them that everyone has twenty-four hours in the day and no one can say, "I have less time than he does."

Usually this completely fills the second session. However, if you have time left, you could give them the Time Management Tips handout. Since it will look like too much print to them, go around the room and have them each read one, allowing them to strike strange poses such as standing on one leg or curling up in a ball as they read.

Questions they should be able to answer: How accurate were you in guessing how much time different activities take? How was your actual pie chart different from your ideal one? What is one time management tip that you could put into place next week?

How Much Time It Takes

The following five activities are activities you will be involved with for your entire life, whether you like it or not. Time-management experts have estimated how much time these activities may take over a lifetime. Can you guess?

Looking for something you have lost

(a) 6 months (b) 1 year (c) 2 years

Doing housework

(a) 2 years (b) 3 years (c) 4 years

Eating

(a) 2 years (b) 6 years (c) 10 years

Waiting at stoplights

(a) 6 months (b) 1 year (c) 2 years

Waiting in line

(a) 2 years (b) 3 years (c) 5 years

(Answers: 1. b, 2. c, 3. b, 4. a, 5. c)

6 months

(cut)--

1 year

(cut)--

2 years

(cut)--

3 years

4 years

(cut) -

5 years

(cut) -

6 years

(cut) -

10 years

LOOKING

FOR

SOMETHING

YOU'VE LOST

EATING

DOING

HOUSE-

WORK

WAITING

AT

STOP-

LIGHTS

WAITING

IN

LINE

Your 24 Hours

Divide the pie charts into fractions showing how much time you think you actually spend and should ideally spend on such activities as: sleeping, eating, sports, homework, television, video games, computer, telephone, chores, and other. (School is already marked.)

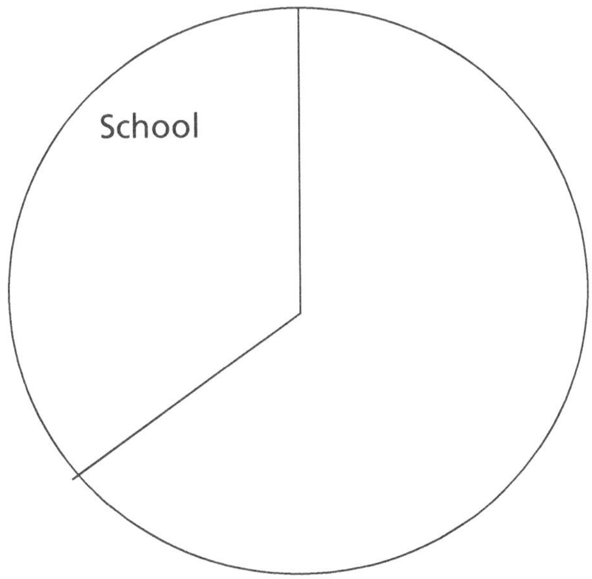

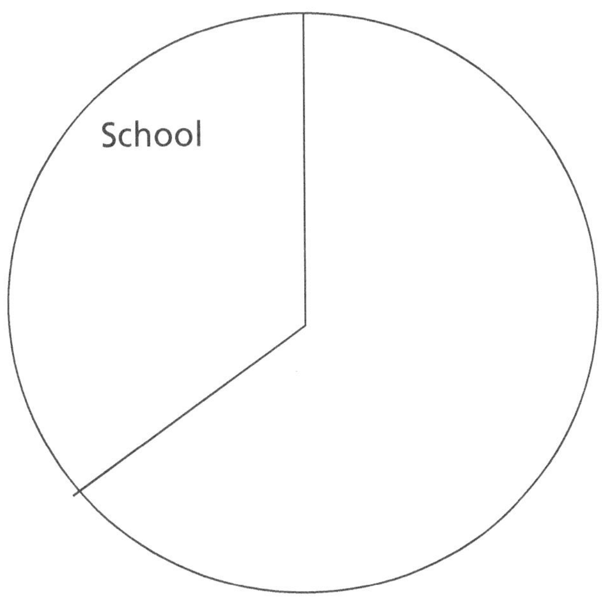

Time Management Tips

1. MAKE LISTS! Always write down your homework each day in an assignment book. Place a star beside assignments that are due the next day.

2. PLAN AHEAD when you have projects due. You may have more time this week than next week. So get started NOW!

3. Take advantage of CLASS TIME to do homework if your teacher allows it. If you have questions about the homework, this is a great time to ask.

4. Have a set STUDY TIME each day and stick to it! Schoolwork should be your #1 priority.

5. Once you have started an assignment, try to FINISH it before starting another one. This helps keep you organized.

6. PACK your book bag the night before. Remember lunch money, gym clothes, signed forms, school supplies, and your HOMEWORK.

7. LIMIT yourself to 30 minutes of telephone talking or texting. Combine your phone time with a simple chore like folding laundry or walking the dog.

8. Keep paper and pen handy in your pocket or purse so that you can JOT NOTES or make lists of things you need to do.

9. READ whenever you go somewhere in the car (if you do not get carsick). This is valuable time that many students forget to use!

10. Watch out for the giant time-robber: TELEVISION. Limit yourself to one program a day. If you have sports practice or a meeting, consider that as your television time for the day. Try one day a week as a "T.V.-Free" day.

11. When you have a chore to do, DON'T ARGUE about it. That wastes time. Just do it!

12. Take a few minutes of time just for FUN! Then you won't mind the work that must be done.

Session 3 Topic: Organization

Session 3 Supplies: For students—Book bags (maybe), Copies of blank calendar, Pencils; For leader—Folders in bright colors (if possible, enough to give one to each student), a locker organizer, several binders of various styles—especially those with accordion-style dividers or separate sections and pockets, sticky notes of various sizes (if possible, enough to give them some), calendars and date books of various sizes, desk organizers

Session 3 Content:

If you didn't have time for the Time Management Tips sheet at the last meeting, you may want to start this session by having students read them aloud. Remember to make it more fun by allowing each to assume a silly pose while reading a tip. The session on time management bridges over nicely to organization. Being disorganized is a major problem among nearly all students diagnosed with ADD (Kutscher, 2002). They urgently need help.

If possible, try to schedule this session during the last period of the day and suggest that students bring their book bags. Link this session to the last one by stating that they'll be able to manage their time better and find things more quickly if they are organized. Show each organization aid item you have brought and explain its use. Point out organization facets of their school-issued agenda or assignment notebook that they may have never bothered to notice. Let them know that organization extends beyond school work to home by suggesting they separate clothing items by drawer and even label those if they need to.

Then give each group member a copy of the blank calendar page to complete in class. Have them fill in the dates for the current month—they will actually think that is fun. Then ask them to write in items beyond the ordinary daily ones, such as when book reports and projects are due. Ask them to add soccer games and practices, music lessons, and other community events—anything that is not a daily activity.

Ask those who brought book bags to empty them in various corners on the floor or on the table. Insist that they throw away trash (candy wrappers, broken pencils, wadded paper). Those who did not bring book bags can assist those who did by helping them discard items and by making suggestions for ways to better organize.

Give each member a brightly colored folder and call it an "all-purpose" folder. Tell them to use it to deposit all their homework in upon completion that night. Suggest that they take it to all classes, turning in all homework as they move through the day. Then it should go home empty to be refilled for the next day. Tell them it is also a good place to put permission forms or tests requiring parent signatures. Also, if you have plenty, give them some sticky notes to keep.

Questions they should be able to answer: How organized do you consider yourself? Which organization aid items that you saw today would help you become better organized? What type of organization system do your teachers recommend? How full is your calendar? How would you describe your book bag—messy or orderly? What should you do with the "all-purpose" folder?

Sun	Mon	Tue	Wed	Thu	Fri	Sat

Session 4 Topic: Study Skills, Goal Setting

Session 4 Supplies: For students—Copies of Yes, You Can Study; Index cards, Pencils; For leader—Tape recorder with tape and microphone (or more sophisticated technology, if you like)

Session 4 Content:

Study Skills for ADD students are not all that different from those for other students, though it should be emphasized that it usually takes ADD students more time to complete their work. In particular, homework can be problematic. While many educators are taking a long, hard look at homework in general—how beneficial it is and how much is too much (Vatterott, 2009)—it is still very much an integral part of grading in most schools. One and one-half to two hours seems to be a fair amount of time to spend each night on homework for middle school students, though major tests and big projects may necessitate increasing that time on occasion (Robin, 2008). Some students are appalled at the suggestion of that amount of time—after all, it interferes with video games and television! Others (typically the more diligent ones) say they spend three and four hours per night on school work. If they are assessing the time correctly, that sounds excessive. A parent/teacher conference to discuss the situation should be scheduled. Distribute copies of the Yes, You Can Study sheet, and ask students to take turns reading a statement into a tape recorder or similar device. Let them be silly, affecting British accents or Donald Duck voices. Then play the tape for them, and they'll laugh at how they sound. A recording device can be much more than a prop for the group session, though. Explain that this is a helpful way to study. For example, they could record their science chapters or vocabulary words and play them back several times before a test.

Then move to the Goal Setting activity. Hand out the index cards and pencils. Ask them to write down all their subjects and current grades (or what they had at the last report period). Then ask them to jot beside that list the grades they could set as realistic goals for the next grading period. Don't let them put all As unless that is truly realistic for them. Then ask them to write on the back of the card which study skill tip(s) they plan to use to reach their goals. Ask for volunteers to share this info with the group.

Questions they should be able to answer: Which of the study skills tips that you learned today will you plan to use during the next week? Did you like the way you sounded on the recording device? How realistic are the goals you set for your grades? How would improved grades affect your daily life?

Yes, You Can Study

1. Plan to take a 10-minute BREAK for every hour of studying. Research shows that most students need a break after 45–50 minutes of studying.

2. Always WRITE down homework assignments. Don't trust your memory. Have you noticed that adults make lists all the time?

3. Ask for the PHONE NUMBERS of one or two responsible classmates in each class so you can check on assignments and ask for help after you get home.

4. OVERESTIMATE THE TIME it will take you to prepare for major tests and projects. Don't wait until the day before to begin.

5. Have a SET study time each day, flexing as needed with your extracurricular activities. Most ADD students need one and a half to two hours for homework.

6. If you do not need 2 hours for your homework, spend part of that time REVIEWING class notes and skimming chapters that the teacher has gone over in class.

7. Try to study the SAME SUBJECT at the SAME TIME each day. This creates a habit of doing that subject at that time and it will seem easier for you.

8. CHECK over the work you are about to turn in. You will catch the careless errors instead of letting the teacher do so.

9. Write down all your grades in a SPECIAL PLACE as you receive them so that you know where you stand in each class. Don't be caught by surprise!

10. Use TRICKS to help you. Example: HOMES = Great Lakes (Huron, Ontario, Michigan, Erie, Superior). Make up your own!

11. Set goals that are RIGHT for you. Don't aim for the A/B Honor Roll until you have begun to move Fs to Ds to Cs.

12. Don't make EXCUSES for poor grades. Don't use your ADD as an excuse. Take control! Even if you don't reach the Honor Roll, you can make improvements. No one should settle for an F!

Session 5 Topic: Impulse Control

Session 5 Supplies: For students—Copies of Responding Appropriately Scenarios; For leader—Copy of Appropriate or Annoying Choices Game cut into small (1" × 3") pieces, 10 large (at least 11" × 14") sheets of construction paper, Basket

Session 5 Content:

To begin, read each part of the Responding Appropriately Scenarios sheet and ask students to formulate inappropriate and appropriate responses. Elaborate on the topic by asking if they can recall specific incidents when they know they responded in an inappropriate manner. Discuss the importance of being aware of not only their feelings but also those of others.

Then play the Appropriate or Annoying Choices Game. This would make an acceptable board game, but that is definitely not the ADD way. These students would rather be the board pieces themselves, in motion. This activity gets loud and is best done outside on a day that is not so windy that your construction paper flies away. Set the ten sheets of construction paper one beside another to form a straight line, or curve it if you prefer. Put the small strips of paper with the behavior choices on them in the basket. Then decide who is going first and ask that student to draw a strip of paper from the basket. The student must read aloud the statement and take the appropriate step(s). For example: When Tyler asked me to stop drumming on my desk, I stopped immediately. Go forward 1 space. Another example: I made duck noises while the substitute was talking. Go back 1 space. Free space means exactly that: the student moves forward a step, just as life in general sometimes offers us smooth passage. If the student draws one which states he must go back a space and he hasn't made it onto the construction paper yet, then he just remains behind the starting line until his next turn when hopefully he'll be able to advance. To add more zip to this, allow them to act out those statements that lend themselves to charades. If the basket is empty before anyone has reached the tenth step or finish line, recycle them. They'll want to play on through even if it means hearing the statements twice. They'll have great fun while recognizing that negative or distracting choices can set them back.

Questions they should be able to answer: When have you responded inappropriately and been punished for it? Why is it important to consider the feelings of others? How did playing the game make you more aware of how your behavior affects both you and others?

Responding Appropriately Scenarios

1. Mrs. Brown returned your test marked with an F. You had studied for that test for two hours. You will be grounded for weeks.

   Inappropriate responses:

   Appropriate responses:

2. Jason told you he liked your haircut. You think your hair looks horrible.

   Inappropriate responses:

   Appropriate responses:

3. Megan told Mr. Green that you were kicking her chair. You were sent to the back of the room to write twenty-five sentences. You *were* kicking the chair, but you felt the punishment was severe.

   Inappropriate responses:

   Appropriate responses:

4. Anna thinks she can sing really well but she actually sounds bad. She wants you to sing with her in the talent show and keeps bugging you to practice with her.

   Inappropriate responses:

   Appropriate responses:

5. Mark's dad is dying of cancer. His mother has been sick, too, and has to have surgery next week. He starts talking to you about it on the bus.

   Inappropriate responses:

   Appropriate responses:

6. Both you and your friend Brandon tried out for football together but you didn't make it. He was talking really loud about how many touchdowns he ran in the scrimmage game. It seemed like he wanted to be sure you heard.

   Inappropriate responses:

   Appropriate responses:

Appropriate or Annoying Choices Game

I clicked my pen until the girl behind me complained. Go back 1 space.	I lost my temper and cursed at the teacher. Go back 3 spaces.
When Tony asked me to stop drumming on my desk, I stopped immediately. Go forward 1 space.	I jumped up and down in lunch line until the lunch ladies scolded me. Go back 1 space.
I did shoulder rolls when I felt like I just had to move. Go forward 1 space.	I coughed loud during Greg's presentation but apologized later. Go forward 1 space.
I crumpled up my paper and threw it at Sandy. Go back 1 space.	I took off my sock and scratched my foot during class. Go back 1 space.
I whistled during class. Go back 1 space.	I twirled around in my chair. Go back 1 space.
I made duck noises while the substitute was talking. Go back 1 space.	I made the Honor Roll for the second time this year. Go forward 2 spaces.
I asked permission to go to the restroom when I needed to move around. Go forward 1 space.	I wanted to crack my knuckles but squeezed a stress ball instead. Go forward 1 space.

I kept talking to Alex and got bumped to another class. Go back 2 spaces.	I jumped up and touched the ceiling as I went down the hall. Go back 1 space.
I organized my locker by cleaning out junk and using a shelf organizer. Go forward 2 spaces.	I got up to sharpen my pencil when I felt like I couldn't stay still another minute. Go forward 1 space.
I ran circles around my desk when the teacher left the room and somebody told on me. Go back 1 space.	When I caught myself looking out the window, I snapped back to attention. Go forward 1 space.
I rolled my eyes at the teacher. Go back 1 space.	I rolled my pencil all over my desk. Go back 1 space.
I started on my project the week before it was due. Go forward 2 spaces.	I turned in all my homework on time for an entire week. Go forward 2 spaces.
I zipped my jacket up and down to annoy Matt. Go back 1 space.	I sang out loud while the teacher was talking. Go back 2 spaces.
I hit Roberto when he teased me about having ADD. Go back 2 spaces.	I threw my medication in the trash can because I was mad at my mom. Go back 2 spaces.
I blurted out an answer in class. Go back 1 space.	I helped erase the board. Go forward 1 space.

1 free space	1 free space
1 free space	1 free space
1 free space	1 free space
1 free space	1 free space
1 free space	1 free space
1 free space	1 free space
1 free space	1 free space
1 free space	1 free space

Session 6 Topic: Impulse Control, Review

Session 6 Supplies: For students—Squeeze balls; For leader—Copies of Road Signs (I went to the website of the Department of Transportation – Division of Motor Vehicles for my state and found pictures of road signs on pp. 93–94 of the *Driver's Handbook* [North Carolina Department of Transportation Division of Motor Vehicles, 2009]. Then I enlarged and printed each sign to the size of a regular page.); Leader's complete folder (for review)

Session 6 Content:

For this final session, it is ideal to place a little more emphasis on controlling impulsive behavior before moving into the review of previous sessions. The Road Signs activity (Webb & Myrick, 2006) makes it fun. Start by telling them that in a few years they will be behind the wheel of automobiles (legally), and that they may want to start paying attention to road signs now to prepare them for that time. Tell them they must relate the sign to ADD students in a classroom setting. You'll be surprised at how good they are at this. Hold up the signs, one at a time, and let them try to connect them to cues for good classroom behavior. For example: The "Railroad Crossing" sign could mean they should slow down and be ready to stop whatever they're doing. (At my school the letters "RR" stand for "Responsibility Room," a place students go for misbehavior, so this sign has a double meaning for them). Another example: The "Merge" direction arrows could mean they must try to fit in with the rest of the class. One more example: The arrow showing 2-way traffic could mean that learning is a 2-way situation, and that they should be sure to put something into it if they hope to get something out of it.) They will come up with some hilarious stuff. To show you like to play games, too, throw in the "Cattle Crossing" one.

Then, if you have been able to pitch in a few bucks of your own, give each of the students a squeeze ball from the dollar store to help with impulse control in the classroom. Remind them that if the balls end up being tossed around the room, teachers will rightfully confiscate them and you will not give them another.

Reviewing previous sessions is important to remind students of the things they have learned. You may want to do one round of the sentence completion statements from the initial meeting. Then touch lightly on information from the sessions on time management, organization, study skills, and impulse control. Ask them to tell you what they remember about each session. At the end, ask students to name two things they have learned or ideas they'd like to continue to explore as a result of being in the group. They will want the group to continue but you will have earned a deep sigh of relief. Be proud, you have managed to conduct a group that can sometimes prove to be difficult! As you bid them goodbye, let them know that they are still welcome to check in with you whenever they need to during the remainder of the year.

Now take a moment's rest before embarking on another group adventure ...

Questions they should be able to answer: Which road sign was your favorite? How would you describe the purpose of the road sign activity? How can you use a squeeze ball in an appropriate manner (avoiding having it taken away)? What do you remember about each group session? What are some of the obstacles an ADD student faces? How can those obstacles be overcome?

Warning Signs

Regulatory Signs

DO NOT STOP ON THE TRACKS reminds the driver **not to stop on the railroad tracks for any reason**

R
R

Evaluation of ADD + (Plus) Group

Rate yourself by circling the number which corresponds with how you evaluate each statement.
1 = Not at all, 2 = A small amount, 3 = Average amount, 4 = More than average, 5 = Very much

1. I felt comfortable discussing having ADD in the group.

   1..................2..................3..................4..................5

2. I learned ways to help me manage time better.

   1..................2..................3..................4..................5

3. I learned ways to help me become more organized.

   1..................2..................3..................4..................5

4. I learned a new study skill.

   1..................2..................3..................4..................5

5. I learned to set realistic goals for my grades.

   1..................2..................3..................4..................5

6. I learned to recognize appropriate and inappropriate responses to situations.

   1..................2..................3..................4..................5

7. I learned to recognize impulsive actions and their consequences.

   1..................2..................3..................4..................5

8. I grew closer to group members during the course of the group.

   1..................2..................3..................4..................5

Suggestions for making the group better: ____

____

References

ADDitude: Living Well with Attention Deficit. (2011) *How many people have ADHD?* Retrieved March 22, 2011, from http://www.additudemag.com/adhd/article/688.html

Centers for Disease Control and Prevention. (2010, November 10). *Attention-Deficit Hyperactivity Disorder data and statistics in the United States.* Retrieved March 22, 2011, from http://www.cdc.gov/ncbddd/adhd/data.html

Hallowell, E. & Ratey, J. (1994). *Driven to distraction.* New York: Touchstone.

Fredrikson, J. (2011, October 13). *Do you know how much of your life is spent waiting in lines and doing housework?* Retrieved May 19, 2011, from http://juliafredrikson.wordpress.com/2007/10/13/do-you-know-how-much-of-your-life-is-spent-waiting-in-lines-and-doing-housework/

Kutscher, M. (2002). Schoolwork and ADHD. *PediatricNeurology.com.* Retrieved April 20, 2011, from http://www.pediatricneurology.com/schoolrx.htm

North Carolina Department of Transportation Division of Motor Vehicles. (2009, May). *Driver's handbook.* Retrieved May 4, 2011, from http://www.ncdot.gov/dmv/driver_services/drivershandbook/download/NCDL_English.pdf

Robin, A. (2008). Helping your adolescent with ADHD get their homework done. *Attention Deficit Disorder resources.* Retrieved April 9, 2011, from http://www.addresources.org/?q=node/616

Vatterott, C. (2009). *Rethinking homework: Best practices that support diverse needs.* Alexandria, VA: ASCD.

Webb, L. & Myrick, R. (2006). A group counseling intervention for children with Attention Deficit Hyperactivity Disorder. *LD Online.* Retrieved April 9, 2011, from http://www.ldonline.org/article/A_Group_Counseling_Intervention_for_Children_with_Attention_Deficit_Hyperactivity_Disorder

Witmer, D. (2011). ADD and ADHD Statistics. *Parenting teens – parents of teenagers find help raising teens.* Retrieved March 22, 2011, from http://parentingteens.about.com/cs/addadhd/a/add_stats.htm

Chapter 3

Asperger Boys Club (ABC)

Asperger Boys Club (ABC) Group Outline

I. Introductory Information/Brain Differences
   A. Purpose, Outline, Schedule, Rules
   B. Study of Brain Differences
II. Communication
   A. Space Considerations
   B. Voice/Tone and Eye Contact
   C. Art of Conversation: Starting, Maintaining, and Ending
III. Relationships
   A. Initiating a Relationship
   B. Responding to Rejection
IV. Anger Management
   A. Aggressive, Passive, and Assertive Communication
   B. Cooling Down Methods
   C. Visit from Service Dog
V. Perception of Others/Uniqueness
   A. Response Scenarios
   B. Self-Appreciation
VI. Summary/Everyday Situations
   A. Review of Prior Sessions
   B. Discussion of Situations through Coping Game

Asperger Boys Club (ABC) Group Sessions

Session 1 Topic: Introductory Information, Study of Brain Differences

Session 1 Supplies: For students—Copies of outline and schedule; For leader—Brain diagram, Actions list cut into strips, Basket, Head of cabbage, Two bags of marshmallows (large and small ones), Toothpicks

Session 1 Content:

To begin, ask members to introduce themselves to the group, giving their names and adding which grade or team they belong to. You may want to model that for them: "I am Mrs. Efird, eighth grade counselor." Explain that the purpose of the group is to help them improve social skills (with high school in mind, for my group). Distribute copies of the outline and the schedule. Tell students about group rules, confidentiality, and other basic information such as how they will be reminded of the meetings and how to respectfully ask teachers for makeup work.

Show group members a copy of the brain diagram with these areas marked: frontal lobe, parietal lobe, temporal lobes, occipital lobe, and cerebellum. If you are artistic, draw it larger on the whiteboard. Explain in simple terms what each section is noted for. The frontal lobe is responsible for planning, organizing, problem solving, and emotions. The parietal lobe is associated with sensation such as touch, temperature, and pain. The two temporal lobes are responsible for distinguishing sounds and smells as well as short-term memory. The occipital lobe is connected with visual reception and distinction of colors and shapes. The cerebellum manages coordination, movement, and balance. This is too much information for them to be expected to learn, but they will most likely be fascinated with the topic. (One of my students knew far more about the subject than I did and wanted to elaborate on the various brain parts. However, if you think this material is too involved for your group, you could simply skip this whole paragraph—including the brain diagram—and discuss only the following paragraphs.)

Tell them the group is going to focus on differences in functioning of the left and right sides of the brain. Generally, the left side is associated with being more logical, analytical, and organized. The right side is linked with being more visual, intuitive, and creative. Give an example of both by providing directions to one's house. A left-brained person might say that you should drive one mile down Main Street heading west and then turn right onto Ninth Street, going to house number 1408. A right-brained person may state that you should drive downtown past the hardware store and then turn at the big cemetery, going to the house with the bay window on the shady side of the street. Tell them that certain brain differences have been found in persons having Asperger Syndrome, with areas that are overdeveloped in some regions and underdeveloped in others (McAlonan et al., 2002). It is known that many people with Asperger Syndrome exhibit certain cognitive strengths (Chiu & Hagerman, 2010). At this point, ask group members to share one thing they are especially good at, expecting answers leaning toward the logical and analytical side of the brain such as figuring out computer problems, putting together puzzles, and solving math equations. They may want to start lengthy monologues about their specialty subjects, which you will need to curb due to time considerations.

Then produce the head of cabbage on which you have labeled "left" and "right" with a felt tip marker (or you may want to label the five regions of the brain mentioned earlier). They will laugh at the idea of the cabbage being a brain, but a medium-sized cabbage head can approximate the actual size if you pull some of the outer leaves off. Set the bags of marshmallows and the toothpicks on the table. Show them the basket full of paper strips with various actions such as "developing an interest in robotics" or "making friends with someone." You will need to demonstrate this activity for them. Draw a slip from the basket and decide if the action stated is something that would typically be associated with the left side or the right side of the brain. Then decide if it would be something that would be highly developed or minimally developed in the brain of someone with Asperger Syndrome. If it is something that would often be well-developed, then pick up a big marshmallow. If it is an action that would likely be minimally developed, choose a small marshmallow. Take a toothpick and spear the strip of paper with it, topping it with the appropriate-size marshmallow, and push it into the cabbage brain on the proper side (left or right).

Take turns until a large portion (or all, if you have time) of the strips have been drawn. Allow them to decide for themselves if it is an activity which would be substantially or modestly developed in the brains of people with Asperger Syndrome. Expect diversity of opinion. Remind them that there are individual differences in everyone, regardless of diagnosis, and that we may be guilty of stereotyping a bit to make a point. They will have fun playing with the cabbage, and it will look pretty peculiar by the time you finish. (Using the marshmallows isn't absolutely necessary, as you could do the activity without distinguishing between what is minimally and what is significantly developed if you wanted.)

Remember that this may be their first exposure to some of the scientific evidence of brain differences in people with Asperger Syndrome. Examining the cabbage at the end of the activity should reinforce that those differences include strengths as well as weaknesses. Remind them that students having Asperger Syndrome can vary as much in personality and aptitude as students without, but it is important for them to recognize the special gifts that often come with the diagnosis.

Questions they should be able to answer: Do you have a specialty topic of your own? What are the specialty topics of others in the group? What is an example of an activity that would be associated with the left side of the brain? The right side? What are your thoughts on the brain differences found in those diagnosed with Asperger Syndrome?

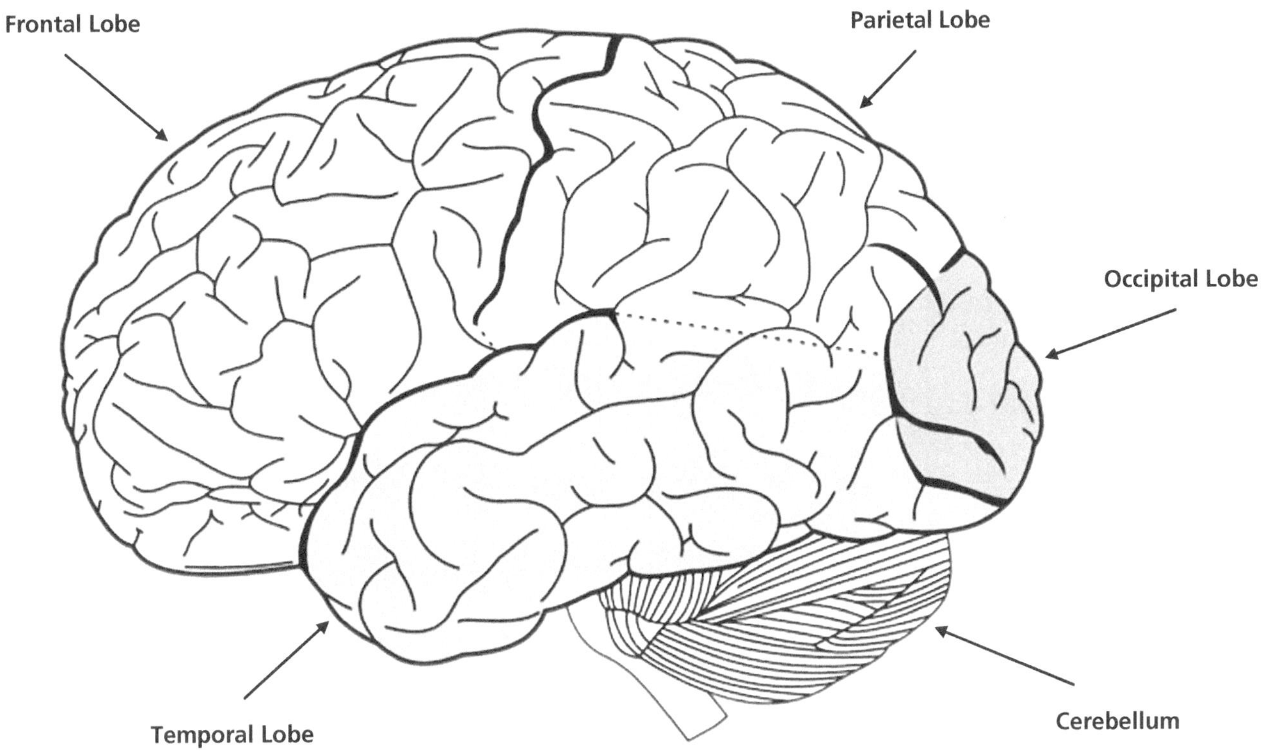
Frontal Lobe
Parietal Lobe
Occipital Lobe
Temporal Lobe
Cerebellum

Actions

Solving math equations

Understanding mathematical geometric figures

Memorizing dates of Civil War battles

Following a complicated cake recipe

Observing varying lines in a pattern

Creating a world of outer space aliens

Asking someone out on a date

Engaging in horseplay

Playing games with younger children

Maintaining a friendship over the years

Making friends with someone

Chitchatting at a party

Developing an interest in robotics

Eating with good manners

Hiding your feelings

Using profanity

Being a teacher's assistant

Talking with adults

Playing sports involving balls

Playing chess or board games

Dancing

Having the school day schedule changed around

Writing a story about another world

Stretching the truth

Learning the steps to a cheer

Learning the words to a song

Singing

Rejecting others who are not like me

Fending off bullies

Fighting

Obeying teachers

"Getting" a joke

Participating in a science experiment

Drawing

Asking a peer to go to the game with you

Session 2 Topic: Communication

Session 2 Supplies: For leader—Copies of Conversation Scenario Skits, Hula hoop

Session 2 Content:

At the second session you may want to remind them of group rules, confidentiality, and any other logistical concerns regarding the schedule.

Communication is all-important, and this is one area where students with Asperger Syndrome may particularly need help. Start with space considerations. Explain that moving too close to another individual can cause uneasiness. Demonstrate the proper distance between individuals engaged in conversation by dropping a hula hoop around each one (McCalley, 2010). (It would be fun if you had enough hula hoops for everyone so that they could go outdoors and try playing with them for a few minutes.) No one is likely to forget the image of keeping a hula hoop-distance away.

Next, talk about using eye contact rather than looking at the ceiling or somewhere else. It is wise to explain the difference in making eye contact and outright staring at someone, which could cause discomfort to others. Ask them to practice making eye contact within the group when talking and listening. Then discuss the importance of voice tone and word emphasis, giving the following example: *I* love you, I *love* you, I love *you*. Ask them how they interpret those three simple statements when a different word is emphasized. (Or maybe you'd be more comfortable and elicit fewer snickers if you used *You* are smart, You *are* smart, You are *smart*.) Voice tone may be a more difficult facet of communication for them to modify. Compare a statement using variation in voice tone with one that sounds flat. Encourage each to repeat the statement, trying voice variation.

The art of conversation begins at the beginning, of course. Demonstrate how to start a conversation by using simple scenarios such as those included in this session, or make up your own. One example involves inviting a classmate to eat lunch, and there are responses for both positive and negative results. Explain how to wait for a pause before interjecting your own comments, so that you are not interrupting. Give examples of casual conversation topics, such as shared classes, current events, recent holidays, school sports. Talk about how to look for signs that you have been talking too much, especially if you find yourself discussing your specialty topic. These could include the listener checking his watch, sighing loudly, attempting to change the subject, or just looking away from the speaker (Crow, 2011). At some point all conversations end. You may need to point at a clock and say, "Oh, it's almost time for class." To show that you have enjoyed the interaction, a short but optimistic closing statement is in order, such as "See you in civics tomorrow," or "Good luck on your biology test."

Questions they should be able to answer: What is the advantage in keeping a hula hoop-distance away from another person? What is the advantage of maintaining proper eye contact when talking and listening to someone? Could you distinguish the different meanings a statement took on when different words were emphasized? Could you determine the differences in the various scenarios of starting, maintaining, and ending conversations?

Conversation Scenarios Skits: Starting

1. Joseph is walking down the hall toward the cafeteria and notices a classmate beside him.

   Joseph: Hi. I think I've seen you in second period civics class.

   Ricardo: Yeah.

   Joseph: That teacher makes me laugh.

   Ricardo: It's my favorite class.

   Joseph: Hey, I'm going to go through the fast food line. Do you want to sit together?

   Ricardo: Sure. I usually try to sit over by the windows.

   Joseph: See you there.

2. Joseph is walking down the hall toward the cafeteria and notices a classmate beside him.

   Joseph: Hi. I think I've seen you in second period civics class.

   Ricardo: Oh, yeah?

   Joseph: That teacher makes me laugh.

   Ricardo: Hmmm.

   Joseph: Hey, I'm going to go through the fast food line. Do you want to sit together?

   Ricardo: Uh, I usually meet some friends at lunch.

   Joseph: Oh, okay. See you in class.

3. Kyle's biology teacher is often a few minutes late in starting class, and most students seize this opportunity to talk. He notices the boy sitting on his left usually reads during that time.

   Kyle: Looks like Mr. Jones is late again. I've noticed you use this time to read.

   David: (looks over at Kyle) I like this wizard series.

   Kyle: Oh, I've heard of those but haven't read them. Which one is that?

   David: The fifth.

   Kyle: I've got a book report coming up. Maybe I'll try one of those.

   David: The library has three copies.

4. Kyle's biology teacher is often a few minutes late in starting class, and most students seize this opportunity to talk. He notices the boy sitting on his left usually reads during that time.

   Kyle: Looks like Mr. Jones is late again. I've noticed you use this time to read.

   David: (keeps reading) Yeah.

   Kyle: Maybe I should try reading now, too. I've got a book report due soon.

   David: (keeps reading, makes no comment)

   Kyle: Oh, well. Sorry to bother you. He opens his biology notebook and resolves to try talking with the student on his right the next day.

Conversation Scenarios Skits: Maintaining

5. Joseph and Ricardo are talking at lunch, and Joseph picks up on a cue that he has dominated too much of the conversation.

   Joseph: And I really liked the way Mr. Crane explained the differences in our economy and England's. Who would have thought that using the euro created so much chaos?

   Ricardo: (looking out the window) Yeah, but I'm tired of talking about class.

   Joseph: Uh, yeah. Me, too. Have you seen the advertisements for the Cirque de Soleil show?

   Ricardo: Yeah, I'm trying to talk my parents into taking my brother and me.

   Joseph: Wow. I wonder if the trapeze acts are as cool as they look.

   Ricardo: I'll be sure to tell you if I go.

   Joseph: Great. I'd love to hear about it.

6. Joseph and Ricardo are talking at lunch, and Joseph realizes too late that he has monopolized the conversation.

   Joseph: And then I take the Apache version and convert it to the PDF format. That's the coolest part. First, you have to align the documents so that there are no…

   Ricardo: (looking out the window) Uh, you lost me a long time ago.

   Joseph: But it's so simple. You reboot, clear the memory, change the hard drive to…

   Ricardo: I see Carl over there. I need to ask him something. (rising to leave)

7. Kyle checks out one of the wizard books and brings it to class to read when time permits.

   Kyle: You were right about this author. He's fantastic.

   David: Wait until you read the next one.

   Kyle: Do you need to read them in order?

   David: Absolutely. They won't make much sense if you don't.

   Kyle: I'm at the part where the hamsters have morphed into monsters.

   David: Oh, that's a great chapter. But I won't spoil it for you.

   Kyle: Oops, here comes Mr. Jones. Guess we better stop talking.

8. Kyle checks out one of the wizard books and brings it to class to read when time permits.
   Kyle: You were right about this author. He's fantastic. But I found another good series.

   David: (looks up from book) Really?

   Kyle: Yeah, you should read them. I finished the first one last night. It ended with the clones transporting the planet to a new galaxy.

   David: Why did you tell me how it ended? Now I probably won't read it.

   Kyle: Oh, sorry. I wasn't thinking.

   David: I really don't want to talk right now. I only lack three pages to finish this book.

   Kyle: Okay. See you tomorrow.

Conversation Scenarios Skits: Ending

9. Joseph needs to leave lunch early to meet with his English teacher before class starts.

   Joseph: You are so lucky that you got to go see Cirque de Soleil. The way you described it would make anyone want to go.

   Ricardo: Yeah, but I'm not finished. I haven't told you the best part yet. When they darkened the stage and used a mist machine, everyone in the first few rows started screaming and ...

   Joseph: I'm sorry to interrupt, but I have to leave early today. I have an appointment with my English teacher before class starts.

   Ricardo: Oh, whatever.

   Joseph: (rising to leave) I do want to hear the rest of it. Tomorrow, maybe?

10. Kyle and David have been discussing the wizard series books.

    Kyle: I'm so glad you told me about these books. I've actually caught up with you.

    David: So you're waiting on the sixth one to come out, just like me?

    Kyle: Yeah. You know the bookstore is planning a big event that night.

    David: Wouldn't it be cool if we could go stand in line to buy one of the new copies?

    Kyle: I'll ask my mom to take us. Check with your parents tonight and let me know.

    David: That would be great.

    Kyle: Yeah. Why is it that lunch time always flies by so fast? See you tomorrow.

Session 3 Topic: Relationships

Session 3 Supplies: For students—Copies of Working on a Relationship quiz, Pencils; For leader — Life-size cardboard cut-out of girl, Hula hoop, Copies of Facing Rejection in Relationships skits

Session 3 Content:

This group session focuses on forming a close relationship of a girlfriend/boyfriend nature (though I mentioned in my group of eighth grade boys, as I perceived them old enough to consider such information, that some of the material would apply to same gender relationships as well). The desire to have a romantic relationship or to engage in dating is an all-important social phenomenon for nearly all adolescents, those with Asperger Syndrome included. Luke Jackson, a young author who has Asperger Syndrome, wrote that "AS and dating definitely do not mix" (2002, p. 174) in his autobiographical book describing his early adolescent years. Yet he devotes a chapter to relationship tips for those seeking romantic relationships. Developing a loving relationship with someone is often a more difficult task for students with Asperger Syndrome. Finding information to navigate these new waters is not as easy for these students as they are far less likely to obtain information from peers (Attwood, 2009).

To notch up the fun level in this session, I enlarged a photograph of my daughter (she still doesn't know this!) and glued it to a large piece of cardboard. Expect a lot of snickering and outright laughing about the cardboard member of the group. After introducing "her" to the group, hand out copies of the Working on a Relationship quiz. Complete it together, with each taking turns reading a question and the list of answers. They will laugh about the answer choices and find it fairly easy to select the best answers. The first question relates to finding the most likely appropriate lunch table topic when females are present. Another involves selecting the best way to get to know a member of the opposite sex, with the tricky "all of the above" answer being correct.

Then hand out copies of the Facing Rejection in Relationships skits, giving each a turn. This is where your cardboard cut-out girl takes a more active role in the group. Ask the group member playing the male role to address her, with the person playing the female role standing behind her to speak the part. Place the hula hoop around the girl and then around the boy to help them recall proper distances. The skits demonstrate ways to handle rejection in a positive, non-threatening manner. Though the comments of the girl in the skit sometimes trigger anger, the boys are given an assertive answer that does not promote aggression. It is important to point out that nearly all teenagers experience some anxiety when it comes to developing romantic relationships, and that most encounter rejection at some point.

You would be remiss if you ended this session without noting that some adolescents are simply not interested in forming a romantic relationship with another person. Particularly while still in middle school, many choose to keep relationships at the friendship level. Haley Moss, another young author who has Asperger Syndrome, advised not dating in middle school at all because it "could end up ruining a good, solid friendship" (2010, p. 113). And I find this good advice for anyone, Asperger or not!

Questions they should be able to answer: What is a proper distance to keep when speaking with someone in whom you have a romantic interest? What are some positive approaches to try in developing this relationship? What are some negative ones? How easy would it be for you to experience rejection from someone you sought as a romantic partner? Are you ready to pursue such a relationship?

Working on a Relationship

1. There are three girls at your table of eight, and you want to involve them in a conversation. You talk about:
   a. *Star Wars* vs. Star Trek.
   b. dog poop.
   c. NCAA basketball.
   d. how "hot" the student teacher looks.
2. You see a girl whom you want to dance with. She is not dancing with anyone in particular, just along with some other girls in the middle of the crowd. You:
   a. start dancing alongside her and smile.
   b. trip her so she can fall into your arms.
   c. tell her that one of your friends wants to dance with her.
   d. stand near her and stare.
3. You like a girl but she has made it clear that she doesn't like you. You:
   a. threaten to hurt her if she doesn't start to like you.
   b. move on to another girl and hope for better luck.
   c. start a rumor that she "does it" with everyone.
   d. stalk her every minute of the day in hopes she'll change her mind.
4. You want a girlfriend but don't know how to get started. You:
   a. join a club or team that has girls on it.
   b. select a girl who does not already have a boyfriend.
   c. practice a conversation in front of your mirror at home.
   d. try all of the above actions.

Facing Rejection in Relationships

Skit # 1

Boy: Hey, would you like to go out with me?

Girl: Get away from me—NOW!

Boy: You don't have to yell at me.

Girl: I'm sorry. But you're such a loser.

Boy: I don't consider myself a loser. I like who I am.

Girl: Fine, but leave me alone.

Boy: Sounds like a plan. Goodbye. (walks away)

Skit # 2

Boy: Hey, would you like to go out with me?

Girl: Is this some kind of joke?

Boy: No.

Girl: I don't go out with freaks.

Boy: I'm sorry that you see me that way. I guess I was wrong in thinking we might get together. (walks away)

Skit # 3

Boy: Hey, would you like to go out with me?

Girl: Uh, I' rather just be friends.

Boy: Okay. (smiles) We'll just be friends.

Session 4 Topic: Anger Management

Session 4 Supplies: For leader—List of Reactions to Anger or Conflict cut into strips, Basket, Service Dog (if possible)

Session 4 Content:

A session on dealing with anger is especially needed for members of an Asperger Syndrome group, as mounting frustrations may lead to unpleasant meltdowns, which further set them apart socially. These students need a supportive staff member who can help them by validating their feelings and listening with compassion (Attwood, 2007, p. 162). They need a designated safe spot for gaining control of anger outbursts, and the usual place will be the office of the counselor or nurse. Try to create a quiet, cozy space in your office area, perhaps in a darkened nook or corner, and show this place to your group members in advance. Some teachers may have offices attached to classrooms or partitioned carrel-type areas where they can direct a student who needs space to regroup.

Anger creeps into our lives even when we try very hard to not get our feathers ruffled. Though conflict cannot be eliminated from daily life, ways to manage it effectively can be taught and practiced. A discussion of passive, aggressive, and assertive communication will help students recognize how they currently respond to anger. First, definitions are in order:

- Passive—expressing very little of your true feelings; accommodating others to keep the peace.
- Aggressive—expressing your opinions/emotions in a harsh or overwhelming way with little or no regard for others.
- Assertive—expressing yourself honestly by standing up for your rights in a way that does not hurt others.

Then write the words passive, aggressive, and assertive on the whiteboard. Pass the basket with the Reactions to Anger strips and ask each student to draw one and decide under which type of communication it falls: passive, aggressive, or assertive. (Or if you prefer, you could just call out the various Reactions to Anger and allow all to answer together.) For example, ignoring someone calling you a bad name comes under passive. Some reactions may seem to fall under two definitions, or there may be differences in opinion about them. Talk about the pros and cons of each of the reactions. Emphasize the benefit of assertive communication: standing up for yourself and getting your point across without resorting to violence or folding to passivity.

After that discussion, ask the group about their methods of cooling down from anger. They may share unique ways to bring down their rage. Add other methods until you have a good list: counting to fifty, deep breathing, listening to music, pacing, taking a walk, playing a video game, spending time with specialty subject, petting your dog or cat, talking to an understanding person (parent or counselor recommended).

Then, if you are lucky enough to procure a visit from a service dog and handler, let the students interact with the four-legged visitor. The handler may want to give a spiel about the benefits of pet therapy, or you may want to gather some information on your own to present. I told them that sometimes petting a dog can help calm a person and reduce the sadness that may set in after an anger outburst. Children usually enjoy interaction with service animals, which provide a safe, nonjudgmental practice field for working on social skills they can later transfer to people (Shallcross, 2011). In my group, all of the boys owned a dog and were comfortable petting the strange one. They shared their dogs' names and what they liked to do with their dogs (toss balls and Frisbees, run and take walks, and simply talk to them). After the group session, I allowed them the opportunity to go wash their hands before returning to class.

Questions they should be able to answer: Do you know where you can go at school when you feel a temper tantrum or meltdown coming on? What are the definitions of passive, aggressive, and assertive communication? Can you give an example of at least one reaction to conflict that falls under each definition? What are some cooling off methods? Which cooling off method usually works best for you? What did you like (or dislike) about the visit from the service dog?

Reactions to Anger or Conflict

Throwing a temper tantrum

Giving in so there is peace

Arguing loudly with someone

Admitting differences in opinion

Ignoring someone calling me a name

Hitting someone

Listening to other person's point of view

Changing the subject

Saying I am at fault when I do not believe I am

Pouting instead of talking about it

Being open to compromise

Session 5 Topic: Responding to Scenarios

Session 5 Supplies: For students—Copies of Response Scenarios; For leader—Seashells

Session 5 Content:

In this session, group members will experience awareness of how others may perceive certain actions of students diagnosed with Asperger Syndrome. Read each of the Response Scenarios, exploring the pros and cons of what the student in each scenario has done. Ask them to try to imagine how the general population would react to such situations. For example: Tina goes through the day saying as few words as she can. It's a contest for her—she counts the words—and her goal is zero. Ask for their thoughts on how others may respond to her actions. What do they think Tina stands to gain or lose from her behavior? It may be difficult for teens with Asperger Syndrome to recognize how their behavior affects or is perceived by others (Asperger-Advice.com, 2007). Discussing the scenarios may trigger self-recognition in some cases.

Following this activity, focus on the individual uniqueness of the group members. Start your discussion by asking them to name one-of-a-kind things (snowflakes, signatures, fingerprints, DNA, etc.). Hand each of them a seashell and have them examine its shape, shade, markings, etc. Then take them all up in a bag and scatter them on the floor, telling them to find their own seashell. (Since my group was small, I added myself into the mix, plus a few extra shells so it wouldn't be too easy.) They were able to quickly find the correct ones and were eager to explain how they did so.

Then shift discussion to how unique they are as individuals with Asperger Syndrome. Though they share some things with others—same grade, same lunchtime, same books, same wish that summer were here—they have some differences, as they know, that set them apart. Share these encouraging, self-affirming points:

- Recognize that you can do things few others can, using your own style and your own approach (for example: build a robot, write computer code, create a story about an alternate universe).
- Appreciate that you have special gifts of memorization and thinking "outside the box."
- Respect yourself and value your insight.
- Adopt ways to be more accepted by others without losing your distinctive gifts.

A pledge for people with Asperger Syndrome written by Liane Holliday Willey includes such positive-focused points as "I am not defective. I am different," as well as "I am a person who is worthy of others' respect and acceptance," and "I will accept myself for who I am" (Attwood, 2007, p. 31). Ask the group members to respond to those statements, telling how they feel about each one.

Questions they should be able to answer: How difficult was it to recognize the negative consequences of certain behaviors in the scenarios? What is something that makes you unique? What are some of the strong points that are typical of students who have Asperger Syndrome? Which of the pledge statements would you like to develop as a personal motto?

Response Scenarios

How do you think others may respond to the following actions of students diagnosed with Asperger Syndrome?

1. Raymond receives an A on his English paper. He proceeds to say to every student he encounters, "I got an A! I got an A!"
2. Jeremy loves green beans. He loves them so much he wants to pick them up with his hands and cram them into his mouth.
3. Stuart wants Melissa to be his girlfriend so he touches her hair whenever he sees her, even though she tells him to stop bothering her.
4. Tina goes through the day saying as few words as she can. It's a contest for her—she counts the words—and her goal is zero.
5. Leo draws fabulous detailed diagrams of buildings. He loves this so much he slips out his drawing tablet many times during classes to work on them.
6. Jason draws pictures with themes of violence: guns, grenades, and bloody battle scenes. Then he shows them to the people sitting near him.
7. Blake does not make eye contact when he interacts with people. He stares up at the ceiling when they try to talk to him.
8. Ramona hates the idea of wasting water. So she skips showers, won't wash her hands before meals, and yells if she sees someone watering plants.
9. Sergio makes faces at every student he encounters as he walks down the hall. It's a game he plays to see how many will react to him.

Session 6 Topic: Coping Game/Summary

Session 6 Supplies: For leader—Leader's complete folder (for review), Copy of Coping Game cut into small (1" × 3") pieces, 10 large (at least 11" × 14") sheets of construction paper, Basket

Session 6 Content:

A brief review of prior sessions is a fitting way to end your sessions. Ask what they remember about brain differences in people with Asperger Syndrome, and see if they can name a couple of left-brained and right-brained activities. Question them about tips for communication and/or for forming romantic relationships. Quiz them on passive, aggressive, and assertive responses to anger. Remind them of the service dog's visit. Ask if they enjoyed talking through the various dilemmas and scenarios that were covered in class.

Students tend to expect the final session of a group to be a party. Though I disagree with that concept, I do realize that all adolescents need a little fun in their lives, and it is appropriate to experience closure in a positive, affirming mood. Playing the Coping Game allows them to have a good time while learning that all behaviors have consequences.

The game is most enjoyable when weather permits playing outside. Set the ten sheets of construction paper one beside another to form a line or a U-shape. Put the small strips of paper describing coping scenarios in the basket. Then decide who's going first and ask that student to draw a strip of paper from the basket. The student must read aloud the statement and take the appropriate step(s). For example: Carl yelled at the teacher when she came up behind him and tapped him on the shoulder. Go back 1 space. Another example: Edwin asked a friend to go to the game. The friend said he couldn't. Edwin said, "That's okay." Go forward 2 spaces. Free space means that the student moves forward a step: it's a freebie. If the student draws one which states he must go back a space and he hasn't made it onto the construction paper yet, then he just remains behind the starting line until his next turn when hopefully he'll be able to advance. At times there may be multiple students standing on one sheet: cooperative group behavior must prevail.

If the basket is empty before anyone has reached the tenth step or finish line, then recycle them. They will want to continue the game even if they must hear the statements a second time. In the course of the game, stop and reflect each time on why that was a positive or negative coping reaction. Also, at the end, it may be helpful to talk about winning and losing without boasting and whining.

As a final goodbye to the group, you should reassure them that you are available to see them individually as needed for the rest of the school year.

Questions they should be able to answer: What do you remember about each group session? What are some of the obstacles a student with Asperger Syndrome faces and how can they be overcome? How did playing the game make you more aware of how your behavior affects both you and others? What have you learned about other group members?

Coping Game

Carl yelled at the teacher when she came up behind him and tapped him on the shoulder. Go back 1 space.	Edwin asked a friend to go to the game. The friend said he couldn't. Edwin said "That's okay." Go forward 2 spaces.
Jared sat down at lunch. Another kid said, "You can't sit there, stupid." Jared said, "There are no reserved seats In here. This is my seat for now." Go forward 2 spaces.	Mario had just started to do his homework sitting out on the deck, but it began to rain. He cursed. Go back 1 space.
Carl made a B on his paper. He thought he'd make an A. He started to complain to the teacher but decided not to. Go forward 1 space.	Edwin had a large pile of grapes at lunch. He didn't really want to share but he offered some to a kid anyway. Go forward 1 space.
Jared practiced soccer for weeks, hoping to make the team. When he saw the list without his name, he stormed down the hall, got a drink of water and cooled down. Then he went to class. Go forward 1 space.	Mario was reading his novel when he was supposed to be listening to the teacher. She took it away. He kept quiet, taking a few deep breaths to calm down. Go forward 1 space.
Carl heard two kids making fun of him for chewing with his mouth open. He laughed and said, "Sorry – didn't realize I was being gross." Go forward 1 space.	Edwin dreaded his turn to read aloud in class so he practiced in front of his mirror at home to get better at it. In class he messed up on one word. He ran outside when kids laughed. Go back 1 space.
Jared asked a girl out. She said yes. He kissed her right then and there in the cafeteria. She ran away, crying. Go back 1 space.	Mario noticed a new kid in his class. He started a conversation and led him through the lunch line. Go forward 2 spaces.

Carl asked a girl out. She said no. He said, "All right, I'm okay with just being friends." Go forward 2 spaces.	Edwin saw two boys making fun of two disabled students in the gym. He said, "You guys need to stop." Go forward 2 spaces.
Jared won the geography bee. Someone told him only nerds entered the contest. He said, "You can think what you want, but I am proud that I won." Go forward 2 spaces.	Mario made all A's on his report card. The teacher asked him to help tutor another kid in math. He felt shy about it but agreed to. Go forward 2 spaces.
Carl asked his teacher 8 or 9 questions about the English paper they had to write. She said he needed to be quiet in class. He wadded up his paper and pouted. Go back 2 spaces.	Edwin threw up in class, and a few kids laughed. He cried a little in the restroom and then returned. When a kid called him "Stinky Breath," he smiled and said, "You're right." Go forward 2 spaces.
Jared drew a fantastic poster for science class. The teacher hung it on the wall, and someone marked on it. Jacob screamed and went into a temper tantrum. Go back 2 spaces.	Mario built a robot for the science fair. He complained to the judge when he won second place instead of first. Go back 1 space.
Carl loves to bake cakes. Someone told him that was "gay." He replied, "Well, I guess you won't be coming to my café when I grow up." Go forward 1 space.	Edwin realized his math teacher had made a mistake on the board. He told her she was stupid Go back 2 spaces.
Jared brought gum to school and a kid said, "I'll be your friend if you give me some." Jared said, "Sorry, I've already promised to share with someone else." Go forward 1 space.	Mario saw a student he didn't like drop $10 on the floor. He picked it up and handed it to him. Go forward 2 spaces.

1 free space	1 free space
1 free space	1 free space
1 free space	1 free space
1 free space	1 free space
1 free space	1 free space
1 free space	1 free space
1 free space	1 free space
1 free space	1 free space

Evaluation of Asperger Boys Club (ABC) Group

Rate yourself by circling the number which corresponds with how you evaluate each statement.
1 = Not at all, 2 = A small amount, 3 = Average amount, 4 = More than average, 5 = Very much

1. I felt comfortable discussing having Asperger Syndrome in the group.

   1..................2..................3..................4..................5

2. I learned about brain differences in persons with Asperger Syndrome.

   1..................2..................3..................4..................5

3. I recognized some special strengths that I have as a person with Asperger Syndrome.

   1..................2..................3..................4..................5

4. I practiced communication skills emphasized in the group.

   1..................2..................3..................4..................5

5. I learned strategies for forming friendship and romantic relationships.

   1..................2..................3..................4..................5

6. I learned to classify responses to anger and conflict as passive, aggressive, or assertive.

   1..................2..................3..................4..................5

7. I became more aware of how the general population may respond to my actions.

   1..................2..................3..................4..................5

8. I grew closer to group members during the course of the group.

   1..................2..................3..................4..................5

Suggestions for making the group better: ____

____

References

Asperger-Advice.com. (2007). *Asperger teens and friendships*. Retrieved March 20, 2011, from http://www.asperger-advice.com/asperger-teens-friendship.html

Attwood, T. (2007). *The complete guide to Asperger's Syndrome*. London: Jessica Kingsley Publishers.

Attwood, T. (2009, February 20). Romantic relationships for young adults with Asperger's Syndrome and high-functioning Autism. *Interactive Autism network community*. Retrieved March 14, 2011, from http://www.iancommunity.org/cs/articles/relationships

Chiu, S. & Hagerman, R. (2010, April 12). Pervasive developmental disorder. *EMedicine from WebMD*. Retrieved March 12, 2011, from http://emedicine.medscape.com/article/914683-overview#aw2aab6b2b2aa

Crow, K. (2011). Parenting special needs: Ten rules of conversation for Asperger teens. *Families.com*. Retrieved March 14, 2011, from http://special-needs.families.com/blog/ten-rules-of-conversation-for-asperger-teens

Gabbert, C. (2009, April 9). Social support for teens with Aspergers. *Bright hub*. Retrieved August 27, 2011, from http://www.brighthub.com/education/special/articles/31543.aspx

Jackson, L. (2002). *Freaks, geeks & Asperger Syndrome*. London: Jessica Kingsley Publishers.

McAlonan, G., Daly, E., Kumari, V., Critchley, H., van Amelsvoort, T., Suckling, J., et al. (2002). Brain anatomy and sensorimotor gating in Asperger's Syndrome. *Brain: A Journal of Neurology Oxford Journals*, 125, 1594–1606. Retrieved March 12, 2011, from http://brain.oxfordjournals.org/content/125/7/1594.full

McCalley, C. (2010, September/October). Fix six social deficits. *ASCA School Counselor*, *48*(1), 23–25.

McCulloch, C. (2010, December 9). Teaching feelings to Autistic children. *Bright Hub: The Hub for Bright Minds*. Retrieved March 8, 2011, from http://www.brighthub.com/education/special/articles/97040.aspx

Moss, H. (2010). *Middle school: The stuff nobody tells you about*. Shawnee Mission, KS: Autism Asperger Publishing Company.

National Autistic Society. (2011, February 25). *What is Asperger Syndrome?* Retrieved March 8, 2011, from http://www.autism.org.uk/about-autism/autism-and-asperger-syndrome-an-introduction/what-is-asperger-syndrome.aspx

National Institute of Neurological Disorders and Stroke. (2011, February 16). *Asperger Syndrome fact sheet*. Retrieved March 8, 2011, from http://www.ninds.nih.gov/disorders/asperger/detail_asperger.htm

Shallcross, L. (2011, August). Counselor's best friend. *Counseling Today*, *54*(2), 38–41.

Chapter 4

Divorce: Stuck In the Middle[1]

Divorce: Stuck In the Middle Group Outline

I. Introductory Information, Charts
   A. Outline, Schedule, Parent Permission, Rules
   B. Family Status Chart
   C. Feelings Chart
II. Facing Special Pitfalls of Children of Divorce
   A. Problems Unique to Children of Divorce
   B. If Divorce Were a Monster Drawings
III. Being Stuck In the Middle—Skits
   A. Responses That Don't Work: Passive and Aggressive
   B. Responses That Do Work: Assertive
IV. Five Controversial Points of Divorce
V. Looking for Positive and Negatives
   A. What Bugs Ya? Form
   B. What's Cool? Form
VI. Review, Sentence Completion Activity
   A. Review of Prior Sessions
   B. Divorce Sentence Completion Statements Activity

1 Parts of this chapter first appeared in *Counseling Today*, December 2006. Reprinted with permission from American Counseling Association.

American School Counselor Association (ASCA) Standards

Personal/Social Development

Standard A: Students will acquire the knowledge, attitudes, and interpersonal skills to help them understand and respect self and others.

PS:A1 Acquire Self-knowledge

PS:A1.5 Identify and express feelings

PS:A1.12 Identify and recognize changing family roles

PS:A2 Acquire Interpersonal Skills

PS:A2.5 Recognize and respect differences in various family configurations

PS:A2.6 Use effective communication skills

Standard B: Students will make decisions, set goals and take necessary action to achieve goals.

PS:B1 Self-knowledge Application

PS:B1.3 Identify alternative solutions to a problem

PS:B1.4 Develop effective coping skills for dealing with problems

Rationale for Stuck in the Middle Divorce Group

It is safe to say that every school has students who have experienced a divorce or are currently in the middle of that event. Divorce is commonly believed to affect approximately 50% of all marriages in the United States (Divorce.com, 2011). While some children exhibit minimal problems with divorce situations, others have a definite need for intervention.

Dr. Robert Hughes, a professor at Ohio State University who has studied single parenting for twenty years, confirms some of the problems of children of divorce: poorer scores on standardized tests, aggressive behavior, depression, and low self-esteem. Even more alarming, adolescents from divorced homes are more inclined to become involved with drug abuse, sexual activity, and other seriously problematic behaviors such as delinquency and dropping out (At Health Mental Health, 2011). A study done at the University of Arizona indicated that children who experienced divorce counseling after a divorce were less apt to engage in those risky behaviors later as teens (Deal with divorce, 2011).

Students troubled by divorce may be too upset to focus on academics and healthy peer/family relationships. For those, group counseling can be helpful in developing coping skills. The group connects them to a supportive circle of friends with whom they can share their feelings. They learn that, though their new family configurations have many challenges, they can work on adapting to them.

Students signing up for my group are instructed that it is designed for those who are experiencing difficulty with a divorce situation. Each week they pinpoint on a chart their current feelings about their family and share that information with others. They are provided opportunities to practice assertive communication with their parents. They have the chance to express built-up anger and hurt through art, skits, and other activities. After venting, they are directed to a more positive focus. Often another member of the group debunks the myth of the horrid stepparent or puts an affirmative spin on having extra parents around to come to band concerts or transport them to soccer practice. Some share their pleasure in having two birthday celebrations—these *are* kids, after all—and about no longer witnessing fights between parents. Clearly, there is not a school in the nation that could not benefit from offering its students a divorce group!

What Makes It Work

1. Students in divorce/separation predicaments need a venting place for anger. Other feelings emerge, too, such as fear and sadness, but anger carries the most momentum with adolescents.
2. Students with heavy crises going on are not focused in class anyway; missing class to learn coping skills may ultimately improve their academic status.
3. Activities are simple yet they have a desired impact. Divorce groups tend to run by themselves—they don't need much of an agenda.
4. Students link quickly with one another, and having someone in the group who is an outsider/misfit rarely matters to them.
5. Students gain valuable skills in communicating with family members and accepting their situations.

Challenges

1. The biggest problem is the occasional parent who demands to know from you what went on in group. Encourage kids to share topics with their parents, but remind them not to name other kids in the group or quote anyone. If they approach you, give parents the "group is confidential" spiel and tell them they are welcome to a group outline. Assure them that even though students are allowed to "mouth off" or vent, there is a push for a positive resolution/explanation of various issues.
2. Sometimes the passion level of a group member's anger is so strong that profanity emerges. Don't punish for such but don't encourage it either.
3. Occasionally a student will bring up abusive situations at home, spilling more details than you want the other students to hear. Intervene by asking the student to hold that information and see you privately after group.
4. Once in a while, a student's custody situation changes mid-stream and the child must move away. It is difficult for the other group members to accept that someone has moved, and it underlines the instability affecting their lives.
5. Sometimes you will discover that the need for outside counseling for certain students is very strong, yet many families will refuse to seek additional help. You will have to come to grips with this situation and give what you can of yourself to these needy kids.
6. They like to waste star stickers, putting them on their faces and wherever. You'd think it was kindergarten. Cut your sheet of stars so that you only pass out to them exactly the right number.

Stuck in the Middle Group Sessions

Session 1 Topic: Introductory Information, Family Status, Expressing Feelings

Session 1 Supplies: For students—Copies of outline, schedule, and parent permission form; Star stickers; For leader—Family Status Chart, Feelings Chart

Session 1 Content:

To begin, explain general group information: outline, schedule, parent permission forms, and group rules. In particular, confidentiality must be emphasized, as many family matters need to be kept private.

Then show group members the Family Status Chart (on which you have already listed their names in a column), and explain that it is divided into three sections: separated, divorced, and divorced plus (which means there have been multiple divorces). Each of those three sections has a column for living with father, mother, or other. The students are to indicate with a star sticker their living arrangement. If a student's parents share equal physical custody, meaning the student lives one week here and one week there, then place the star on the line straddling the mother and father column. (I direct students whose parents were never officially married to the separated column.) Ask students to position their stars in the appropriate spot, and to share with the group their family status and how long their parents have been divorced/separated.

Then explain the Feelings Chart, which includes these descriptive words: angry, happy, sad, confused, frustrated, hurt, and so-so. You will probably have to define "so-so." Explain to the group that each session will start with completion of the Feelings Chart. As they arrive at group, they are to find their names and place a star in the column of the word that best describes how they are feeling about their families that day. Their feelings about failing math tests or friends turned traitors do not apply—they must relate only feelings pertaining to their family situation. Often they will want to select more than one, but I require them to indicate only one overriding feeling.

Then pass around the Feelings Chart and star stickers, having them place their stars one by one to identify a specific feeling. Ask them to share why they selected that feeling. They may elaborate excessively and you may run out of time without hearing from everyone. Pace the session, reminding them to be concise as needed.

Questions they should be able to answer: What are the topics that will be covered in group? How does the schedule work? What are the group rules? Why is confidentiality important? When is the parent permission form due? What are some of the different family configurations present in the group? What were some of the feelings expressed on the Feelings Chart? What did you learn about each other in the introductory session?

Table 4.1 Family Status Chart

Student Names	*Separated*			*Divorced*			*Divorced Plus*		
	Lives with Mom	*Lives with Dad*	*Lives with Other*	*Lives with Mom*	*Lives with Dad*	*Lives with Other*	*Lives with Mom*	*Lives with Dad*	*Lives with Other*

Table 4.2 Feelings Chart

Student Names	*Angry*	*Happy*	*Sad*	*Confused*	*Frustrated*	*Hurt*	*So-So*

Session 2 Topic: Special Problems of Children of Divorce

Session 2 Supplies: For students—Star stickers, Construction paper, Pencils; For leader—Feelings Chart, Whiteboard, Marker

Session 2 Content:

At the second session, and at all ensuing sessions, begin with the Feelings Chart. Cut this off after ten minutes or group members may stay on this topic the whole session, and you have so much to cover! Ask them to generate specific problems of children from divorced families—not problems affecting students in general. Write these on the whiteboard or allow them to take turns writing. You will hear about problems of this nature: custody fights, child support issues, visitation rules, split vacations, financial need, conflicting rules, and biased treatment of step-siblings. They will want to talk volumes about these things.

Then move to the art activity: drawings depicting “If Divorce Were a Monster.” With anger being a primary feeling at some point in the divorce experience, it is helpful to use art as an expressive outlet (Ferenc, 2011). Tell the students to imagine what divorce would look like if it were a monster, and they will come up with fire-breathing horned ogres stretching children in two or malevolent thunderstorms with jagged lightning and swirling tornadoes. Show them a sample if you feel so inclined, but encourage creativity (no copycats). As they are drawing, encourage them to continue to talk about the issues on the whiteboard. As they finish their pictures, ask them to describe them. Remind them that art is an effective way to express feelings. You may want to suggest that they leave off their names so that you can post the pictures on your office walls.

Questions they should be able to answer: What are some problems children of divorce experience that other students do not? How many of the problems that were mentioned affect you? How does your picture describe divorce? Was it easy for you to depict divorce as a monster?

Session 3 Topic: Stuck in the Middle—Skits

Session 3 Supplies: For students—Star stickers, Copies of Passive, Aggressive, and Assertive Worksheet, Pencils; For leader—Feelings Chart, Copies of the Skits with Passive, Aggressive, and Assertive Responses

Session 3 Content:

After completing the Feelings Chart, explain the terms passive, aggressive, and assertive. You may want to use the definitions below, and then give an example or two of how each type of response can relate to a divorce situation:

- Passive—expressing very little of your true feelings; accommodating others to keep the peace.
- Aggressive—expressing your opinions/emotions in a harsh or overwhelming way with little or no regard for others.
- Assertive—expressing yourself honestly by standing up for your rights in a way that does not hurt others.

Then move to the Skits with Passive, Aggressive, and Assertive Responses. Give copies of a skit to two students who'll play those parts. Give the next skit parts to two other students. They'll think for a moment that you are repeating the skit, but tell them to note the big differences in the child's responses. These skits represent many conflicts that will sound familiar to children of divorce, such as having one parent grill them about the other's new boyfriend or having a parent send unpleasant messages to the other through them. Let them take turns playing the role of parent or step-parent—they love that. Expect some snickering and some pure joy as they shout the aggressive answers. This is truly a venting exercise! Ask them to decide after each skit if the response was passive, aggressive, or assertive. Point out that the assertive manner is going to win them the most satisfaction in the long run.

To be sure they understand, you may want to include the Passive, Aggressive, and Assertive Worksheet activity. Ask them to write their own responses to the two scenarios. Then ask them to share what they have written. Lastly, encourage them to practice being assertive during the next week, not just with their parents but also with their siblings or friends.

Questions they should be able to answer: What is the difference in passive, aggressive, and assertive responses? Have you experienced any of the situations covered by the skits? Can you give a personal example of a situation in which you used one of these responses? Was it easy for you to complete the worksheet?

Skits with Passive, Aggressive, and Assertive Responses

Scenario One

Mom: Your father didn't pay his child support payment again this month. He has probably been out drinking every night. I wonder if he has any idea how much it costs to keep shoes on your feet. If he would just give up a few six-packs a month, it would help.

Melissa: Quit bad-mouthing my father! He may drink too much but at least he doesn't constantly remind me of how much money I cost.

or

Mom: Your father didn't pay his child support payment again this month. He has probably been out drinking every night. I wonder if he has any idea how much it costs to keep shoes on your feet. If he would just give up a few six-packs a month, it would help.

Melissa: I feel hurt when you say those things about Daddy, especially if it's about missing child support checks. I would honestly rather not know. Could you please not share that information with me?

Scenario Two

Dad: Tell your mother she can forget about me keeping you in March when she has that business trip. I'm not changing the schedule because she wouldn't let me have you at Christmas. Tell her I said she will rot in you-know-where before I do her any favors.

Ricardo: Dad, I know you two don't like to talk to each other, but I feel really tense sometimes when you ask me to be the go-between. Can you help me out here?

or

Dad: Tell your mother she can forget about me keeping you in March when she has that business trip. I'm not changing the schedule because she wouldn't let me have you at Christmas. Tell her I said she will rot in you-know-where before I do her any favors.

Ricardo: Okay, I guess I'll tell her. But she isn't going to like it.

Scenario Three

Mom: I want you to ask your father when he's going to start picking you up on time when it's his weekend. I'm sick and tired of us sitting around waiting for him to show up. You ask him when he gets here. I can't talk to the jerk.

Chris: Mom, I really don't want to ask Dad about that. I'm afraid he'll get upset. It would be so much better for me if you would call him or write him a note.

or

Mom: I want you to ask your father when he's going to start picking you up on time when it's his weekend. I'm sick and tired of us sitting around waiting for him to show up. You ask him when he gets here. I can't talk to the jerk.

Chris: I'm sick and tired of you making such a big deal out of him being late. How did I end up with such losers for parents?

Scenario Four

Dad: Tell me about your mother's new boyfriend. What sort of job does he have? What kind of car does he drive? Is he there in the mornings when you wake up?

Allen: Why don't you mind your own business?

or

Dad: Tell me about your mother's new boyfriend. What sort of job does he have? What kind of car does he drive? Is he there in the mornings when you wake up?

Allen: Dad, it makes me feel uncomfortable when you ask me questions about Mom's new boyfriend. I would appreciate it if you could talk directly with her about stuff you want to know. Please try to leave me out of it.

Passive, Aggressive, and Assertive Worksheet

Write responses to the following statements in the appropriate spaces:

1. Mom: I can't believe how bad your report card is. If you don't improve your grades soon, I am going to send you to live with your dad! I don't care how mean your stepmother treats you.

   Passive:

   Aggressive:

   Assertive:

2. Stepdad: I'd play basketball with you but you have such a bad attitude. You obviously got it from your dad. I don't see what your mother saw in him in the first place.

   Passive:

   Aggressive:

   Assertive:

Session 4 Topic: Five Controversial Points of Divorce

Session 4 Supplies: For students—Star stickers, Copies of Five Controversial Points of Divorce; For leader—Feelings Chart

Session 4 Content:

Following completion of the Feelings Chart, be ready for a lively discussion of the Five Controversial Points of Divorce. First, reinforce that differences in opinion are welcome and all responses will be respected. Then ask a volunteer to read each statement, pausing for that student to either defend or oppose the statement. Encourage them to elaborate. You will hear about those who feel like slaves because their dads leave dirty dishes all week for them to clean when it is their weekend to be with him. You will learn there are step-mothers who do not allow them to put their feet on the sofa even though their step-siblings do it all the time. You will hear them say they wish their mothers would not confide in them as friends because it is just too much information for them to handle. The statement about parents staying together for the sake of the children usually brings about the most heated discussion. You can count on everyone wanting to weigh in, ensuring a full session of intensive talk.

Questions they should be able to answer: What is the meaning of controversy? What are some controversial points associated with divorce? Was there a statement that you strongly defended? Was there a statement that you strongly opposed? Were there differences in opinion on every statement?

Five Controversial Points of Divorce

Think about the following statements and decide how you would either defend or oppose them:

1. If I try really hard to be a perfect kid, my parents will get back together.

2. Parents who do not love each other should stay together for the sake of the children.

3. The parent that I visit should not have rules or make me do work.

4. My step-parent has no right to discipline me.

5. I should try to make up for the parent who left by being an emotional support to the parent I am living with.

Five Controversial Points of Divorce

Think about the following statements and decide how you would either defend or oppose them:

1. If I try really hard to be a perfect kid, my parents will get back together.

2. Parents who do not love each other should stay together for the sake of the children.

3. The parent that I visit should not have rules or make me do work.

4. My step-parent has no right to discipline me.

5. I should try to make up for the parent who left by being an emotional support to the parent I am living with.

Session 5 Topic: Negatives and Positives about Current Living Situation

Session 5 Supplies: For students—Star stickers, Pencils, Colored pencils, Copies of What Bugs Ya? and What's Cool? worksheets; For leader—Feelings Chart

Session 5 Content:

Start with completing the Feelings Chart, as usual. Then hand out pencils and the What Bugs Ya? worksheet. Ask group members to list things about their families that they dislike on the ladybug lines. Most can think of negative items with no problem. After sharing information and discussion, hand out the What's Cool? worksheet. Some will struggle to fill even a couple of lines on the butterfly. If their family situation involves two households, they may choose to write what's good about each one on separate sides of the butterfly. Again, ask them to share info. This usually helps them think of more positives, though they are often superficial things like two holiday celebrations or four possible rides to baseball practice. Help them see that even though the positives may be small, they do exist. (If you have colored pencils available, some students like to color these sheets. Coloring is a soothing activity that I believe no one ever really grows out of!) You may want to ask them to omit signing their names on these pictures so that you can post them in your office, along with the monster pictures.

Questions they should be able to answer: What were some of the things about your family situation that you listed as negative? Was it harder to think of things to list that are positive? How were responses different among the group members?

WHAT BUGS YA?

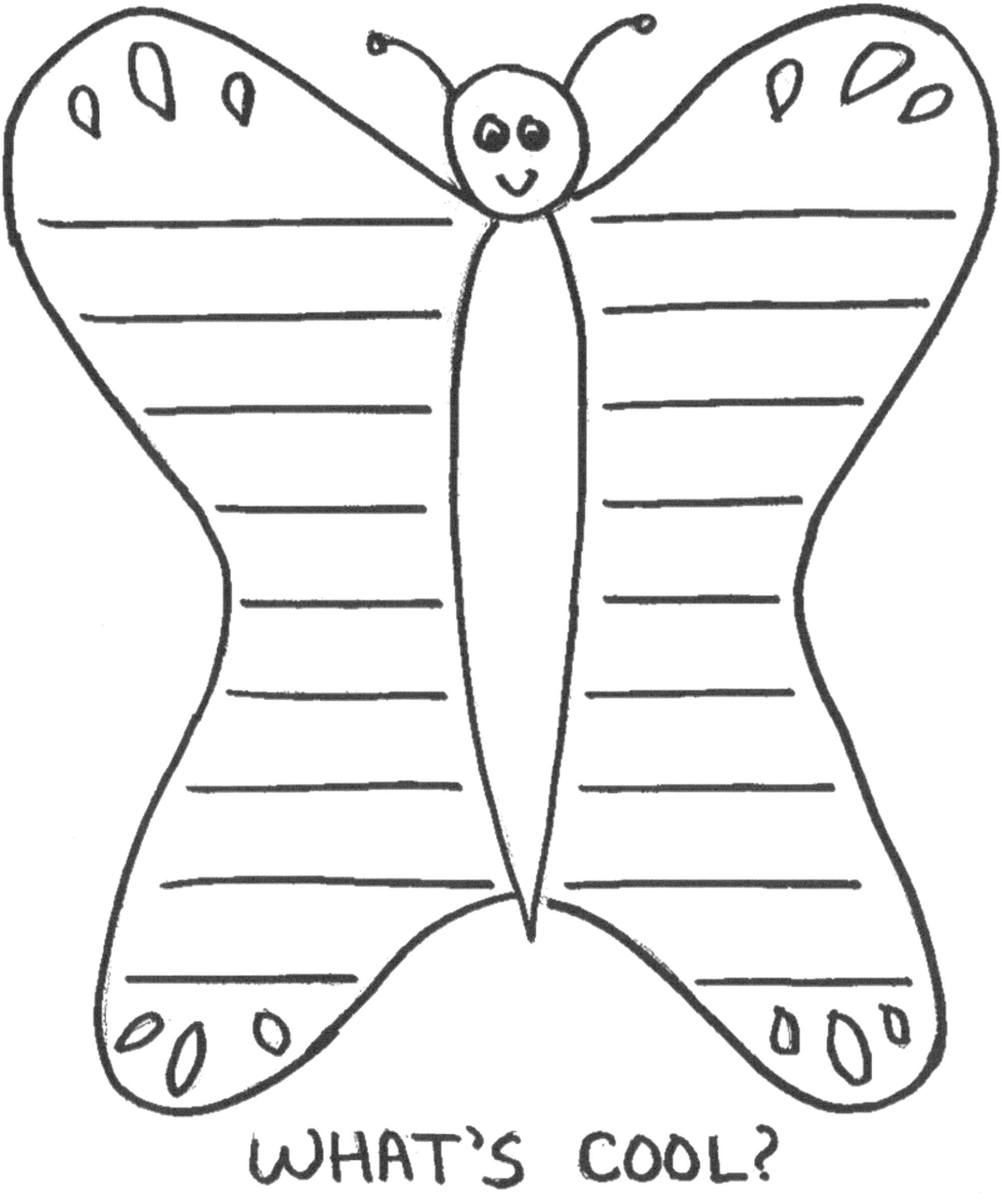
WHAT'S COOL?

Session 6 Topic: Review/Sentence Completion Activity

Session 6 Supplies: For students—Star stickers; For leader—Feelings Chart, Leader's complete folder (for review), Divorce Sentence Completion Statements cut into strips, Basket

Session 6 Content:

After a final completion of the Feelings Chart, review previous sessions. Start at the beginning and ask what they can remember from each session. Emphasize the importance of the session that focused on using assertive language with their parents when "stuck in the middle," and ask if any have put this into practice. Also, it is important to draw the group to a close with members feeling empowered rather than victimized by their family situation. Survivors they are, and will continue to be. Some researchers have found that as many as 75% of children of divorce weathered the storm fine and were able to grow into adults who found personal happiness and career success (Balber, n.d.). Still, closure cannot occur without reassuring your students that you remain available to them as new family crises arise (parent remarrying, birth of sibling, noncustodial parent moving far away). As a final activity, pass the basket with the Divorce Sentence Completion Statements. Discussion will come readily and they will not be ready to end, but there are other groups to offer and many other things you must do!

Questions they should be able to answer: What do you remember about each group session? How difficult was it for you to complete the sentences you drew? How easy was it for you to identify your feelings about your family situation on the chart each week? In what ways have you accepted your family situation?

Divorce Sentence Completion Statements

When I first found out my parents were getting a divorce, I felt ______________________________.

Something I still don't understand about the divorce is ______________________________.

One thing that I miss is ______________________________.

A way that I have changed is ______________________________.

I appreciate my mother for ______________________________.

I appreciate my father for ______________________________.

I can help other students whose parents are divorced by ______________________________.

I wish my mother would be more ______________________________.

I wish my father would be more ______________________________.

When I get married, I plan to ______________________________.

If I could change one thing about myself now, it would be ______________________________.

When my friends learn that my parents are divorced, they ____________________________.

The best thing about my life now is that ____________________________.

When I grow up, I ____________________________.

One good thing about my stepdad is ____________________________.

One good thing about my stepmom is ____________________________.

The worst thing about having divorced parents is ____________________________.

Whenever I become really sad, I ____________________________.

I wish ____________________________.

If I could change one thing about my life, it would be ____________________________.

The best thing about talking to other kids experiencing divorce is ____________________________.

Whenever I become really angry, I ____________________________.

Evaluation of Stuck in the Middle Divorce Group

Rate yourself by circling the number which corresponds with how you evaluate each statement.
1 = Not at all, 2 = A small amount, 3 = Average amount, 4 = More than average, 5 = Very much

1. I felt comfortable discussing divorce issues in the group.

   1.................2.................3.................4.................5

2. I was able to select a feeling word each week to describe my family situation.

   1.................2.................3.................4.................5

3. I was able to recognize problems of divorce that other children do not have.

   1.................2.................3.................4.................5

4. I was able to express my true feelings in a drawing.

   1.................2.................3.................4.................5

5. I learned the difference in aggressive, passive, and assertive responses.

   1.................2.................3.................4.................5

6. I was able to defend or oppose controversial statements about divorce.

   1.................2.................3.................4.................5

7. I was able to list positive as well as negative aspects of my current life.

   1.................2.................3.................4.................5

8 .I grew closer to group members during the course of the group.

   1.................2.................3.................4.................5

Suggestions for making the group better: ____

____

References

At Health Mental Health. (2011, March 28). *Divorce and children: An interview with Dr. Robert Hughes, Jr., Phd.* Retrieved April 10, 2011, from http://www.athealth.com/consumer/disorders/children divorce.html

Balber, L. (n.d.). Should you stay together for your children's sake? *BabyZone | Baby, Pregnancy, Baby Names, and Parenting*. Retrieved April 11, 2011, from http://www.babyzone.com/mom_dad/love_friendship/article/staying-together-for-children

Deal with divorce. (2011). *Divorce counseling can help reduce teen troubles*. Retrieved April 10, 2011, from http://www.dealwithdivorce.com/effects-divorce/divorce-counseling-teen-troubles/06/

Divorce.com. (2011). *Divorce rate*. Retrieved April 23, 2011, from http://www.divorce.com/article/divorce-rate

Ferenc, T. (2011). Managing children's anger about divorce or separation. *Education.com*. Retrieved April 21, 2011, from http://www.education.com/reference/article/Ref_Managing_Childrens/

Chapter 5

Fitness Matters[1]

Fitness Matters Group Outline

I. Introductory Information, Name-Calling, Magic Wand
   A. Outline, Schedule, Parent Permission, Rules
   B. Name-Calling Activity
   C. Magic Wand Activity

II. Acceptance and Problem Solving/Goal Setting
   A. Things You Can/Cannot Change Activity
   B. Completion of Problem Solving/Goal Setting Strategies

III. Uniqueness
   A. Shell activity
   B. Interest Assessment Activity

IV. Building Confidence Through Assertiveness
   A. Definitions of Passive, Aggressive, and Assertive
   B. Scenarios

V. Dieting (Speaker—Dietitian or Nurse)
   A. Counting Calories, Determining Fats
   B. Fad Diets, Healthy Diets
   C. Understanding Food Labels

VI. Searching for Beauty in the Media
   A. Comparing Regular and Plus-Size Women's Magazines
   B. Dangers of Eating Disorders

VII. Health Concerns (Speaker—Nurse)
   A. Overview of Serious Illnesses
   B. Determining BMI, Taking Blood Pressure

VIII. How to Handle Tough Situations
   A. Completion of What Should She Do? Questionnaire
   B. Discussion of Relapse, Depression, Parties

1 Parts of this chapter first appeared in *Counseling Today*, September 2004. Reprinted with permission from American Counseling Association.

IX. Making the Most of Your Appearance (Speaker—Plus-Size Model or Agent)
X. Review/Health Tips
   A. Review of Prior Sessions
   B. Health Tips Discussion

American School Counselor Association (ASCA) Standards

Career Development

Standard A: Students will acquire the skills to investigate the world of work in relation to knowledge of self and to make informed career decisions.

C:A1 Develop Career Awareness

C:A1.3 Develop an awareness of personal abilities, skills, interests, and motivations

Personal/Social Development

Standard A: Students will acquire the knowledge, attitudes, and interpersonal skills to help them understand and respect self and others.

PS:A1 Acquire Self-knowledge

PS:A1.1 Develop positive attitudes toward self as a unique and worthy person

PS:A1.2 Identify values, attitudes, and beliefs

PS:A1.3 Learn the goal-setting process

PS:A1.5 Identify and express feelings

PS:A1.10 Identify personal strengths and assets

Standard B: Students will make decisions, set goals and take necessary action to achieve goals.

PS:B1 Self-knowledge Application

PS:B1.2 Understand consequences of decisions and choices

PS:B1.4 Develop effective coping skills for dealing with problems

PS:B1.9 Identify long- and short-term goals

PS:B1.12 Develop an action plan to set and achieve realistic goals

Rationale for Fitness Matters Group

All you have to do is look around to see the need for this group. Today's adolescents do not run outside to play. They sit by the computer or television for hours on end. Combine that with calorie-laden fast food and maximum-sized sodas, and the result is a high number of overweight and even obese teenagers. Statistics reveal that nearly 20% of adolescents are now classified as obese. In the last thirty years, the rates of both childhood and adolescent obesity have tripled (Centers for Disease Control and Prevention, 2010).

What are the repercussions from this? It is reported that the military commitment of our country may be difficult to fill with volunteers as almost three out of four Americans of recruiting age cannot pass the physical exam (Seidenberg, 2009). How scary is that? Also, projected health costs have the whole country deeply worried. Approximately one third of American adults are considered obese, whereas only 17% of Europeans have weight problems (Reinberg, 2007). Whether overweight or not, physically fit young people are becoming a rarity. Our society needs to look for ways to integrate fitness into our daily lives so that all will embrace it from childhood to old age.

Our First Lady Michelle Obama has publicized and promoted the fight against childhood obesity. Many schools have taken up this cause, but strong efforts from families are needed as well to tackle this problem (Patchell, 2011). Schools should offer more than gym class and sports teams. What about those students who are not particularly athletic? Everyone cannot win a spot on the school basketball team. Overweight adolescents need our help! Physically, they are setting themselves up for becoming heavy adults, putting themselves at high risk for heart disease, diabetes, bone problems, and a whole myriad of other health troubles. Socially, these students face an emotional nightmare, often becoming victims of bullying and falling into self-loathing.

This group attempts to promote fitness in both an informative and invigorating fashion by incorporating classroom sessions and after school workouts. Fitness is the main goal, with weight loss being a possible side benefit. There are optional weekly weigh-in opportunities. Guest speakers in the professions of nursing, nutrition, and modeling are invited to add their expertise to the group. Students acknowledge the negative emotional impact of being obese as they react to common scenarios and societal messages. An important tip is summarized at the exercise session each week. An added benefit of forming a fitness group is that it helps keep the leader fit as well!

What Makes It Work:

1 It is quite trendy right now to emphasize fitness. Everywhere you can find staggering statistics about obese young people.
2. Parents are searching for a way to get their children off the computer for an hour. They can often relate to the pain of being overweight/physically unfit and may try to reinforce your efforts at home.
3. I set up this group in ten sessions rather than my usual six or eight because it takes time for fitness to become a habit (and certainly for weight loss to occur).
4. Students like the unique combination of in-school educational and after school exercise sessions. There may be some students who need and want the educational component but cannot stay for the after school exercise sessions. I would include them in anything they can manage to attend.
5. Since this group necessitates parents picking up students after school, you will need parent notification beyond the standard permission form. (I have included a sample letter.)

6. This information is geared toward a girls-only group. If you choose to conduct a boys' group, then you would need to revamp the focus of some educational sessions, plus you would need to search for exercise videos that include males (many don't). Mixing boys with girls in this group would be extremely difficult due to the sensitivity of the subject.
7. You should have a requirement that students in this group be at least fifteen pounds overweight according to their pediatrician, parent, or height/weight tables (though this is difficult to determine since usually such tables are for adults). The group is designed for overweight girls, and though anyone can have improved fitness as a goal, much of the material would not be suitable for average- or small-sized students.
8. Students have the opportunity to weigh at each weekly classroom meeting, though it is totally optional. You may find that many of the girls do not have scales at home and are quite excited about the chance to weigh weekly. Numbers are kept private between the girl and the leader, unless the girl chooses to share her weight with others.
9. Students have the opportunity to hear information from experts (nurse, dietitian, plus-size model), and having guest speakers keeps the interest level high.
10. For the exercise sessions, use DVDs (or whatever technology is currently in vogue). Look for variety in your exercise styles: kickboxing, zumba, aerobics, salsa dancing, hip-hop, yoga, walking. Do not use the same video two weeks in a row, though it's perfectly fine to repeat the use of one several times in the ten weeks. It is always easier for them to follow the routines the second time it is viewed. Allow them to bring in videos of their own, but you may want to take them home to preview and search for the best parts.
11. Materials are no-cost or low cost if you happen to have some videos of your own. Also, you can check them out of the public library for free.
12. You may want to ask female physical education teachers or coaches to co-lead the group with you. They know what to do in case of simple injuries, and they can add interest to the exercise regimes.
13. Laugh a lot together about the mistakes you will make in trying to follow the exercise routines, and snicker about the Barbie-doll figures of certain physical fitness video stars. Their perfection can be annoying!
14. Hopefully, students make exercise a habit and learn lifelong health tips.

Challenges:

1. Recruiting girls for this group cannot be arranged in your usual public way due to embarrassment about weight issues. (Other students might point at overweight students and tease them about their need to join.) You may want to put up posters and signs in the hallways to solicit members. The signs could direct them to the guidance office, where you could post the standard insurance weight tables beside the sign-up sheet.
2. You do not want students in your group who are at risk for eating disorders. Emphasize the dangers.
3. Students may feel uncomfortable being in a group focusing on being overweight. It is challenging to be blunt about the hazards of obesity and yet remain supportive of a positive self-image. Students need to recognize the fact that most women will fall quite short of society's ideal shape and size.
4. Students may be disappointed if they do not lose any weight in the ten weeks. Emphasize that exercising one time a week in the group will never be enough! They must develop the habit of finding exercise time on their own.

5. Watch out for the slackers—the kids who join because anyone can and maybe they want their picture in the yearbook but they have no intention of moving any muscles beyond those required for breathing. Or perhaps, like many adults, they want to be fit and trim but lack the discipline to set into motion the practices that will help them achieve their goals.
6. Beware the exhibitionists—there are always a few who want to wear very short shorts and sports bras to exercise. They hope to catch the eye of the boys lingering after school or running laps through the building at their own team practices. If yours is a conservative school (or if you just wish it were), stick to school dress code and suggest they wear their gym clothes.
7. You may end up with a medical emergency. Keep a phone nearby.
8. You may end up with a technology emergency—a DVD player that just won't work. Be sure to have a backup plan, even if it's as simple as walking laps throughout your school hallways or circling the field where the football team is practicing.
9. As with any after school activity, you may have parents who fail to pick up their children on time. To avoid becoming overly frustrated, carry a book bag of paperwork you can complete while you wait for that last car to drive up.

Date

Dear Parent:

Your daughter ______________________________ has indicated an interest in being in a support group for girls who want to become more physically fit. This group will meet once a week for ten weeks during classes on a rotating schedule. There will also be an after school exercise component on Mondays each week for those students who are able to find their own transportation.

Students signing up for this group must be at least fifteen pounds overweight by pediatric or health insurance tables. We intend to set realistic goals for losing weight as we address health, diet, exercise, and social functioning. Other topics of discussion will be self-esteem issues, relapsing, dealing with teasing, and other concerns. In addition, we plan to have speakers such as the school nurse and a representative from a plus-size modeling agency. The after school sessions will include a variety of exercises ranging from aerobic DVD's to simply walking laps.

If you have questions about the group, please call me at 704-455-4700. Students may not join the after school exercise group without being in the in-school support group. However, since all students may not be able to find transportation, they are allowed to join the in-school group without joining the after school workout sessions.

Please sign below if you would like for your daughter to join. Return the forms by Thursday, September 15. Our first after school meeting will be Monday, September 19, in the open area by the cafeteria.

Sincerely,

Debra Efird,
Counselor

****

I give permission for my daughter ________________________ to join the support group. If she joins the after school sessions on Mondays, I will be able to provide transportation at 5:15.

______________________________________ ________________

(Parent signature) (date)

Fitness Matters Group Sessions

Session 1 Topic: Introductory Information, Name-Calling, Magic Wand

Session 1 Supplies: For students—Copies of outline, schedule, and parent permission form; Small strips of paper, Pencils; For leader—Trashcan, Magic Wand

Session 1 Content:

To begin, go over the usual introductory information such as the outline, schedule, and parent permission form. Be sure to emphasize the importance of parents picking them up on time if they plan to participate in the after school exercise session. When discussing group rules, you will want to highlight being sensitive to the feelings of other group members. It is important to note that the purpose of the group is to help them achieve a higher level of fitness, which may or may not lead to weight loss.

Then conduct the Name-Calling activity. Set a trashcan in the middle of the room. Give each student a strip of paper and ask her to write a name she has been called before. Then go around the circle and have each read aloud the word she has written. Then have them, one by one, step to the center of the room, crumple or tear the paper and toss it in the trashcan. Talk about how it feels to treat that word as the trash it is, throwing it away from your life. Expect words such as these: fatso, lard-butt, slob, elephant, hippo, gross, plus some profanity.

Then proceed to the Magic Wand activity. (A ruler or pencil covered with aluminum foil with a glitter-covered paper star glued to the end works fine.) Ask each student to take turns shaking the wand over the girl next to her. Then ask each to respond how she would be different if the wand truly had magic powers. This is a very personal exercise, and some will take it very seriously while others will laugh it off. Among the answers you will probably hear: desiring to be a smaller size, becoming popular, looking pretty, finding a boyfriend, and even being smart.

Questions they should be able to answer: What are the topics that will be covered in group? How does the schedule work? What are the group rules? When is the parent permission form due? What are some of the negative names that members of the group have been called? What were some of the responses in the Magic Wand activity? What did you learn about others in this introductory session of the group?

Session 2 Topic: Acceptance and Problem Solving/Goal Setting Strategies

Session 2 Supplies: For students—Copies of Things You Can/Cannot Change and Problem Solving/Goal Setting Strategies, Pencils; For leader—Scale, Index cards

Session 2 Content:

Begin the session by reflecting back on the Magic Wand activity from last week. Reinforce that though it is helpful to dream, real change usually comes through hard work. At this session, the focus is on identifying what can be changed and seeking results through goal setting.

Then give students the Things You Can/Cannot Change handout and pencils. Ask them to complete it individually and then read over it aloud. Expect a little low-key disagreement about whether or not some things really can be changed.

Offer an opportunity to weigh in a private corner of the room. Explain that they will have the chance to do so each week from now on but are welcome to decline as well. Some may need your help operating the scale. Ask the girl to write the date and their weight on an index card and give it to you for safekeeping. Most of them will probably want to weigh, and some may even broadcast their numbers.

Next, hand them the Problem Solving/Goal Setting Strategies worksheet. Ask each to write a realistic weight loss goal and viable strategies. You may want to write on the whiteboard the step-by-step process of problem solving:

1. State the specific problem or concern and what goal you want to reach.
2. Brainstorm strategies to address the problem or reach the goal.
3. Evaluate strategies and narrow to two or three to try.
4. Set a time for a trial period. (Suggest eight weeks so that they can report back to the group at the final session.)
5. Evaluate how well the problem was solved or goal was reached. (to be completed later)
6. Revamp plan/goal if needed. (to be completed later)

Questions they should be able to answer: What were some of the differences in opinion about whether or not things could be changed? Did you choose to weigh? If so, was your weight what you expected it to be? How easy was it to generate strategies for the goal-setting activity? How realistic is your weight loss goal?

Things You Can/Cannot Change

Read the following statements. If it is something you can change, put a Y for yes in the blank. If it is something you cannot change, put an N for no in the blank.

_____ 1. You made an F in Science on your last report card.

_____ 2. You hate eating salads for lunch.

_____ 3. Your uncle died last summer.

_____ 4. You smoke cigarettes.

_____ 5. Your best friend is Jessica.

_____ 6. Your boyfriend dumped you and dated your best friend.

_____ 7. You choose to ride the elevator rather than walk up the stairs.

_____ 8. You are African American.

_____ 9. Your favorite snack is a pack of M&M's.

_____10. You live on Eastway Drive.

_____11. You wear your coat to hide your size.

_____12. You want to live in a mansion by the ocean.

_____13. You are failing math.

_____14. Your mother is an alcoholic.

_____15. Your favorite color is green.

_____16. You are the oldest child in your family.

_____17. Your sister is thin.

_____18. You have brown eyes.

_____19. Your dog ate your homework.

_____20. You are overweight.

Problem Solving/Goal Setting Strategies

1. State the specific problem or concern and what goal you want to reach:

____

____

2 Brainstorm solutions to address the problem or reach the goal:

____

____

____

____

____

3. Evaluate strategies and narrow to 2 or 3 to try:

(1) ____

(2) ____

(3) ____

4. Set a time for a trial: ____

5. Evaluate how well the problem was solved or goal was reached:

____

____

6, Revamp plan/goal if needed:

____

____

Session 3 Topic: Uniqueness

Session 3 Supplies: For students—Copies of Interest Assessment worksheet; For leader—Seashells (or rocks), Scale, Index cards (from before)

Session 3 Content:

The focus of this session is the uniqueness of each individual. Start your discussion by asking group members to name one-of-a-kind things (snowflakes, signatures, fingerprints, DNA, etc.) Use any items that look very similar for the uniqueness activity: seashells, rocks, or even apples would do. Hand each of them a seashell and have them examine its shape, shade, markings, etc. Then take them all up in a bag and scatter them on the floor, telling them to find their own seashell. Almost without fail, each will be able to find her own seashell. Ask several students to briefly explain how they identified the correct seashell.

Then shift talk to how unique they are as individuals (appearance, personality, abilities, likes and dislikes, etc.). And though they share some things with others—same desire to lose weight, same struggle with name-calling—they are still one-of-a-kind. There are several points to make:

- You can express your individuality through clothing and hairstyles.
- You may want to accept being larger than others instead of constantly trying to assimilate.
- You can learn to respect yourself and value your performance in school and the community.

Then complete the Interest Assessment worksheet. Ask them to share some of the things in which they excel. Ask if they think any of these talents or interests may lead to future careers, and encourage them to expand on the topic. Suggest they note who has selected similar choices.

Questions they should be able to answer: How are you different from others in the group? How are you alike? What are your interests? What things do you excel in? Who shares some of your talents and interests?

Interest Assessment

Mark the following items that you like to do or think you are good at doing:

_____Singing	_____Building things
_____Drawing	_____Reading aloud
_____Working with plants	_____Doing math
_____Cooking meals	_____Writing
_____Working in a group	_____Organizing things
_____Being a leader	_____Acting in a play
_____Working with your hands	_____Creating things
_____Designing things	_____Greeting people
_____Working independently	_____Cleaning house
_____Convincing people to see things your way	_____Making jewelry
_____Giving a speech	_____Playing sports
_____Following directions	_____Painting the house
_____Taking care of children	_____Directing others
_____Learning a foreign language	_____Following orders
_____Working without a lot of rules	_____Working in an office
_____Paying attention to details	_____Selling things
_____Doing school projects	_____Teaching others
_____Working with animals	_____Dancing
_____Working outside	_____Helping sick people
_____Working on the computer	_____Leading exercises

Session 4 Topic: Building Confidence Through Assertiveness

Session 4 Supplies: For students—Copies of Passive, Aggressive, and Assertive Scenarios; For leader—Scale, Index cards (from before)

Session 4 Content:
This session focuses on building self-esteem by teaching students assertive behavior. They may be somewhat unaware of how often they respond to others in less productive passive and aggressive ways. Present the following definitions of passive, aggressive, and assertive:

- Passive—being a pushover, being too fearful to express your own opinion or seek your rights, accommodating others just to keep the peace.
- Aggressive—being too demanding or intimidating, expressing your opinion in an overwhelming fashion which does not consider the feelings of others.
- Assertive—expressing your feelings honestly and standing up for your rights without hurting others.

Then give each girl a copy of the Passive, Aggressive, and Assertive Scenarios. Ask the girls to take turns reading them aloud and decide together if the person acted in a passive, aggressive, or assertive manner. One example of an assertive response involves Nikki's comment to a friend who suggests she might procure a boyfriend if she lost weight. Another example of an assertive response has Maya choosing to seek the help of her counselor in dealing with some name-calling students. Ask group members to offer alternative responses to each scenario, encouraging them to seek an assertive mode when handling such situations.

Questions they should be able to answer: What are the differences in passive, aggressive, and assertive responses? How easy was it for you to identify which response was exhibited in each scenario? What type of response do you usually make? Do you want to share a similar story or situation and how you responded?

Passive, Aggressive, and Assertive Scenarios

1. Tiffany tried to make her way down the crowded hall. Someone bumped her and caused her to bump into Jason. He turned toward her and snarled, "Hey, watch it, Fatso. There's no room in these halls for a double-wide load." Several boys around Jason laughed. Tiffany cursed at Jason, and then he cursed back. Tiffany told him she'd get her older brother to check on him and his friends after school. Jason and the boys said they'd be ready. Rumors flew around all day about a big fight.

2. Gina heard the "moo" sounds behind her when the young, skinny substitute teacher faced the board. She knew the boys behind her were making fun of her, not someone else. They had done it before when teachers were unlikely to hear. Gina put her head down on her desk when her eyes became teary. She tried to imagine herself walking in a beautiful snow-covered forest with no one else around.

3. Nikki's best friend Alex was talking about her newest boyfriend. She went on and on about it until she realized Nikki wasn't saying anything. "You know, Nikki, you could get a boyfriend, too, if you'd just lose weight." Nikki took a deep breath and replied, "Maybe so, but it's not that easy to do. And I think there's probably a guy out there somewhere who won't mind me being heavy."

4. Krista had on a new outfit. She looked good in it and she knew it, even though she'd had to go up a size. Jessica saw her and said, "Krista, you're looking good today, girl." Krista replied, "I don't look good and you know it. I'm way too fat."

5. Two small-sized boys pushed at Maya when she stopped at her locker. One said, "I thought she'd be soft like the Pillsbury dough boy, but she's not." The other one said, "Maybe she's Shamu instead." They laughed and ran away. Maya started to chase them but decided to take time to cool down. She went straight to the counselor, who went over several options for handling the situation with her.

6. Erin selected a piece of chocolate cake to go along with her meal in the cafeteria line. A girl behind her said, "You don't need that." Erin turned around and smashed the cake on top the girl's spaghetti.

Session 5 Topic: Dieting (Speaker—Dietitian or Nutritionist)

Session 5 Supplies: For students—Copies of Reference List of Healthy Diet Information (plus any brochures, charts, or articles provided by speaker); For leader—Several cans and packages of foods, Scale, Index cards (from before)

Session 5 Content:

For the best information on dieting, ask a dietitian or nutritionist to lead this session. Your school nurse would suffice, though you will want to use her again in a later session. Hopefully, the speaker will bring relevant brochures for the girls to take home.

If you are unable to procure a professional in this field, you can find pertinent information yourself by researching the Internet. Explain the difference in counting calories and fat grams (Livestrong.com, 2011). Provide the girls with copies of the Reference List of Healthy Diet Information so that they can access extensive food charts—copying these would take excessive amounts of paper! Plan to reserve a computer lab for part of the period (especially if you are unable to find a speaker) and allow them to look up calories and fat grams of the foods they are interested in. Share information about various fad diets (Fad Diet.com, 2011), noting how impractical and ridiculous many of them are. Then focus on sensible dieting. Emphasize such points as eating a variety of colorful fruits and vegetables daily, limiting sugar and salt intake, increasing fiber with whole grains, and simply following a policy of moderation (Helpguide.org, 2011).

Spend a few minutes examining food labels on the cans and packages you have brought to class. Help them make sense of the labels (U.S. Food and Drug Administration, 2011). Teach them to be cautious of the claims made on the front cover of some packages. Also point out what is considered a proper portion of certain foods. Note how food companies have increased the packaged size and restaurants have enlarged serving sizes of foods over the years (Centers for Disease Control and Prevention, 2006).

Questions they should be able to answer: What is the difference in counting calories and determining fat grams? Can you name some high calorie and high fat foods? Can you name some low calorie and low fat foods? What did you think of some of the fad diets? Can you list some healthy eating tips? How important is it to read food labels?

Reference List of Healthy Diet Information

Mike's Calorie and Fat Gram Chart for 1000 Foods
http://www.caloriecountercharts.com/chart1a.htm
The Calorie Counter
http://www.thecaloriecounter.com/
Low Carb - Carbohydrate Counter/Fat Gram Counter
http://www.cellhealthmakeover.com/1.html
Healthy Eating
http://www.helpguide.org/life/healthy_eating_diet.htm
Reading and Understanding Nutrition Labels
http://www.fda.gov/food/labelingnutrition/consumerinformation/ucm078889.htm

Session 6 Topic: Searching for Beauty

Session 6 Supplies: For leader—A collection of teens' or women's magazines, being sure to include something similar to Radiance, World of Curves, and Plus Model Magazine, which are designed for plus-size women; Scale, Index cards (from before)

Session 6 Content:

Distribute magazines—it is all right to ask them to share if you don't have enough—and look through them. Ask the girls to compare models in the typical women's magazines with the plus-size ones. Point out the beauty in both. Talk about women on television and in movies also. They should be able to name celebrities who struggle with weight issues as well as thin stars. Point out unrealistic societal ideals.

Discuss the dangers of eating disorders such as anorexia and bulimia. Sufferers of these disorders generally see themselves as fat no matter how thin they may become. Those with anorexia restrict their food intake to the point they become exceedingly malnourished. Bulimics engage in binge eating but then force themselves to throw up, which can result in damage to the esophagus as well as their teeth. They also tend to abuse laxatives, which can lead to intestinal distress and kidney problems. Whether anorexic or bulimic, sufferers can develop heart failure (National Institute of Mental Health, 2010). Be certain that group members understand the consequences of these conditions.

Questions they should be able to answer: What similarities and differences do you find in typical models and those who are plus-size? Who are some celebrities that you think are too thin? Who are some celebrities that you think are too heavy? How realistic are societal ideals regarding weight? What are the differences in anorexia nervosa and bulimia?

Session 7 Topic: Health Concerns (Speaker—Nurse)

Session 7 Supplies: (whatever the speaker brings—blood pressure cuff, hopefully!) For leader – Scale, Index cards (from before)

Session 7 Content:

For this session you truly need the school nurse, or perhaps you could contact a local nursing school and ask a few students to come. If you are absolutely unable to obtain a professional in the field, then you will need to talk to them yourself about the many health concerns of obesity: diabetes, heart disease, stroke, and even certain forms of cancer (Weight-control Information Network, 2007). They will enjoy figuring out their body mass index (BMI), which is the ratio of height to weight and can be determined by referencing a chart specifically for children and teens (Centers for Disease Control and Prevention, 2011). If the nurse brings a pressure cuff, she can check the blood pressure of each girl. Hopefully, she will bring useful handouts as well. Encourage group members to ask questions.

Questions they should be able to answer: What are some of the diseases or conditions associated with being overweight? What is your body mass index? What is your blood pressure reading? What do the two numbers measuring blood pressure mean? How can you attempt to avoid the illnesses mentioned earlier?

Session 8 Topic: How to Handle Tough Situations

Session 8 Supplies: For students—Copies of the What Should She Do? worksheet; For leader—Scale, Index cards (from before)

Session 8 Content:

Complete the What Should She Do? worksheet, either together or individually. Go over each situation and talk about the pros and cons of each possible answer. There may be multiple acceptable answers for each scenario. The questions address the turmoil facing girls struggling with weight issues and the difficult decisions they must make in daily life. One example involves feelings aroused when a friend wins a race to lose five pounds. Another example relates what may happen when a girl trying to lose weight actually gains pounds. As you go through the scenarios, encourage group members to offer supportive ideas.

Discuss in detail situations that present obstacles to weight loss: relapse, depression, and parties. You may need to define relapse: to fall or slip back into a former pattern of behavior, to backslide. If a girl has been following a nutritious diet for weeks and then eats large amounts of unhealthy foods for a whole weekend, one could say she has relapsed from her diet. The term "depression" is likely to be more familiar, but they may need to know some of the symptoms: extended feelings of sadness, lack of energy, sleep disruptions, crying for unknown reasons, loss of interest in activities that were formerly enjoyed, and changes with eating patterns. As far as parties are concerned, most people agree that everyone needs the occasional celebration and can allow an exception or two in their diets for such events. Ask group members to share how they have responded to the situations of relapse, depression, and special celebrations.

Questions they should be able to answer: How easy was it to choose answers for the questions on the worksheet? What does it mean to relapse? What are symptoms of depression? How do you handle parties and other celebrations involving food? How can you offer support to each other?

WHAT SHOULD SHE DO?

1 Megan lost two pounds since the last weigh-in. She should:
   a. Eat an ice cream sandwich in celebration.
   b. Encourage herself to exercise to lose a few more pounds.
   c. Buy a new pair of jeans one size smaller as an incentive.
   d. Cry because two pounds isn't very much.

2. April gained two pounds since the last weigh-in. She should:
   a. Eat an ice cream bar because she might as well give up.
   b. Exercise more often to make up for gaining weight.
   c. Buy a new pair of jeans one size larger just in case.
   d. Shrug her shoulders because two pounds isn't very much.

3. Christina is going to a big wedding that promises to have a lavish buffet. She should:
   a. Take her own yogurt and try not to be noticed while she eats.
   b. Drink a glass of water prior to the buffet.
   c. Select very small portions of "danger" foods.
   d. Eat whatever she wants because it's a party.

4. Tiffany has to bring a snack for the Multicultural Club. She should:
   a. Bring potato chips and soda because that's what everybody likes.
   b. Bring low-fat baked chips and a diet drink because it won't hurt anybody.
   c. Complain about a club serving refreshments at school and tempting her to eat.
   d. Offer to give a club presentation on dieting and weight loss.

5. Katie and Keisha were racing to see who could lose 5 pounds first. Katie won, and Keisha got mad and stopped speaking to her. Katie should:
   a. Approach Keisha with encouraging words.
   b. Share with the group how she lost her 5 pounds.
   c. Avoid Keisha by not coming to group.
   d. Eat everything in sight to gain weight so Keisha will be her friend again.

Session 9 Topic: Making the Most of Your Appearance (Speaker—Modeling Agent or Model)

Session 9 Supplies: (whatever the speaker may bring) For leader—Scale, Index cards (from before)

Session 9 Content:

To make this an effective session, you need to contact a plus-size modeling agency for a speaker. If a model is unavailable (which actually happened to me), ask the modeling agency representative to bring sample portfolios of plus-size models. The girls can examine some of the photo shoots of the model while listening to the speaker. Clue the speaker in advance that you'd like for her to focus on the need to accept one's body but work toward a fitter, healthier one. She should acknowledge that everyone was not meant to be a size four, but that all people can take steps to improve their health and appearance. Also, you may want to suggest that she emphasize the importance of good grooming, posture, and presentation. Ask her to share healthy ways that the agency recommends for its models to stay in shape.

Questions they should be able to answer: What did you learn about plus-size modeling? Did you find any of the models attractive? What are some tips for making the most of one's appearance?

Session 10 Topic: Review/Heatlh Tips

Session 10 Supplies: For students—Copies of Health Tips; For leader—Scale, Index cards (from before), Leader's complete folder (for review)

Session 10 Content:

Recap each of the previous sessions, asking them what points they remember. Save time at the end to go over the Health Tips sheet, which is a summary of all the tips that were discussed briefly during the after school exercise sessions. Allow them one last time to weigh, and return index cards for them to keep. Ask if some girls want to share their weight loss progress. Remind them that the weekly workout with the group should be a jumpstart for them establishing a regular pattern of daily exercise. Leave them with encouraging words and a reminder that they can see you individually as needed throughout the year.

Questions they should be able to answer: What do you remember from each session? What was your favorite session? Which speaker did you like best? How do you feel about your size? In what ways have you changed since joining this group? Were you able to note any weight loss over the course of the group? What are some health tips that you can begin to follow right now?

Health Tips

1. Drink lots of water.

2. Exercise can be fun: dance while you dust, sweep playfully.

3. When you feel down about something, call an understanding friend instead of going to the refrigerator.

4. Do not believe that the word "natural" means something is safe for everyone. A lot of health store items are meant for adults only.

5. Eat Halloween candy! In other words, don't deny yourself treats. Just use moderation.

6. Drink lots of milk and spend a little time out in the sunshine to be sure you are getting adequate calcium and Vitamin D.

7. Don't smoke!

8. Seek professional help if you recognize that you may be developing an eating disorder such as anorexia or bulimia.

9. Accept compliments with grace. Don't say, "I think I look fat in these jeans."

10. Enjoy the holiday season, but use a small plate at buffets. Again, remember moderation is the key.

Evaluation of Fitness Matters Group

Rate yourself by circling the number which corresponds with how you evaluate each statement.
1 = Not at all, 2 = A small amount, 3 = Average amount, 4 = More than average, 5 = Very much

1. I felt comfortable being in the group of overweight students.

   1.................2.................3.................4.................5

2. I was able to distinguish between things I can and cannot change.

   1.................2.................3.................4.................5

3. I learned to set realistic goals and have a plan for reaching them.

   1.................2.................3.................4.................5

4. I was able to recognize that I am a unique, worthy person.

   1.................2.................3.................4.................5

5. I learned the difference in passive, aggressive, and assertive responses.

   1.................2.................3.................4.................5

6. I can name health problems associated with being overweight.

   1.................2.................3.................4.................5

7. I learned about unrealistic societal expectations of beauty.

   1.................2.................3.................4.................5

8. I grew closer to group members during the course of the group.

   1.................2.................3.................4.................5

Suggestions for making the group better: ____

____

References

Centers for Disease Control and Prevention. (2006, May). *Do increased portion sizes affect how much we eat?* Retrieved April 23, 2011, from http://www.cdc.gov/nccdphp/dnpa/nutrition/pdf/portion_size_research.pdf

Centers for Disease Control and Prevention. (2010, June 3). *Healthy youth! Childhood obesity*. Retrieved March 28, 2011, from http://www.cdc.gov/HealthyYouth/obesity/

Centers for Disease Control and Prevention. (2011, February 15). *Body Mass Index*. Retrieved April 24, 2011, from http://www.cdc.gov/healthyweight/assessing/bmi/

Fad Diet.com. (2011). *30 ways to lose the same 5 pounds.* Retrieved April 23, 2011, from http://www.faddiet.com/

Helpguide.org. (2011). *Healthy eating.* Retrieved April 23, 2011, from http://www.helpguide.org/life/healthy_eating_diet.htm

Livestrong.com. (2011). *Calories vs. fat grams*. Retrieved April 23, 2011, from http://www.livestrong.com/article/379498-calories-vs-fat-grams/

National Institute of Mental Health (NIMH). (2010, August 24). *Eating disorders*. Retrieved April 24, 2010 from http://www.nimh.nih.gov/health/publications/eating-disorders/complete-index.shtml

Patchell, B. (2011). Adolescent fitness. *BellaOnline – The voice of women*. Retrieved March 28, 2011, from http://www.bellaonline.com/articles/art68582.asp

Reinberg, S. (2007, October 2). Obesity driving rising US health costs. *Health news, discussions, articles, and resources*. Retrieved March 29, 2011, from http://news.healingwell.com/index.php?p=news1&id=608776

Seidenberg, J. (2009, November 15). Poor physical fitness now affecting military. *Suite101.com: Online magazine and writers' network*. Retrieved March 29, 2011, from http://www.suite101.com/content/poor-physical-fitness-now-affecting-military-a166468

U.S. Food and Drug Administration Home. (2011, March 11). *How to understand and use the nutrition facts label.* Retrieved April 23, 2011, from http://www.fda.gov/food/labelingnutrition/consumerinformation/ucm078889.htm

Chapter 6

Good Grief

Good Grief Group Outline

I. Introductory Information, Sentence Completion Activity
   A. Outline, Schedule, Parent Permission, Rules
   B. Sentence Completion Activity
II. Stages of Grief
   A. Kubler-Ross Model
   B. Feelings Poster
III. Handling Loss
   A. Different Levels of Loss: Possessions, Pets, People
   B. Mural of Losses
IV. Things People Say and Do
   A. Negative or Hurtful Statements/Actions
   B. Positive or Helpful Statements/Actions
V. Sharing Your Loved One through a Collage
VI. Mementoes, Review
   A. Sharing of Mementoes
   B. Review of Prior Sessions

American School Counselor Association (ASCA) Standards

Personal/Social Development

Standard A: Students will acquire the knowledge, attitudes, and interpersonal skills to help them understand and respect self and others.

PS:A1 Acquire Self-knowledge

PS:A1.4 Understand change is a part of growth

PS:A1.5 Identify and express feelings

PS:A1.10 Identify personal strengths and assets

PS:A1.11 Identify and discuss changing personal and social roles

PS:A1.12 Identify and recognize changing family roles

Standard B: Students will make decisions, set goals and take necessary action to achieve goals.

PS:B1 Self-knowledge Application

PS:B1.4 Develop effective coping skills for dealing with problems

Rationale for Good Grief Group

Grief reactions in adolescents, as in adults, can vary from barely observable to wide-open wailing. As children reach adolescence, every emotion can be compounded, with grief being no exception. They are old enough to understand the finality of death (National Library of Medicine, 2011), just as they are reaching the point in time when the likelihood of experiencing the deaths of grandparents is increasing. No longer can they be shooed outside to play while adults mourn a death; students eleven and above demand their grief be acknowledged.

Grief groups with adolescents provide a safe, comfortable environment in which teens can express feelings among others who are also wrestling with the troubling emotions surrounding death. Alongside peers, they discover that their feelings are normal, and they are provided activities to work through the unfamiliar process of grief (Thompson, 2011). Interaction with other teens who are also hurting or angry or confused can be very beneficial as teens push through the unsettling journey of grief (The Healing Place, n.d.). In a group, adolescents are given ample opportunity to tell others their sad stories without being told to hush or cheer up. They are offered reassurance that the severity of their emotional pain will lessen (Wolfelt, n.d.). Being in a support group can hasten their return to focusing on the things non-grieving teens concentrate on: peer relationships, grades, sports, clubs, and other normal facets of adolescent life.

At my first group meeting, students are told that the general goal of the group is to move them to a point where they are experiencing less pain associated with the death. Upon hearing those encouraging words, relief and hope are often visible in their faces, along with a measure of doubt. Activities are designed to acquaint students with normal grieving phases and allow them to openly express whatever conflicting and challenging feelings they harbor. They draw losses on mural paper, make colorful collages, and bring in special mementoes. While they are doing those things, they talk, talk, talk about every aspect of the death: funeral services, cremation, family squabbles, unusual last wishes, and so on. As they become more comfortable in articulating their emotions, they are able to lend mutual support. Students in these groups typically grow close to one another as they suffer together in their quest for healing.

What Makes It Work:

1. There is a deep need to help young adolescents cope with grief. Many times their parents dismiss their reactions to death, thinking of them as too young to feel the pain of grief.
2. Students learn that they are not alone: there are others in their unfortunate state.
3. Students in this group bond tightly with one another. As in the divorce group, where emotions are also keenly felt, it doesn't seem to matter if a student is an outsider or misfit.
4. It helps if you, too, have experienced grief on several levels, but it is not a necessity in leading this group. If you have had some serious loss in your life, then participate in everything they do, including drawing on the mural and making a collage. They will be able to see you modeling the work it takes to move through grief.
5. Hopefully students reach a comfort level in talking through their grief and can move on to a less troubled state.

Challenges:

1. Sometimes students sign up for grief group when the deceased person is their neighbor's brother's girlfriend. Or their great-grandmothers. You will probably want to limit the group to regular grandparents (or, of course, step-grandparents). The way to handle this is to screen everyone who signs up by having a brief individual conference in advance of the group starting. If they do not meet your criteria, don't just leave them hanging. Give them the Guidelines for Dealing with Death information (a copy is included here), and tell them they can see you individually as needed. Judging someone's grief level can be difficult. Sometimes students will sign up with bona-fide dead relatives, but still they have only a very tenuous link to the deaths: an uncle who lived across the country and the student only saw him once and that was four years ago. You may try to convince the student that he would not fit in well with those suffering a closer, deeper grief. Hand him the grief information (as mentioned above). But you need to realize that you could misjudge the level of grief and exclude someone who should have been served.
2. At various points in time your own grief may make it extremely tough to share in the activities of grief group. A totally unexpected death of one of your own friends or relatives may throw you for a loop, but that experience will also deepen your level of compassion for your students.
3. Six weeks of grief group is a very short time. Some need longer. If you limit your group to six weeks, recommend Hospice or other grief group counseling for students demonstrating a serious need.

Guidelines for Dealing with Death

1. TALK it out. Find a friend or relative who will listen. If possible, find someone who has also experienced a death.

2. ACCEPT your sadness. Let the tears flow. If we cannot cry about death, then what are tears for? Allow some time for being alone with your grief.

3. CELEBRATE what that person meant to you. Review your life with that person by looking at old photos or family videos. Remember the good times and laugh.

4. FINISH unfinished business. Write a letter to your family member who died. Tell that person what you wish you had said and done and what you wish you had not said and done. You may want to tell that person what you wish he or she would have said and done to you. Seek forgiveness and be forgiving. Read your letter at the gravesite or at a private place where you will be undisturbed.

5. CREATE! Write stories, poems, or songs expressing your sorrow. Keep a journal or draw pictures illustrating your feelings.

6. TAKE CARE of your physical needs. Try to eat well and stay in a normal sleep pattern. Exercise to help prevent depression and work out your angry feelings.

7. STAY INVOLVED with activities. Connect with other people through sports, church, school events, and clubs.

8. MAKE a memorial for the person. You may want to select a special charity to give some of your allowance to or light a candle on holidays in memory of the person. Keep a picture of the person in a special place in your room.

9. VOLUNTEER. Help others and your own pain will become smaller.

10. SEEK HELP from your counselor if you feel overwhelmed. Things will get better for you!

Good Grief Group Sessions

Session 1 Topic: Introductory Information, Sentence Completion Activity

Session 1 Supplies: For students—Copies of outline, schedule, and parent permission form; For leader—Copy of Grief Sentence Completion Statements cut into strips, Basket, Tissues

Session 1 Content:
At the first meeting, start with a simple discussion of schedule, outline, parent permission, and group rules. You may want to note that tears are quite possible and totally permissible in this group. You may also want to point out that there is likely to be some laughter: they will not be sitting around in a circle throwing damp tissues into the trashcan (though you should have a box of tissues within reach). Tell them that the goal of the group is to work through the pain so that eventually they will feel less hurt associated with their grief.

Next, ask them to identify whom they are mourning, how long ago that person died, and whether it was a sudden death or an "expected" one. Even stating those stark facts about a death can be unsettling for some. Then start the Grief Sentence Completion Statements activity. Place the strips in the basket and have each one draw one at a time. Remember that some of the thoughts generated by the sentence completion statements are quite difficult to talk about. Give them the opportunity to "pass" if they do not feel comfortable responding.

Questions they should be able to answer: What are the topics that will be covered in group? How does the schedule work? What are the group rules? When is the parent permission form due? How easy was it for you to express your loss? How easy was it for you to complete the sentences you drew? What did you learn about each other in the introductory session?

Grief Sentence Completion Statements

When someone says, "I know how you feel," I ______________________________.

My worst fear about death is ______________________________.

When I am around other people who are grieving, I feel ______________________________.

When someone you love has died, holidays seem ______________________________.

When I feel lonely, I ______________________________.

When I see other members of my family cry, I feel ______________________________.

The idea of going to a funeral makes me ______________________________.

The person I feel most comfortable talking about the death with is ______________________________.

Sometimes I pretend ______________________________.

Sometimes I feel so bad I could ______________________________.

I feel better when ______________________________.

When I'm afraid, I ____.

The worst thing about dying is ____.

I wish ____.

I hope ____.

I cry when ____.

When someone really listens to me talk about the death, I feel ______________________.

When I take the time to cry, I ____.

One thing I regret is ____.

I would compare the pain of grief to ____.

One thing I could do to make the person who died proud of me would be ______________.

One thing I really want to accomplish in my life is ______________________________.

If only I could ____.

Session 2 Topic: Stages of Grief

Session 2 Supplies: For students—Star stickers; For leader—Whiteboard, Marker, Poster paper, Tissues

Session 2 Content:

Open the session by discussing Elizabeth Kubler-Ross's famed work (Kessler & Kubler-Ross, 2011). Write (or ask students to write) the five stages on the board: denial, anger, bargaining, depression, and acceptance. Talk about each as you go, giving examples of how grieving persons might demonstrate each stage. Ask if group members can identify having experienced some of the stages. Be sure to explain that all grieving people do not go through all the stages, and that the order of experience is not necessarily as listed.

Then ask them to brainstorm a list of descriptive feeling words that may go with grief and write them on the piece of poster paper, calling it the group's Feelings Poster. They will think of some but are likely to need a little help from you. Expect words such as frustrated, lost, afraid, miserable, worried, dazed, confused, furious, annoyed, disappointed, disturbed, hurt, betrayed, neglected, discouraged, curious, tense, guilty, calm, relieved, peaceful, content, and so on. Then hand them a page of stickers and tell them to put stars by the feelings they have had or are currently feeling about the death. It will be interesting to see where the bulk of the stickers land.

Questions they should be able to answer: What are the stages of the Kubler-Ross model? Which stages have you experienced so far? What are some of the feelings that you identified with on the Feelings Poster?

Session 3 Topic: Handling Loss

Session 3 Supplies: For students—Mural paper, Markers, Pencils; For leader—Tissues

Session 3 Content:

The focus of this session is on loss in general. Begin by talking about short-term minor losses, such as when the electrical power goes off during a storm. Ask the students if they become angry or frustrated when the power loss means they can't play on the computer. Or do they find it adventurous to sit around by candlelight with their families? Another example of loss is when they lose game time, such as if the coach pulls them out or only sends them in briefly.

Lead them next to losses of possessions, such as when you misplace a jacket or a friend borrows a book or CD for too long. Point out that sometimes an item that you thought was lost forever is returned. Other times you give up and purchase a substitute item.

Then move the discussion to the death of pets. Nearly every child can relate to this experience. Though one may obtain another puppy, she won't be the same as "Molly." Point out that though pets are irreplaceable, many who have enjoyed owning a cat or dog will eventually choose to provide a loving home for another one. Ask the group members to share the names of the pets they've lost.

Then guide them to the deepest level of loss, that of the people they are mourning. Allow them to acknowledge how this level of loss is different from others. It is more difficult because it is long-term and there is no one who can be substituted for the person they lost. After some have shared their feelings about this loss, cover the table with mural or bulletin board paper and place a pile of markers and pencils in the middle. Ask them to draw items representing all levels of losses they've experienced, such as earrings that went down the drain, bikes that were stolen, toys that were lost, cats and dogs and other pets that died. Ask them to draw that person they lost, or just things that remind them of the person—such as Grandfather's pipe, Mother's fuzzy blue robe, a cousin's favorite food. Before the session is over, allow time for each to explain his drawings. Then tape the mural on the wall in the group room or your office if you have space, or roll it up and store it in the corner until the last session when you will cut out each student's section and return it to the artist.

Questions they should be able to answer: What does loss mean? What are some of the minor losses you've experienced? Did you eventually obtain another pet after the death of one? How are those losses different from the loss of a person? How easy was it for you to draw pictures pertaining to your losses and to describe them to the others?

Session 4 Topic: Things People Say and Do

Session 4 Supplies: For leader—Whiteboard, Marker, Tissues

Session 4 Content:

During this session, ask group members to generate a list of the harmful and helpful things people say and do when responding to their grief. Allow them to write the comments on the whiteboard. First, focus on the statements or actions that people find negative: "I know how you feel" and "Don't cry." Then list the helpful things, such as "I'm thinking about you" and "I'm sorry." Explain that what may soothe some may be upsetting to others, but any answer is acceptable because you are talking about your opinions. Many people like a long hug. Others like someone who will lighten up the mood and make them laugh. Most everybody appreciates having someone simply stand by and be there for them.

Sometimes this discussion ventures into the religious realm, which is one in which school personnel must be wary. You may need to let them know that religion is not something that you can discuss in detail, but that if they are connected to a religion, they may want to seek the aid of their own religious leaders. You may want to point out that many claim religious beliefs help them work through their grief. You may also want to state that it is normal to pull away from or be furious with their religion during some stages of grief, but that most people return to their spiritual beliefs at some point and find comfort in them.

Questions they should be able to answer: What were some of the harmful comments people made to you upon the death of your loved one? What were some of the helpful things people said and did? What were some of the differences in opinions among group members?

Session 5 Topic: Sharing Your Loved One through a Collage

Session 5 Supplies: For students—Pre-cut magazine pictures, Construction paper, Scissors, Glue; For leader—Tissues

Session 5 Content:

It's time to make a collage. (You will find it most helpful to bring a pile of pictures you have already cut in order to save time.) Ask group members to find pictures that remind them of their loved one. As they work, talk about funerals and funeral homes. It's a subject adolescents are often very into, and it opens them right up, as this is not something their parents want to talk about. There is great variety in the way people formally mark a person's death, with individualized differences making the event more personal. Encourage them to share unique details of the funerals they experienced. Also, you may want to share information about cultural differences among African-American, Latin American, Christian, Muslim, and Buddhist services (Hazell, 2010).

At the end of the session, ask group members to share their finished collages, explaining why they chose certain pictures. Then ask them to bring a photograph or memento of their loved one to the next session, which is the last one. Let them know that they can drop off special items in your office that morning if their parents are reluctant to allow them to be responsible for treasured articles all day. They can return to your office at the end of the day to pick them up.

Questions they should be able to answer: How easy was it for you to find pictures relating to your loved one? How easy was it for you to share information about your collage with the others? What are your thoughts about funerals and funeral homes?

Session 6 Topic: Mementoes, Review

Session 6 Supplies: For students—Personal items (they bring in themselves, and you should, too), Star stickers; For leader—Leader's complete folder (for review), Students' work to return (mural pictures and collages), Feelings Poster (made in second session)

Session 6 Content:

At the sixth and final session, share photographs or mementoes. Allow time for proper appreciation of each person who has died. Then do a brief review of all sessions. It is helpful to start with a round of sentence completions drawn from the basket, just as you did in the very first session. Then show the Feelings Poster again, giving them more stickers in case they have new feelings to mark. In particular, ask if any are feeling less pain as a result of being in grief group. Give back to each of them the cut-out section of the loss mural that they drew. Remind them that they have been coping with losses all their lives, some petty and some serious. Being in group has enhanced their ability to respond to others disturbed by grief in uplifting rather than annoying ways. As you return the collages, praise their ability to present their loved ones so descriptively. Talk about how the experience of grief has enriched them, making them more compassionate toward others who may suffer loss. And, finally, point out that having somewhere to go with their grief—the group—has pushed forward their healing even if they do not recognize it yet. If they continue to feel the need to see you, make yourself available or refer them to Hospice grief counseling.

Questions they should be able to answer: What memento did you bring? How easy was it for you to share your memento with the others? What do you remember about each session? Do you feel less pain in your grief journey now than when you started this group?

Evaluation of Good Grief Group

Rate yourself by circling the number which corresponds with how you evaluate each statement.
1 = Not at all, 2 = A small amount, 3 = Average amount, 4 = More than average, 5 = Very much

1 I felt comfortable discussing my grief in the group.

1.................2.................3.................4.................5

2. I was able to understand the various stages of grief.

1.................2.................3.................4.................5

3. I was able to recognize and pinpoint feelings I have had at different points in my grief.

1.................2.................3.................4.................5

4. I was able to draw a variety of losses I have experienced and survived.

1.................2.................3.................4.................5

5. I learned some helpful things to say and do for others experiencing grief.

1.................2.................3.................4.................5

6. I was able to share info about my loved one with others through the collage.

1.................2.................3.................4.................5

7. I believe the group has helped me feel less pain and hurt.

1.................2.................3.................4.................5

8. I grew closer to group members during the course of the group.

1.................2.................3.................4.................5

Suggestions for making the group better: ____

____

References

Hazell, L. (2010). Funeral customs—Cross-cultural funeral rites. *Funeralwise.com.* Retrieved May 9, 2011, from http://www.funeralwise.com/customs/cross-cultural-funerals

Kessler, D. & Kubler-Ross, E. (2011). *The five stages of grief.* Retrieved April 24, 2011, from http://grief.com/the-five-stages-of-grief/

National Library of Medicine – National Institutes of Health. (2011, March 28). *Discussing death with children: MedlinePlus medical encyclopedia.* Retrieved April 13, 2011, from http://www.nlm.nih.gov/medlineplus/ency/article/001909.htm

The Healing Place. (n.d.) *Grief support for teens and their families.* Retrieved August 27, 2011, from http://www.thehealingplaceinfo.org/grief_support_teens.html

Thompson, T. (2011). Adolescent grief group activities. *Natural remedies – the natural choice.*Retrieved March 24, 2011, from http://www.nativeremedies.com/articles/adolescent-grief-group-activities.html

Wolfelt, A. (n.d.). Helping teenagers cope with grief. *Hospice.* Retrieved March 24, 2011, from http://www.hospicenet.org/html/teenager.html

Chapter 7

Juvenile Diabetes: Living with JD[1]

Living with JD Group Outline

(Please note: I use JD as an abbreviation for Juvenile Diabetes throughout this work.)

I. Introductory Information, Sentence Completion Activity
    A. Outline, Schedule, Rules
    B. Sentence Completion Activity
II. How JD Impacts School Life
    A. Discussion of School Setting
    B. Dealing with Focus on Food
III. How JD Impacts Family Life
IV. The Me Who's Not About Diabetes Collage
V. What's On the Horizon
    A. Official Diabetes Information Sources
    B. Emergency Preparedness
VI. Guest Speaker
VII. Attitudes in Special Situations/JDRF Campaign
    A. Living with JD Game
    B. JDRF Campaign
VIII. Summer Situations, Review
    A. Being Aware of Vacation Hazards
    B. Review of Prior Sessions

1 Parts of this chapter first appeared in *Diabetes Self-Management*, September/October 2009. Reprinted with permission. Copyright 2009 R.A. Rapaport Publishing, Inc.

American School Counselor Association (ASCA) Standards

Academic Development

Standard A: Students will acquire the attitudes, knowledge, and skills that contribute to effective learning in school and across the life span.

A:A3 Achieve School Success

A:A3.5 Share knowledge

Career Development

Standard A: Students will acquire the skills to investigate the world of work in relation to knowledge of self and to make informed career decisions.

C:A1 Develop Career Awareness

C:A1.3 Develop an awareness of personal abilities, skills, interests, and motivations

Personal/Social Development

Standard A: Students will acquire the knowledge, attitudes, and interpersonal skills to help them understand and respect self and others.

PS:A1 Acquire Self-knowledge

PS:A1.5 Identify and express feelings

PS:A1.10 Identify personal strengths and assets

Standard B: Students will make decisions, set goals and take necessary action to achieve goals.

PS:B1 Self-knowledge Application

PS:B1.4 Develop effective coping skills for dealing with problems

Standard C: Students will understand safety and survival skills

PS:C1 Acquire Personal Safety Skills

PS:C1.11 Learn coping skills for managing life events

Rationale for Living with Juvenile Diabetes (JD) Group

Type 1 Diabetes, also known as Juvenile Diabetes, is a life-changing, incurable diagnosis. It is estimated that three million Americans have Type 1, with eighty per day being diagnosed (Juvenile Diabetes Research Foundation, 2010). The health hazards from having diabetes are severe: possible amputations, heart disease, blindness, stroke, and kidney failure. The vast majority of people diagnosed with diabetes have Type 2, which can sometimes be prevented with attention to a healthy lifestyle. Of the people diagnosed with diabetes, only 5% of them have Type 1 (American Diabetes Association, 2010). Sometimes people with Type 1 are erroneously accused of having somehow contributed to their diagnosis from reckless or unhealthy behaviors, but Type 1 comes on suddenly and is not preventable.

People affected by JD never get a break from it. As friends wolf down pizzas, sodas, and ice cream at school and community functions, the child with JD must perform mathematical calculations multiple times a day to figure out what he or she can safely eat. Having a support group for these students gives them an opportunity to connect with others who also face the daily grind of living with diabetes. They bond quickly as they commiserate but also lift each other up with shared tips and techniques about their diagnosis.

In this group students experience sessions on how diabetes affects school life and family life. Current research findings are discussed. They play a game in which both positive and negative consequences of their actions regarding diabetes are exemplified. A guest speaker (usually an older teen who is managing his or her diabetes well) is invited for one session. There is also a session in which discussion of diabetes is forbidden, turning the focus to other facets of their lives. The final session provides special information related to summer concerns and ends with encouragement for members to join the support group again next year.

What Makes It Work:

1. This group would not be solicited as the others, of course. The best place to obtain your list of diagnosed students is from the school nurse, as she is the staff member most closely connected to these students. Send a letter (see the sample included here) to parents BEFORE meeting with these students!
2. Most kids with JD have never before had the opportunity to be in a group and are very excited to have their concerns acknowledged. The diagnosis has suddenly taken on a slightly positive aura.
3. Parents are very happy that someone is recognizing the special obstacles their children face.
4. You may want to include the school nurse in several (or all) group sessions.
5. Members realize they are not the only ones coping with this disease, and they form a close tie with each other.
6. Students receive emotional support and learn strategies to cope with this condition.

Challenges:

1. At many schools you may not have enough students diagnosed with JD to warrant having a group. You would probably need at least four students. (One year I had nine!)
2. Since having a disease or condition such as JD is very personal health information, it is possible that some parents and/or students would prefer to not participate in such a group.
3. Most likely your students will be from different grade levels and thus scheduling needs to reflect that. It may work best to run this group in either the first or last period of the day to best accommodate multiple grade levels and not clash with lunch schedules. In order to keep these students from missing so much class in a short period of time, it is ideal to develop this as a yearlong group that meets monthly. That way the meetings are spaced far apart, and the first and last period teachers hardly notice the students missing their classes. My school runs a traditional calendar schedule, starting school in late August. I begin this group in October, giving the students time to adjust to the demands of the new school year, and continue it through May for a total of eight sessions.
4. When compared to the general population, these students may suffer a higher rate of absenteeism (though I have not found this to be true with my students).
5. When compared to the general population, it is more likely that a student in this type of group could become very seriously ill or even die. This would be extremely difficult for other group members.

Date

Dear Parent of ____,

For the fifth year, I am conducting a support group for students at CC Griffin who have been diagnosed with Juvenile Diabetes – Type 1. The group will meet for forty-five minutes once a month during the school day. Students will miss class but will be allowed to make up work. I have set up the first group meeting for Friday, October 7, from 3:15–4:00.

The group will give students a chance to share feelings about having this diagnosis and learn how others manage to cope. It will be most helpful for them to realize that they are not alone in our school. Our school nurse may come to some meetings.

In the past the group has been a lot of fun, and I hope to have all of those students returning to the group plus any new ones. If you have questions, please call me at 704/455-4700. Please complete the form below and return it to me by Friday, September 24.

Sincerely,

Debra Efird
School Counselor

++

Student Name____

_____ Yes, my child has permission to be in the group.

_____ No, I do not want my child to participate in the group.

____ ______________

Parent signature Date

Living with JD Group Sessions

Session 1 Topic: Introductory Info, Sentence Completion Activity

Session 1 Supplies: For students—Copies of outline and schedule; For leader—Copy of JD Sentence Completion Statements cut into strips, Basket

Session 1 Content:

Begin with the usual introductory information explaining the outline, schedule, and group rules. Then ask the members to tell the others in the group at what age they were diagnosed with Juvenile Diabetes – Type 1.

Then move into that great conversation starter, the JD Sentence Completion Statements activity. Allow students to pass or redraw another slip if they do not feel comfortable answering the one they draw first. Take your time, allowing students to elaborate on their own statements and those of others. With this being a multi-grade level group, care must be taken to ensure that younger students do not feel intimidated by older ones.

Questions they should be able to answer: What are the topics that will be covered in group? How does the schedule work? What are the group rules? How easy was it for you to complete the sentences you drew? What did you learn about each other in the introductory session?

JD Sentence Completion Statements

People think you are ______________________________ if you have diabetes.

I want to tell my friends who don't have diabetes that ______________________________.

When I hear someone talking about diabetes, I ______________________________.

When my blood sugar levels are good, I feel ______________________________.

When I hear the word diabetes, I ______________________________.

One thing I hate about the hospital is ______________________________.

I wish things were like they were before I was diagnosed because ______________________________.

Sometimes I'm afraid that ______________________________.

When my blood sugar levels are not good, I feel ______________________________.

When someone says, "I know how you feel," I ______________________________.

The person I feel most comfortable talking about diabetes with is ______________________________.

When I am around other people with diabetes, I feel ______________________________.

When I see other kids eating what they want, I feel ______________________________.

The idea of pain makes me ______________________________.

If I could be any kind of doctor, I would be a ______________________________.

When I hear my parent tell someone else about my having diabetes, I feel ______________.

When I first learned I had diabetes, I ______________________________.

One thing I like about the hospital is ______________________________.

When I see my parent upset about my diabetes, I feel ______________________________.

When I go to the doctor about my diabetes, I feel ______________________________.

What I hate most about having diabetes is ______________________________.

Sometimes I hate waking up in the morning because ______________________________.

The best thing about being around other kids with diabetes is ______________________.

Session 2 Topic: How JD Impacts School Life

Session 2 Supplies: For students—Copies of When It Seems That Food Makes the World Go Round worksheet, Pencils

Session 2 Content:

A good place to start: how JD affects life at school. Be sure that they understand their right to check blood sugar levels or to see the nurse at any time they need. Ask them to share how they feel about having to miss part of class to check in with the nurse. Ask how they catch up with the class. Encourage them to discuss how prolonged episodes of abnormal sugar levels could affect their grades. Talk about the pros and cons of being separated from others or having special modifications during testing. Find out what worries them most about school.

Then move the discussion to food. No matter where anyone goes, food will be at the center of many events throughout life. It will be important for them to learn to deal with this in a healthy manner, not just as students but as adults. Distribute the When It Seems That Food Makes the World Go Round worksheet and pencils. One example covers the various actions a student could take when faced with snacks at an after school club meeting. Complete it together, asking which answer choice each selected. Allow for differences in opinion. Encourage them to share an additional answer if they think of something on their own.

Questions they should be able to answer: What are your rights as a student with Juvenile Diabetes? What are some of the special problems students with JD face in school? Do you feel comfortable with how your school accepts your special needs as a student with JD? What are some appropriate ways to handle food-driven social situations?

When It Seems That Food Makes the World Go Round ...

1. Jonathan's chess club always has snacks during the meeting. Students take turn providing refreshments, and most bring regular sodas and high-calorie sweets. Jonathan should:

    a. eat nothing and sulk.

    b. eat all of it and take a risk.

    c. bring his own snacks.

    d. bring in healthy snacks when it is his turn.

2. The homeroom that wins the door decorating contest gets a free pizza party. Elizabeth knows that she may not be able to participate in the party because her blood sugar levels have been very irregular lately. She should:

    a. do a bad job on her part of the decorations on purpose so that her class will not win.

    b. approach her principal about providing other incentives besides food, such as thirty minutes outside or an extra library period.

    c. take her own food and smile if her team wins.

    d. eat just as much as she wants and not worry about it.

3. After school the kids hang out at the ice cream shop on their way home from school. Mark wants to join them but has trouble with self-discipline regarding ice cream. Mark should:

    a. go straight home and forget about hanging out.

    b. eat a healthy snack before he gets there so he won't be tempted by the ice cream.

    c. suggest that the kids hang out at the convenience store instead where there is a variety of food and drinks to choose from.

    d. ask for a free sample only.

Session 3 Topic: How JD Impacts Home Life

Session 3 Supplies: For leader—Copies of sheets labeled Activities, Food, Money, and Siblings (cut into strips, using different colors for each category); Basket

Session 3 Content:

In this session you will address how having JD affects home life. Start by putting the labeled strips in a basket. Ask each student to pull a strip. The student must tell how having JD affects that particular aspect of his home life. For example: If the student pulls a strip labeled "money," he must talk about an incident or something in general about how JD affects family finances. He may reveal that he has overheard his mother complaining about the cost of insulin. Or he may say that his family is saving money for a new pump.

To keep the activity more mysterious, don't tell them on the first round that the colors mean anything. On the second round, clue them in to the fact all yellow strips are about money, all blue ones are about food, etc. That way they can exercise more choice in selecting the general area they want to comment on in subsequent rounds. With the strip labeled "food," you'll hear comments about not always being able to eat what everyone else in the family is having or the trouble their mothers go to just to cook something special for them. With the strip labeled "activities," you may have responses about the whole family canceling fun plans due to the child having low blood sugar. With the strip labeled "siblings," you can expect to stir up some anger. They'll report on siblings who taunt them while snacking on candy bars or those who scream in jealousy over all the attention the diagnosed child gets. This activity sparks shared laughter and helps bond the students even closer.

Questions they should be able to answer: What are some of the home problems presented by JD in the areas of food, money, activities, and siblings? How easy was it for you to think of examples for the topics you pulled from the basket?

ACTIVITES

(cut)- -

ACTIVITIES

(cut)- -

ACTIVITIES

(cut)- -

ACTIVITIES

FOOD

(cut)- -

FOOD

(cut)- -

FOOD

(cut)- -

FOOD

MONEY

(cut)--

MONEY

(cut)--

MONEY

(cut)--

MONEY

SIBLINGS

(cut)- -

SIBLINGS

(cut)- -

SIBLINGS

(cut)- -

SIBLINGS

Session 4 Topic: The Me Who's Not About Diabetes Collage

Session 4 Supplies: For students—Pre-cut (to save time) magazine pictures, Construction paper, Glue, Scissors

Session 4 Content:

If you time it right, your fourth session may fall in January, which is always a time for new beginnings. This session underlines the value in focusing on the many other facets of their lives. On the door of your group room, place a sign that says "Live-abetes" and instruct the students that they cannot utter the word "diabetes" during this entire session. If someone says the "d" word, instate a silly punishment, like running three laps around the table or singing "The Star-Spangled Banner" as a solo.

Carefully state that they are going to create The Me Who's Not About Diabetes collage. (Maybe you can spell "diabetes" and that won't count against you.) Pile the pictures and other supplies on the table within reach of all. Urge them to select pictures that they think represent them now and in the future so that their thoughts are directed forward to possible careers. Most students enjoy talking about what they want to be when they grow up. When they have completed their work, ask them to show their collages and share the reasons for their choices.

Questions they should be able to answer: What are some aspects of your life that have nothing to do with JD? Was it fun to eliminate thoughts of diabetes from the group session? Were you able to see the others in a different light?

Session 5 Topic: What's On the Horizon

Session 5 Supplies: For leader—Current Internet articles from websites of American Diabetes Association and Juvenile Diabetes Research Foundation, Whiteboard, Marker

Session 5 Content:

At this session talk about what is new on the horizon medically. First ask them if they have information to share regarding any recent developments in the search for a cure or for better management of diabetes. It is wise to caution them about claims of cures. Assure them that their doctors will know when something helpful has been approved. It is important to talk hopefully about some of the research results. Show them any current articles of interest you have found from researching these reputable websites: American Diabetes Association (www.diabetes.org) and Juvenile Diabetes Research Foundation (www.jdrf.org). Share those web addresses by writing them on the board. This is also a good time to mention the national Juvenile Diabetes Research Foundation (JDRF) drive that is held in the spring in most communities and is often supported by schools. If your community has a march, give group members the date now so that they can start thinking about joining the walk.

Just for fun, ask them to imagine some funny cures, and they'll laugh themselves silly. What if scientists discover that green "M & M's" are the magic bullet? What if a mixture of chopped caterpillars and birdseed is the cure—would they eat it?

Another topic that ties in somewhat with medical news is the need to be fully prepared in the case of natural disasters and emergencies. Though there are often warnings about the approach of some dangerous storms or situations, other events such as a hazardous waste spill or a stray tornado can catch people off guard. In the event of a sudden evacuation, students need to be sure they have a set of diabetes supplies ready to transport with them. Even a prolonged power outage can create problems in keeping insulin at the correct temperature (Katzki & Katzki, 2009). Ask group members to check with their parents about such emergency planning.

Questions they should be able to answer: What are some legitimate sources of information about diabetes? What are some hopeful research findings? What can you do in your school and community to promote research for the cure? What might be an insanely ridiculous cure? Do you have a diabetes care kit set aside for emergencies? Have you ever experienced an emergency situation in which you were without the items you needed to manage your diabetes?

Session 6 Topic: Guest Speaker

Session 6 Supplies: Guest Speaker (really!), For leader—Sample Questions for Speaker cut into strips, Basket

Session 6 Content:

Time for a breath of fresh air! Seek a guest speaker who is a high school or college student coping successfully with JD. If none are available, an adult speaker will do, but preferably someone fairly young so that he or she can better relate to the group members. Ask your school nurse to contact her cohort at a nearby high school to locate someone suitable, or perhaps you could arrange this counselor-to-counselor. It is advisable to schedule this meeting at the end of the school day for the convenience of the high school student. If there are transportation problems, perhaps you or his parent or the school nurse could bring him. It's a good idea to prepare the Sample Questions for Speaker that your group members can ask in case they suddenly freeze up about asking questions. Cut the sample questions into strips and throw them into that faithful basket to add a little intrigue.

Questions they should be able to answer: How does the guest speaker cope with JD? What special challenges has the speaker overcome? Were you inspired or encouraged by anything the speaker said?

Sample Questions for Speaker

1. Do you have to miss much school or work due to your diabetes?

2. When do you tell friends or coworkers that you have diabetes?

3. Is it hard for people to understand that you are not contagious?

4. Do your parents still ask you about your sugar readings all the time?

5. What is your most embarrassing moment with diabetes?

6. Does your blood sugar level affect your driving?

7. Do you check your blood sugar in front of people?

8. What is your biggest fear of diabetes?

9. Is it hard for a person with diabetes to maintain a romantic relationship?

10. Are you planning to go to college or continue your education in some way?

Session 7 Topic: Attitudes in Special Situations

Session 7 Supplies: For leader—Copy of Living with JD Game cut into small (1" × 3") pieces, 10 large (at least 11" × 14") sheets of construction paper, Basket, Copy of JDRF Announcement

Session 7 Content:

By now your students know you and each other well. It is a good time to talk about choosing the attitude that will go with the special situations they find themselves in day after day, even if it means stepping on their toes a bit. Playing the Living with JD Game makes it fun. You need a little space, as you will be setting the ten sheets of construction paper one beside another to form a line (which can curve if you like) and the students will be moving toward the finish line. Put the small pieces of paper with various JD situations on them in the basket. Indicate who's going first and ask that student to draw a strip of paper from the basket. The student must read aloud the statement and take the appropriate step(s). For example: You can laugh or joke about your diabetes sometimes. Go forward 1 space. Another example: You fudge your true numbers because you know your parents won't like them. Go back 2 spaces. Free space means one step forward with no conditions attached. If the student draws one which states he must go back a space and he hasn't made it onto the construction paper yet, then he just remains behind the starting line until his next turn.

If the basket is empty before anyone has reached the tenth step or finish line, then recycle them. They will not want the game to end. They will laugh even as they recognize and admit their occasional negative choices. Let the group freely express and chide one another, but keep it from becoming vindictive.

If your school operates on a traditional calendar and you have started your group at the first of the school year, then it is now the time of year for the nationwide JDRF fundraising drive. If your school supports this cause, it is a great opportunity to promote the positive side of being "special" for your students with Juvenile Diabetes. Ideas for fundraising include having an annual talent show with all proceeds benefitting JDRF. Other ideas are raffles for goods that have been donated and regular collections in classrooms. Group members can make the drive much more meaningful to other students if they speak on school video announcements or at assemblies. (A sample brief announcement is included.) If a march is held near you, make this a group project. Even if only a few members can participate, it is still a way to lift up the cause.

Questions they should be able to answer: What are some situations in which you may have exhibited a negative attitude regarding managing your diabetes? How can you provide emotional support for each other in these situations? When have you demonstrated a positive attitude regarding managing your diabetes? What are some things you can do as a group to support the JDRF campaign?

Living with JD Game

You are embarrassed when your mother acts terribly overprotective when you go on the Scout camping trip. Go back 1 space.	You forget to make adjustments at lunch and your numbers go high when you get home, ensuring your parents will yell at you. Go back 1 space.
You don't tell your mom when you run out of snacks at school. Go back 1 space.	You use your diabetes as a shock factor, telling classmates "I might die tonight." Go back 2 spaces.
You remember to check your blood sugar levels accurately for a whole week because your dad rewards you when you do a good job of managing them. Go forward 1 space.	You decide to irritate your parents by running up your numbers on purpose. Go back 2 spaces.
You answer curious classmates who ask questions about your diabetes in a nice way. Go forward 1 space.	You make up all the class work you miss when you have to sit in the nurse's office because of being low. Go forward 2 spaces.
You make a strong effort to stay physically fit by eating right and exercising. Go forward 2 spaces.	You pass out in class because you choose to ignore your warning signs. Go back 1 space.
Your parents can trust you to make adjustments independently. Go forward 2 spaces.	You choose to do your health class report on JD to educate others and make an easy A. Go forward 1 space.

Your principal wants you to lead the school JDRF campaign. Go forward 2 spaces.	The school nurse asks you to help a newly diagnosed student cope with his situation. Go forward 2 spaces.
You stick a kid with a needle because he's been annoying you when you check your blood sugar levels in class. Go back 3 spaces.	You fudge your true numbers because you know your parents won't like them. Go back 2 spaces.
You share your school snacks with another diabetic who has run out. Go forward 1 space.	You do not use your diabetes as an excuse for not doing homework. Go forward 1 space.
You do not talk about your diabetes excessively around your classmates. Go forward 1 space.	You accept the fact that many social functions revolve around food, and you try to participate in your own way. Go forward 1 space.
You can laugh or joke about your diabetes sometimes. Go forward 1 space.	You have hope that diabetes will be cured in the next ten years. Go forward 2 spaces.
You manage to pass all your classes even though you are hospitalized several times. Go forward 2 spaces.	You eat way too much of the wrong things because you are feeling sorry for yourself. Go back 2 spaces.

1 free space	1 free space
1 free space	1 free space
1 free space	1 free space
1 free space	1 free space
1 free space	1 free space
1 free space	1 free space
1 free space	1 free space
1 free space	1 free space

JDRF Announcement

My name is ______________________________ and I have Juvenile Diabetes, also known as Type 1 Diabetes.

People with Type 1 Diabetes do not get it from eating the wrong things or not exercising enough. They do not catch it from someone. Sometimes genetics plays a role in who gets diabetes. Most of the time there is no explanation why some people get it and some don't.

I've had Juvenile Diabetes since I was ____ years old.

It could happen to your brother or sister or friend.

It could happen to you.

Please support JDRF. Help find a cure.

Session 8 Topic: Summer Situations, Review

Session 8 Supplies: For students—Copies of evaluation form, Pencils; For leader—Leader's complete folder (for review)

Session 8 Content:

At the eighth and final meeting (it's almost summer!), it is time to discuss important matters that may come up during the months that group members are away from school. Ask them to share any special situations that they anticipate, such as travel concerns. Note how time changes and flight schedules can make handling their diabetes problematic, just as being out of a regular routine during long days at the beach can require adjustments. Also, some students may have had a nurse nearby for eight hours a day while in school and now they must depend on themselves or parents to help monitor their levels. Different sleeping and eating patterns may require important adjustments.

Also encourage them to seek information, printable handouts, or even a "pen pal" (with parent approval, of course) over the summer from the Juvenile Diabetes Research Foundation web site (www.jdrf.org).

Then do a brief review of earlier sessions, reminding them of previous topics and activities. As with other groups that are ending, remind them that you are always available for individual counseling as needed. Encourage returning students to join your group again next year when you'll provide a whole new slate of sessions. (Get to work!)

Questions they should be able to answer: What are some special situations that arise with summer? What are some sources of support you can seek in the summer? What do you remember about each session? How has this group been helpful to you?

Evaluation of Living with JD Group

Rate yourself by circling the number which corresponds with how you evaluate each statement.
1 = Not at all, 2 = A small amount, 3 = Average amount, 4 = More than average, 5 = Very much

1. I felt comfortable discussing having diabetes in the group.

   1.................2.................3.................4.................5

2. I understand how having diabetes impacts my school life.

   1.................2.................3.................4.................5

3. I recognize how having diabetes impacts my family.

   1.................2.................3.................4.................5

4. I recognize that there are many facets of myself that have nothing to do with diabetes.

   1.................2.................3.................4.................5

5. I learned good sources for diabetes information.

   1.................2.................3.................4.................5

6. I recognize the need to express my emotions about having diabetes.

   1.................2.................3.................4.................5

7. I understand the special diabetes management situations that may come up in summer.

   1.................2.................3.................4.................5

8. I grew closer to group members during the course of the group.

   1.................2.................3.................4.................5

Suggestions for making the group better: ____

____

References

American Diabetes Association. (2010). *Diabetes Basics Type 1*. Retrieved March 26, 2011, from http://www.diabetes.org/diabetes-basics/type-1/

Juvenile Diabetes Research Foundation International. (2010, December). *Type 1 Diabetes: Dedicated to finding a cure*. Retrieved March 26, 2011, from http://www.jdrf.org/index.cfm?page_id=102585

Katzki, D. & Katzki, L. (2009, September/October). Disaster preparedness: It's never too early to plan ahead! *Diabetes Self-Management, 26*(5), 27-31.

Chapter 8

Latina Pride[1]

Latina Pride Group Outline

I. Introductory Information/Academic Focus
   A. Outline, Schedule, Parent Permission, Rules
   B. Academic Report

II. Who Are You? Collage

III. How You Fit In: Expectations/Dilemmas

IV. Acceptance: Things You Can/Cannot Change

V. Looking to the Future/Career Awareness
   A. Academic Progress Report
   B. When I Am 23 Activity
   C. Occupations Study

VI. Relationships with Friends/Boyfriends

VII. Cultural Celebrations

VIII. Review/Game
   A. Review of Prior Sessions
   B. Academic Progress Report
   C. Latina Situations Game

1 Parts of this chapter first appeared in *Counseling Today*, November 2007. Reprinted with permission from American Counseling Association. That article also appeared in Silhouettes, the e-journal of National At-Risk Education Network, September 2008, reprinted with permission from NAREN.

American School Counselor Association (ASCA) Standards

Academic Development

Standard A: Students will acquire the attitudes, knowledge, and skills that contribute to effective learning in school and across the life span.

A:A3 Achieve School Success

A:A3.5 Share knowledge

Standard B: Students will complete school with the academic preparation essential to choose from a wide range of substantial post-secondary options, including college.

A:B2 Plan to Achieve Goals

A:B2.1 Establish challenging academic goals in elementary, middle/jr. high, and high school

Career Development

Standard A: Students will acquire the skills to investigate the world of work in relation to knowledge of self and to make informed career decisions.

C:A1 Develop Career Awareness

C:A1.1 Develop skills to locate, evaluate, and interpret career information

C:A1.3 Develop an awareness of personal abilities, skills, interests, and motivations

Personal/Social Development

Standard A: Students will acquire the knowledge, attitudes, and interpersonal skills to help them understand and respect self and others.

PS:A1 Acquire Self-knowledge

PS:A1.2 Identify values, attitudes, and beliefs

PS:A1.5 Identify and express feelings

PS:A1.12 Identify and recognize changing family roles

Standard B: Students will make decisions, set goals and take necessary action to achieve goals.

PS:B1 Self-knowledge Application

PS:B1.9 Identify long- and short-term goals

Rationale for Latina Pride Group

It is generally known that the Latino population is the largest and fastest growing minority group in the United States. Nearly 52% of Latinas become pregnant as teenagers. Latina teens are three times more likely to become pregnant than non-Hispanic white girls (The National Campaign, 2011). Pregnancy complicates a teen's life dramatically and may lead girls and their boyfriends to drop out of school. The ramifications for our country are clear to see: a large proportion of our population will remain undereducated if this trend continues.

In 2008, the Latino dropout rate across the United States averaged at 18% for students in the 16–24 age range (National Center for Education Statistics, n.d.). Some statistics indicate there is a considerable difference in the dropout rates of native-born Hispanic students and immigrant-born ones, with those who have received their education in the United States having a far lower dropout rate than those who immigrate. Still, the rate is higher than other minority populations. It is also noted that low English proficiency correlates closely with the dropout rate. But even in those who have achieved proficient English, the Hispanic dropout rate is still problematic (Jones & Bou-Waked, 2007).

The Pew Hispanic Center (2011) noted that many Latino students drop out to work. Unfortunately, the income they produce usually leaves them in poverty. Continuing their education offers them much more economic opportunity in the long run, but it is difficult if their families have a history of valuing work over education.

How do we curtail the quick exit through the school doors of our Latino students? Offering support groups for them is one intervention that school counselors can provide. When providing a group with a focus on multicultural concerns, one must become more self-aware by examining one's own cultural biases. It is vital to acknowledge and respect cultural differences. Allowing Latino students a place to come together contributes to their comfort level at school. In a group they can share concerns with others who understand the difficulties they face in trying to straddle life between two cultures.

In this group, there are sessions to discuss scenarios which deal with relationship problems, dilemmas of fitting in, and acceptance of change. One session is dedicated to discussing how their families have blended American and Latino holidays. The importance of academic success and future careers are emphasized. Besides lively discussions, they experience fun activities such as making a collage and playing a game. More than anything, they have a place to belong.

What Makes It Work:

1. This group can be either selected or solicited, depending on your numbers of Latinas. One good way to determine membership is by using students connected to the English as a Second Language program, whether it is by active classroom participation or merely consultation. Depending on how much you want to take on, you could expand this to fit your school by having several sections. Or you could limit it to just one grade level; for example, only seventh graders in the group. You may choose to do a mixed-gender class, but you would need to tweak the agenda somewhat since this one is designed for girls.
2. It gives them an opportunity to belong to something. Holding the group during school hours eliminates the transportation problem that prevents many of these students from becoming actively engaged in their schools.

3. It provides them with moral support as they face increasingly harsh attitudes about immigration. We must always remember that these students did not choose where they live.
4. It gives them a chance to learn conflict resolution skills to deflect the negativism often shown to minorities. If fights can be prevented because students can vent their feelings in a group, we are accomplishing much!
5. It gives them the chance to relax and speak a little Spanish if they so desire without someone demanding that English be spoken. (Think how relieved you feel when you're traveling in a foreign country and you hear someone speaking English. For a few moments, life is easier.)
6. It gives these students a connection to staff members, which is something they may not ordinarily seek on their own. We all need support, and students facing dual identities especially need help.
7. Hopefully, the girls gain a sense of the importance of academics and goal setting as well as a feeling of belonging.

Challenges:

1. Scheduling can be a problem with multi-grade level groups as you may be limited to conducting the group in either the first or last 45 minutes of the day. In order to keep in good stead with teachers, you may want to make this a monthly group rather than a short-term weekly one so that teachers don't become concerned about the frequency of them missing class. I do this group as a monthly one, starting in October and ending in May, for a total of eight sessions.
2. Students may be afraid to join if they are undocumented. At the initial meeting, tell them that there will be no questions about their immigration status. Sometimes in the course of group discussion students will reveal this information. Be sure that it is kept confidential.
3. Language problems are certainly possible. If you speak Spanish well or have a co-leader who is bilingual, this will alleviate situations in which someone gets stuck due to language difficulties. However, the vast majority of students have adequate English skills to get something out of the group, and they can help the few others who may need some translation. Be sure to make copies of the parent permission letter in Spanish and English. (I have included a parent letter in Spanish that was developed by a fluent friend—I hope it is error-free.)
4. There is a generally perceived idea that Latinos have attendance problems. In all my years, this is simply an unfounded stereotype.
5. Due to the controversy surrounding immigration issues, some administrators and other staff may prefer no special assistance be given to Latino students. Unless you are micromanaged by your administration, you might start the group without seeking permission and then present information after the fact listing it alongside all the other groups you are conducting.

15 de septembre, 2011

Estimados Padres de______________________________________:

Quisieremos ofrecer un grupo de sosten para las estudiantes Latinas en nuestra escuela. El grupo comienza en octubre y termine en mayo. Nos encontramos un vez cada mes y cambiaramos la hora del dia para que ellas no falten la misma clase cada vez que nos reunimos.

Las Latinas en los estados unidos pueden encontrar problemas y desafios en su vida que son diferentes de las ostras estudiantes. Tenemos planeado actividades divertidas que acentuan la importancia de la educacion y que tambien ayuden su hija en la escuela.

Por favor firme abojo dando permiso que su hija participle en este grupo. Devuelva esta forma a la Senora Efird en la oficina de las consejeras.

Sinceramante,

____

Debra Efird, Consejera

____ ________________

Firme de los padres la fecha

Latina Pride Group Sessions

Session 1 Topic: Introductory Information, Academic Focus

Session 1 Supplies: For students—Copies of outline, schedule, and parent permission form in Spanish, Index cards, Pencils; For leader— Spanish dictionary (just in case)

Session 1 Content:

It's especially invitational to welcome group members in Spanish and maybe throw out a few other Spanish phrases here and there if possible. Keep a Spanish dictionary nearby, but you probably won't need it. Most of them will be fairly fluent in English, and they can lean on each other to check their understanding. In the beginning the students will naturally be questioning why they have been pulled together for a meeting. After explaining the purpose of the group, which is to create a setting in which they can discuss various issues about living in two cultures, you will probably sense a current of excitement. Most will be eager to have a chance to talk about their lives, and, of course, be given a valid excuse to miss class.

First you must explain the schedule, parent permission requirement, outline, and rules. For everything that is written I use only English, with the exception of the parent permission letter. It is also important to discuss the concept of confidentiality. It is important to assure them that no questions will be asked about the documentation status of their families.

To keep administration comfortable, it is ideal for your group to have some academic focus (however minimal). Hand out index cards and pencils and ask them to write down their most recent grade averages in all subjects. Then ask them to set a goal for the next grading period, whether it is to maintain the current grade or improve it, and write it beside the current grade. Then take up the cards to bring back at a later date.

Questions they should be able to answer: What are the topics that will be covered in group? How does the schedule work? What are the group rules? When is the signed parent permission letter due? How easy was it for you to set academic goals?

Session 2 Topic: Who Are You? Collage

Session 2 Supplies: For students—Pre-cut (to save time) magazine pictures, Construction paper, Glue, Scissors; For leader—Spanish dictionary

Session 2 Content:

Making a collage is an easy way for students to relax and feel comfortable in a group. Place the pictures and other materials in a pile in the middle of the table and invite them to choose the ones that appeal to them or describe them. Also ask that they choose pictures that show their career interests. Even if you cannot find many pictures of Latinos to include in your stash, it probably won't bother them. As they are working, encourage conversation among group members to help them bond. Perhaps ask them for the "high" and "low" points of the week to encourage them to start talking.

When they have completed the collages, ask group members to share with others the reasons for their choices of pictures. This activity helps the girls get to know one another, which is especially helpful if they are spread across several grade levels.

Questions they should be able to answer: How easy was it for you to find pictures that represented your life? Were you unable to find pictures to represent certain things you wanted to include? What did you learn about others in the group?

Session 3 Topic: How You Fit In: Expectations/Dilemmas

Session 3 Supplies: For students—Copies of How You Fit In Scenarios; For leader—Spanish dictionary

Session 3 Content:

Distribute copies of the How You Fit In Scenarios sheet, asking group members to read each scenario aloud and discuss it. It makes this activity more fun if you retype them using the names of your group members in the stories (though names have been changed for this work). These scenarios cover divisive topics such as when family values conflict with personal wants and needs. Ask them to note the controversy they face when their new culture clashes with their old one. Each situation generates much discussion, as they are very familiar with these issues. Encourage them to brainstorm alternative solutions.

Take the example about Florinda's mother needing her to accompany her to a doctor's appointment during school hours to translate symptoms of her illness. Florinda is torn between the importance of school attendance and family loyalty. Responses to this scenario may include trying to identify someone else who could accompany Florinda's mother, such as another sibling who has a better attendance record or perhaps a cousin who can take off work for a few hours. Or someone might suggest that Florinda write down a list of all her mother's symptoms in English for her to give to the doctor, with a request for the doctor to write his comments as well. Another girl may say she should tell her teachers about her dilemma because that might make them more sympathetic to her situation and thus more willing to help her catch up.

If there is time, ask them to tell of other similar situations that they have personally encountered.

Questions they should be able to answer: What are some of the special situations facing Latinas that other students do not experience? What are some ways in which your family's culture conflicts with American culture? Were there others in the group who shared your same issues?

How You Fit In Scenarios

Rosa has a weekend job helping sell food at the flea market. The boss needs her to work on a school day because of a special event. Rosa will receive double pay, but she knows she has two tests that day at school.

Florinda's mother has a doctor's appointment at 9:30 Tuesday morning. She needs Florinda to translate while she describes her illness to the doctor. Florinda has missed 14 days of school already, but she knows her mother needs her.

Zitlali had a great idea for her science project. She wrote such a fine report that Liliana wants to copy it. Zitlali knows it isn't right, but she doesn't want to lose her as a friend and she knows Liliana is failing science.

Eneida has been a friend of Felisa for a long time. Eneida thinks she should tell Felisa that she smells bad, but she knows that Felisa's family sometimes struggles to pay the power and water bills. Felisa is very sensitive and gets her feelings hurt easily.

Bernice wants to go to her best friend Maria's 13th birthday party, but she is expected to go with her family to a cousin's wedding the same day. She doesn't know how to talk about it with either Maria or her parents.

Even though Giovanna is on probation for stealing from a store, she took money from a teacher's purse when she was out of the room. Suleyma saw her do it and was very surprised that her friend would take such a risk. When the teacher suspected Giovanna, Suleyma wondered if she should jump in and take the blame.

Guadalupe's aunt, who lives in Mexico, sent her a plane ticket to visit her this summer. Guadalupe doesn't feel comfortable visiting in her former home because her old friends there treat her differently now.

Session 4 Topic: Acceptance: Things You Can/Cannot Change

Session 4 Supplies: For leader—Copy of Things You Can/Cannot Change (cut into strips), Basket, Spanish dictionary

Session 4 Content:

Introduce this session by asking group members if they can think of things they can change and things that they cannot alter. They may struggle with the concepts, but they will understand once you start the pass-the-basket activity. Put the strips you have cut from the Things You Can/Cannot Change sheet into the basket, and ask group members to pull one at a time and indicate their answer. Some of these items are a little tricky and may trigger controversy. Expect some good-natured disagreement. For example: You made an "F" in science last quarter. (No, you cannot change it; the grade is a "done deed." However, you could work on making a higher grade for next quarter.) Another example: Your best friend is Felicia. (Yes, this can change as you might decide you like Eneida better.) At the end of the session, they should be aware of the things in their own lives that they can change or improve. They should also realize that some things cannot be changed and must be accepted.

Questions they should be able to answer: How easy was it for you to decide if an item could be changed or not? How important is it to realize what can be changed and what cannot be? What were some of the items that students had a variety of opinions on?

Things You Can/Cannot Change

You do not know how to bake a cake.

You missed 22 days of school last year.

You hate green beans.

You made an F in science first quarter.

Your best friend is Felicia.

Your dog ate your homework.

You know only a little Spanish.

Your father drives his car while drunk.

Your uncle died last summer.

Your mother yells at you when you do not help with dinner.

You have brown eyes.

You are failing math.

You smoke cigarettes.

Your friends make fun of your shoes or coat.

Your hair is short and curly.

You are lucky when playing cards.

Your boyfriend is Rodrigo.

You want to live in a big brick house.

You are the oldest child in your family.

Your dad works at the poultry farm.

You live on Pine Street.

You babysit on Friday nights.

You are Latina.

Session 5 Topic: Looking to the Future/Career Awareness

Session 5 Supplies: For students—Copies of When I Am 23 worksheet, Pencils; For leader—Index cards (from before), Copy of Occupational Outlook Handbook (Bureau of Labor Statistics, 2009), Spanish dictionary

Session 5 Content:

At this session, start by having group members look over the index cards they completed at the first session. Ask them to update the cards with their current grades. Encourage them to talk about their progress.

Distribute the When I Am 23 worksheet and ask them to complete it as you go along, reading aloud each statement and answer choices. This activity sparks a lot of buzz among the girls as they imagine their futures. Some of the terms such as "soup kitchen" or "Crisis Assistance" may need explanation. When they inevitably choose to drive a new car, own a house, and eat at nice restaurants, ask them how they are going to do this. It is time for that age-old question: "What do you want to be when you grow up?" As they report their career goals, ask them if they know what sort of training would be needed for those jobs. Pick up a copy of the Occupational Outlook Handbook, 2010–11 Edition (Bureau of Labor Statistics, 2009), and ask each girl to read aloud some of the detailed information about a career choice.

Note the value of being bilingual in the world of work and encourage them to maintain their use of Spanish. You may also want to make them aware of the existence of college information especially for Latinas (Hispanic College Fund, 2011).

If possible, you could enhance this session by booking a computer lab. Then they could explore career and college information by examining the online version of the Occupational Outlook Handbook at http://www.bls.gov/oco/ and the Hispanic College Fund at http://www.hispanicfund.org/. It's never too early to begin thinking about education beyond high school!

Questions they should be able to answer: How hard was it for you to imagine what life would be like at age 23? Was it clear that everyone needs a life plan in order to avoid some of the disastrous answer choices? What are your career goals? What sort of training or experience do you need to achieve those goals? What is a special advantage of being bilingual? What is a source of assistance for college-bound Latinas?

When I am 23

1. I will go places by
   a. Driving my new car.
   b. Catching a city bus.
   c. Calling a friend for a ride.
   d. Driving a beat-up junk car that works only sometimes.

2. I will wear clothes from
   a. Upscale stores at the mall.
   b. Discount stores.
   c. Yard sales.
   d. Crisis Assistance Clothing Closet.

3. I will have a job
   a. With my own private office.
   b. In a fast-food restaurant.
   c. In a factory that is noisy and crowded.
   d. That is only temporary and then I don't know what I'll do to pay bills.

4. I will go out to eat once a week at
   a. An expensive Italian restaurant.
   b. A fast-food restaurant.
   c. My mother's house.
   d. A soup kitchen.

5. I will celebrate Mother's Day by

    a. Going to visit my mother and being thankful that I have delayed having children.

    b. Receiving handmade cards and hugs from my four children ranging in age from ten months to seven years old.

    c. Patting my pregnant tummy as I prepare to have my first child.

    d. Being jealous of other people's children because I have developed a sexually transmitted disease that has made me infertile.

6. I will be sleeping

    a. In my own apartment or house.

    b. At my mother's house.

    c. At a homeless shelter.

    d. In a crack house.

7. I will be sleeping with

    a. My husband.

    b. My teddy bear.

    c. My 57th lover.

    d. An IV stuck in my arm in a hospital bed, dying from AIDS.

8. Other ideas about being 23: ______________________________

____

____

____

Session 6 Topic: Relationships with Friends/Boyfriends

Session 6 Supplies: For students—Copies of Relationship Problems Scenarios; For leader—List of Latino holidays (homework), Spanish dictionary

Session 6 Content:

Distribute the copies of Relationship Problems Scenarios, having students take turns reading them and choosing how to handle them. There will be some giggles during this session, which is, of course, reassuring. These scenarios cover such issues as pressure for intimacy, conflicting viewpoints from parents about dating, and families valuing marriage at a young age. Encourage them to look at a variety of responses to each situation.

Homework! For the next session, assign each student to make a two-three sentence oral report on a Latin American holiday. Be sure that someone is assigned the quinceanera, preferably one that has an older sister or cousin who has recently experienced this coming of age event for girls at age fifteen. (Look ahead to Session 7 for list of holidays.)

Questions they should be able to answer: What are some conflicts Latinas find in intimate relationships? What are some conflicts regarding parental views on dating and marriage? How hard was it for you to come up with a suitable response to the scenarios? Which holiday will you be reporting on at the next session?

Relationship Problems Scenarios

Barbara and Candace tell their parents that they are going to an all-night skate event at the community center. They tell Ana that they are actually planning on leaving with two high school boys at midnight. Ana is worried about them.

Isabel is planning to break up with her boyfriend. She tells Felicia, who promises not to tell. Then Felicia tells the boy, who turns around and breaks up with Isabel first. Isabel is furious with Felicia.

Melea is pregnant and her uncle is the father. She is afraid to tell her dad because he might kill the uncle and be sent to prison for the rest of his life. She doesn't know whom to talk to.

Dora likes her boyfriend, but he is pushing her to have an intimate relationship. She does not want to lose him, but she does not feel ready for that step.

Clara and Elena both like Erick. He has been flirting with both of them. They are getting mad at each other for flirting back.

Angela wants to go to college. Her boyfriend wants her to drop out of school at age 16 and get married. She loves him, but she has always dreamed of being a nurse.

Tania's parents beat her over very small mistakes. Tania's 17-year-old boyfriend is very kind to her. He promises he will take care of her if they run away together. He says he has friends in Texas that they can live with. Tania is tempted but afraid.

Session 7 Topic: Cultural Celebrations

Session 7 Supplies: For leader—Mexican Holidays list, Spanish dictionary

Session 7 Content:

Ask the students to present information about the holidays they were assigned. Some will not have done their homework, which means, hopefully, you did yours! Included here is a minimum of information about typical holidays in Mexico (MEXonline.com, n.d.), but you may want to do further research. Though some of the group members may be from countries other than Mexico, it is likely that many of their holidays are similar. You will probably find that at least two or three of the students are familiar with every one of the holidays and can add their own family's personal expression of the special days. Ask about the dual cultural celebrations they encounter in their homes and if the American and Latino influences mix well. All will want to talk about quinceanera plans, even if it is several years away.

Also talk about summer vacation, which is rapidly approaching if you are conducting this as a monthly group on a traditional school calendar. Ask members to discuss the pros and cons of making a return visit to the countries of their heritage.

Questions they should be able to answer: What are some Latino holidays that your family celebrates? Which American holidays does your family celebrate? What are positive and negative reasons for visiting your country of heritage?

Mexican Holidays

(from http://www.mexonline.com/holiday.htm)

January 1: Ano Nuevo (New Year's Day) is an official Mexican holiday.

January 6: Dia de los Santos Reyes (Day of the Holy Kings) is the day when the three Wise Men arrived to meet the baby Jesus. Christmas presents are exchanged then.

January 17: Feast Day of de San Antonio de Abad (Animal Blessing Day) is a day when animals are allowed to enter the Catholic Church to be blessed.

February 2: Dia de la Candelaria (Candlemas) is a religious holiday that may include dancing, bull-fights, and parades. Candles are blessed on this day.

February 5: Dia de la Constitucion (Constitution Day) is an official holiday honoring the Constitution.

February 24: Dia de la Bandera (Flag Day) is a day to honor the Mexican flag.

February/March: Carnaval (Carnival) is a five-day celebration that occurs before the onset of Lent. It is a time of vivacious celebration, with streets closed for dances and parades.

March 19: Dia de San Jose (St. Joseph's Day) is a religious holiday.

March 21: Birthday of Benito Juarez celebrates a famed national hero and former President.

March/April: Semana Santa (Holy Week) is the week that ends Lent and includes Good Friday and Easter Sunday. A fun custom involves breaking eggs filled with confetti over the heads of loved ones and friends.

May 1: Primero de Mayo (Labor Day) is a national holiday similar to Labor Day.

May 3: Dia de la Santa Cruz (Holy Cross Day) is a day when construction workers set crosses on buildings under construction and have picnics there. Fireworks, too!

May 5: Cinco de Mayo (Fifth of May) is a day honoring victory over the French army at the Puebla de los Angeles. Many U.S. citizens have begun to note this day.

May 10: Dia de los Madres (Mother's Day) is very important in Latino culture.

June 1: Dia de la Armada (Navy Day) is an official holiday.

June 24: Dia de San Juan (Saint John the Baptist Day) is a religious holiday. A fun custom involves jokingly dunking people in water.

June 29: Fiesta of Saint Peter and Saint Paul is a religious holiday.

September 16: Mexican Independence Day commemorates the day that the Mexican revolution against Spanish rule began.

October 12: Dia de la Raza is a day to celebrate the arrival of Christopher Columbus in the Americas.

November 1 & 2: Dia de los Muertos (Day of the Dead) is a famous celebration in which the dead are honored by parties held in cemeteries.

November 20: Mexican Revolution Day is an official holiday marking the Mexican Revolution of 1910.

December 12: Dia de Nuestra Senora de Guadalupe (Day of Virgin of Guadalupe) is an important religious holiday honoring the Patroness of the Americas and is a celebration of the Virgin Mary, mother of Jesus.

December 16: Las Posadas is a religious celebration complete with candlelit parades to nativity scenes.

December 25: Navidad (Christmas) is a religious holiday that coincides with the celebration of Christmas in the U.S.

Quinceanera (15th birthday) is a lavish coming of age party held for girls turning fifteen to signify that soon they will be women. It starts with a religious ceremony and then becomes a lively reception with music, dancing, and celebration.

Session 8 Topic: Review/Game

Session 8 Supplies: For leader—Leader's complete folder (for review), Index cards (from before), Copy of Latina Situations Game cut into small (1" × 3") pieces, 10 large (at least 11" × 14") sheets of construction paper, Basket, Spanish dictionary

Session 8 Content:

At the eighth and final session, briefly review the previous sessions. See how much they can remember from each session's topic.

Bring out the index cards for setting academic goals again and ask for volunteers to report progress. Give one last reminder about the importance of grades.

The last activity is the best! Playing the Latina Situations Game means you need room to move around, as you will be lining ten sheets of construction paper one beside another to represent steps on a board game with the girls being the game pieces. Put the small pieces of paper with various Latina situations on them in the basket. Choose who is going first and ask that student to draw a strip of paper from the basket. The student must read aloud the statement and take the appropriate step(s). For example: Esmeralda started a babysitting group in her neighborhood which included Latina, African American, and white girls. Go forward 1 space. Another example: Fabiola started a rumor that Lydia told a racist joke. Go back 2 spaces. Free space means exactly that: the student moves forward a step without having to do anything, which sometimes happens in life (but don't count on it). If the student draws one which states she must go back a space and she hasn't made it onto the construction paper yet, then she just remains behind the starting line until her next turn. If the basket is empty before anyone has reached the tenth step or finish line, then recycle them. They don't mind hearing the statements twice. Pause during each move for students to recognize the significance of the steps they are taking, both forward and backward.

In closing, remind them of your availability to see them about concerns on an individual basis.

Questions they should be able to answer: What do you remember about each session? Have you been able to meet your academic goals that were set at the first meeting? What did you learn from steps you and others took (forward and backward) in the Latina Situations Game?

Latina Situations Game

Fabiola asked her teacher for the work she missed during the Latina group. Go forward 1 space.	Esmeralda brought up her math grade from a D to a B. Go forward 2 spaces.
Ana wanted to go to the school basketball game but she talked back to her mother so she was not allowed to go. Go back 1 space.	Lydia wanted to try out to be an officer in Beta Club but was afraid no one would vote for a Latina. Go back 1 space.
Paola had hoped for Honor Roll but made all C's on her report card. She was so sad that she decided to stop trying. Go back 1 space.	One day Guadalupe brought her Mexican flag to school and saluted it during the Pledge of Allegiance. Go back 1 space.
Zuri shared notebook paper with an African American girl who had once been her enemy. Go forward 1 space.	Felicia got mad at a friend who reported to the counselor that she had been badly beaten by her father. Go back 1 space.
Nina taught two white girls in her neighborhood how to salsa dance. Go forward 1 space.	Tia brought homemade enchiladas as her "show & tell" project for class. Go forward 1 space.

Marie organized a neighborhood babysitting service that included African American, white, and Latina girls. Go forward 2 spaces.	Rosie started a rumor about an African American boy beating up a Latino to stir up some excitement. Go back 2 spaces.
Eneida turned in her brother's old science project instead of doing her own because she had no poster paper. Go back 1 space.	Barbara went out with a 20-year-old man because he promised to take her to Puerto Rico to visit her grandma. Go back 2 spaces.
Martha chose to write her persuasive Language Arts paper on why she thought building a wall at the US/Mexico border was not a good idea. Go forward 1 space.	A boy told Rita that his dad couldn't get a job because the Mexicans took all of them. She calmly said, "That has nothing to do with me and you." Go forward 2 spaces.
Dora walked into class late and the teacher said, "You people are always late." Dora stormed out of the room. Go back 1 space.	When a white girl called her an "illegal alien," Cecilia went to the counselor instead of cursing her. Go forward 2 spaces.
Florinda did not have money for a field trip, so she stayed home from school instead of asking for financial help. Go back 1 space.	Mercedes refused to work in the group the teacher put her in because there were no Latinos in it. Instead she worked alone. Go back 1 space.

1 free space	1 free space
1 free space	1 free space
1 free space	1 free space
1 free space	1 free space
1 free space	1 free space
1 free space	1 free space
1 free space	1 free space
1 free space	1 free space

Evaluation of Latina Pride Group

Rate yourself by circling the number which corresponds with how you evaluate each statement.
1 = Not at all, 2 = A small amount, 3 = Average amount, 4 = More than average, 5 = Very much

1. I felt comfortable discussing issues related to being Latina in the group.

   1.................2.................3.................4.................5

2. I practiced setting realistic academic goals.

   1.................2.................3.................4.................5

3. I recognize there are things that can and cannot be changed.

   1.................2.................3.................4.................5

4. I was able to discuss special issues related to belonging to two cultures.

   1.................2.................3.................4.................5

5. I learned good sources of career information.

   1.................2.................3.................4.................5

6. I learned to think more seriously about my future.

   1.................2.................3.................4.................5

7. I learned to value the cultural celebrations of my heritage.

   1.................2.................3.................4.................5

8. I grew closer to members during the course of the group.

   1.................2.................3.................4.................5

Suggestions for making the group better: ____

____

References

Bureau of Labor Statistics, U.S. Department of Labor. (2009)., *Occupational outlook handbook,* 2010–11 Edition, Bulletin 2800. Superintendent of Documents, U.S. Government Printing Office, Washington, DC, 2006. (also online at http://www.bls.gov/oco/)

Hispanic College Fund. (2011). Retrieved April 26, 2011, from http://www.hispanicfund.org/

Jones, M. & Bou-Waked, R. (2007, November 12). School choice and Hispanic dropouts. *National Center for Policy Analysis*. Retrieved March 27, 2011, from http://www.ncpa.org/pub/ba602

MEXonline.com. (n.d.). *Mexico's official and religious holidays*. Retrieved April 26, 2011, from http://www.mexonline.com/holiday.htm

National Center for Education Statistics (NCES) Home Page. (n.d.). *Fast facts.* Retrieved April 26, 2011, from http://nces.ed.gov/fastfacts/display.asp?id=16

Pew Hispanic Center. (2011). *Hispanic youth dropping out of U.S. schools: Measuring the challenge*. Retrieved March 27, 2011, from http://pewhispanic.org/newsroom/releases/release.php?ReleaseID=5

The National Campaign to Prevent Teen and Unplanned Pregnancy. (2011, February). *Teen pregnancy and childbearing among Latino teens*. Retrieved March 27, 2011, from http://www.thenationalcampaign.org/resources/pdf/FastFacts_TPChildbearing_Latinos.pdf

Chapter 9

Relational Aggression: Friends and Important Relationships (FAIR)

Friends and Important Relationships (FAIR) Group Outline

I. Introductory Information

- A. Outline, Schedule, Parent Permission, Rules
- B. Sentence Completion Statements

II. Recognizing Responses

- A. Definition of Passive, Aggressive, and Assertive
- B. Skits: Victims and Villains

III. Making Decisions

- A. Consequences
- B. FAIR Game

IV. Recognizing Worth

- A. Uniqueness, Seashell Activity
- B. Interest Assessment

V. Handling Anger

- A. When I Am 23
- B. Calming Methods
- C. Forgiveness/Apologies

VI. Examining Friendship/Review

- A. Relationship Dilemmas
- B. Review of Sessions

American School Counselor Association (ASCA) Standards

Career Development

Standard A: Students will acquire the skills to investigate the world of work in relation to knowledge of self and to make informed career decisions.

C:A1 Develop Career Awareness

C:A1.3 Develop an awareness of personal abilities, skills, interests and motivations

Personal/Social Development

Standard A: Students will acquire the knowledge, attitudes, and interpersonal skills to help them understand and respect self and others.

PS:A1 Acquire Self-knowledge

PS:A1.1 Develop positive attitudes toward self as a unique and worthy person

PS:A1.2 Identify values, attitudes, and beliefs

PS:A1.5 Identify and express feelings

PS:A1.6 Distinguish between appropriate and inappropriate behavior

PS:A1.8 Understand the need for self-control and how to practice it

PS:A1.9 Demonstrate cooperative behavior in groups

PS:A1.10 Identify personal strengths and assets

PS:A2 Acquire Interpersonal Skills

PS:A2.1 Recognize that everyone has rights and responsibilities

PS:A2.2 Respect alternative points of view

PS:A2.3 Recognize, accept, respect and appreciate individual differences

PS:A2.6 Use effective communication skills

PS:A2.8 Learn how to make and keep friends

Standard B: Students will make decisions, set goals and take necessary action to achieve goals.

PS:B1 Self-knowledge Application

PS:B1.2 Understand consequences of decisions and choices

PS:B1.3 Identify alternative solutions to a problem

PS:B1.4 Develop effective coping skills for dealing with problems

PS:B1.8 Know when peer pressure is influencing a decision

Standard C: Students will understand safety and survival skills.

PS:C1 Acquire Personal Safety Skills

PS:C1.9 Learn how to cope with peer pressure

PS:C1.10 Learn techniques for managing stress and conflict

Rationale for Friends and Important Relationships (FAIR) Group

The term "relational aggression" first appeared as a result of a study in 1995 by University of Minnesota researchers (Crick & Grotpeter, p. 711), and it took off to the point it is now a mainstream expression. Those researchers defined it as behavior intended to harm someone by damaging or manipulating relationships with others. Unlike most forms of bullying, it is most often perpetrated by females and uses covert tactics of coercion, humiliation, intimidation, and isolation. One of the most celebrated volumes covering this type of aggressive behavior is Rachel Simmons' work entitled *Odd Girl Out: The Hidden Culture of Aggression in Girls,* in which she describes girl aggression as "epidemic, distinctive, and destructive" (2002, p. 3). Her poignant account of girls relentlessly moving in and out of friendships with hopeful spirits rising and then crashing makes one want to step in to stop the damage, but her comprehensive work illustrates that is never as simple as it sounds.

With the widespread use of social networking media in recent years, relational aggression has moved into the cyber-world in astronomical proportions. Contrast the number of online girls claiming to be victims of cyber-bullying with that of online boys: 38% to 26% (Lenhart, 2007). Also, a survey conducted by Cox Communications in 2009 yielded that 59% of cyber-bullies are female, as opposed to 41% being male (Facecrooks Home Page, 2010).

One might think that the most practical way to determine need for a girls' relational aggression group is to review school discipline records, looking for violations by females. However, administrative discipline data is more likely to focus on incidents that are overt behaviors, such as fighting or using profanity or other obvious forms of bullying. Though relational aggression is often considered bullying, it usually skims sneakily just under the radar rather than manifesting itself publicly A more helpful way to both determine group membership and rate the effectiveness of the group is to use a teacher pre- and post-assessment instrument such as those included in this chapter. It incorporates teacher observation of such incidents as girls teasing or taunting, spreading rumors, denying inclusion at the lunch table, and giving the silent treatment.

This group focuses on the complications of relationships with other girls, demonstrating the benefits and hardships of friendship. It is designed to increase awareness of their own relational aggressive behaviors and resulting consequences through participation in and discussion of relevant scenarios, role plays, skits, and a game. In an attempt to increase bonding of group members, they experience a session which focuses on appreciating their uniqueness as well as their commonalities. During one session, they practice techniques to reduce anger and also learn the benefits of forgiveness. Hopefully, the results of your teacher observation post-assessment will reveal that group members engage in fewer negative behaviors during the course of the group and afterwards.

What Makes It Work:

1. What could be more important among adolescent girls than working on relationships? There are mean girls everywhere! And sometimes they are you and me. When the girls realize this, it can be powerful.
2. The girls will probably like referring to it as the FAIR group.
3. Relational aggression is a current buzz word. Your principals will be very excited that you are tackling this problem in the hopes that it leads to fewer discipline referrals in their offices.

4. Relationships with adolescent girls change constantly. Though some girls within your group may be currently feuding, chances are they will be calling each other best friends by your next session. If there is obvious tension, confront it right then and there. Modeling how to deal with this conflict can serve as a teachable moment.
5. If you're working in a middle school which follows the team concept, you may find it helpful to choose all the girls from the same team. After all, the same team shares many social moments: lunch time, study hall, field trips. Since they are together constantly, it is quite important to minimize disruptive conflict.
6. Hopefully they will leave this group choosing to practice relationship skills which avoid aggression.

Challenges:

1. Because of the high numbers of girls who could benefit from such a group, it may be difficult to limit selection. I chose my group based upon my own experiences dealing with girls having peer problems multiple times, plus I asked the team of teachers for their input using the Teacher Pre-Group Assessment of Behavior. Then I narrowed it down to a workable number, inviting a few more than I felt I could comfortably handle, figuring some would decline.
2. It may be an awkward meeting when you call them together for the first time to announce the formation of the group and explain its purpose. They may feel that they have been identified as mean girls.
3. Parents may balk at the idea that their daughters need such a group. My actual experience so far has not proven this true, but I expect that I will encounter such parents at some point.
4. It is possible that some girls may be so vindictive that they are unable to relate in a positive way to others in the group. In that case you may need to ask them to withdraw.
5. You will probably run out of time when you're doing the skits and the role plays because they will be driven to talk, talk, talk about the issues.
6. After they've come a time or two, some may beg you to let their other friends join. It's tough to turn them down, but most counselors would agree that once a group has formed, no newcomers should be allowed.

Teacher Pre-Group Assessment of Behavior

Teacher name ____

Name of student ____

In recent times (perhaps the last 6 weeks), I have observed/witnessed/heard that this student took part in the following negative relational behaviors:
1 = Not at all, 2 = A small amount, 3 = Average amount, 4 = More than average, 5 = Very much

1. Talking negatively about a peer

   1.................2.................3.................4.................5

2. Huddling with peers while pointing or staring at another girl

   1.................2.................3.................4.................5

3. Teasing or taunting a peer

   1.................2.................3.................4.................5

4. Yelling at a peer

   1.................2.................3.................4.................5

5. Attempting to force a peer to sit elsewhere at lunch

   1.................2.................3.................4.................5

6. Starting or spreading a harmful rumor about someone

   1.................2.................3.................4.................5

7. Giving a peer the silent treatment

   1.................2.................3.................4.................5

8. Communicating negative comments through texting or social media

   1.................2.................3.................4.................5

Friends and Important Relationships (FAIR) Group Sessions

Session 1 Topic: Introductory Information, Sentence Completion Activity

Session 1 Supplies: For students—Copies of outline, schedule, and parent permission form; For leader —Copy of Relational Aggression Sentence Completion Statements cut into strips, Basket

Session 1 Content:

Begin with an explanation that the acronym FAIR stands for Friends and Important Relationships. Then you need to inform group members that they were selected based on your own and teachers' observations that they have frequent conflicts with peers. Emphasize that the purpose of the group is for students to become aware of incidents of relational aggression and to learn ways to reduce conflicts with friends. You will need to define relational aggression as behavior intended to hurt someone by damaging or manipulating relationships (Crick & Grotpeter, 1995). Explain that it comes up a lot in "girl drama" episodes, with sneaky tactics such as coercing, humiliating, intimidating, or isolating someone. Then proceed with your explanation of the outline, schedule, parent permission, and group rules.

It is time for the conversation starter, the Relational Aggression Sentence Completion Statements. Pass the basket, having them draw a strip and finish the sentence. Remind them to be respectful of the answers of others even if they disagree with them.

Don't be too alarmed if they are unusually quiet in this first session. They may be struggling with being identified as needing this group and wondering if they are viewed as troublemakers or mean girls. It is also possible that some of the girls have current ongoing issues with other girls in the group. There may be a little hesitancy to speak, much less bond. But that will come, in time.

Questions they should be able to answer: What are the topics that will be covered in group? How does the schedule work? What are the group rules? When is the parent permission form due? How easy was it for you to complete the sentences you drew? What did you learn about others in the group in this introductory session?

Relational Aggression Sentence Completion Statements

When a friend betrays me, I feel ____.

I tell my friends what to do when ____.

I get jealous when ____.

I feel closer to this parent (mother or father): _______________________________________.

When I get mad, I ____.

If someone directs profanity towards me, I ____.

If I were to get into a physical fight at school, my parents would _______________________.

When someone gives me the silent treatment, I ____.

When I argue with a best friend, I feel ____.

I like being a peacemaker because ____.

If I reveal a friend's secret to someone, I feel ________________________________.

I talk too much when ____.

When it comes to solving conflict, I consider myself ___________________________.

When I confide in a friend, I expect ____.

I might scream and yell if ____.

If someone threatens me, I ____.

I argue with my friends about ____.

I feel sad or depressed when friends ____.

When I find out friends are talking about me behind my back, I _________________.

Session 2 Topic: Recognizing Responses

Session 2 Supplies: For leader—Copies of Villains and Victims skits

Session 2 Content:

Though conflict cannot be eliminated from daily life, ways to manage it effectively can be taught and practiced. A discussion of passive, aggressive, and assertive communication will help students recognize how they currently respond to conflict. Use these definitions:

- Passive—expressing very little of your true feelings; accommodating others to keep the peace.
- Aggressive—expressing your opinions/emotions in a harsh or overwhelming way with little or no regard for others.
- Assertive—expressing yourself honestly by standing up for your rights in a way that does not hurt others.

Then hand out copies of the first Villains and Victims Skits to the appropriate number of girls. Give the next skit parts to different students. The skits come in sets of threes, with each one representing a passive, aggressive, or assertive response to a certain situation such as being put down for wearing inferior clothing. Ask the girls to note the big differences in the way certain characters respond. The skits represent conflicts that will be familiar to your students: flirting with another girl's boyfriend, being left out of a party, and feeling isolated at lunch. Let them take turns playing various roles. Expect some joking around and some pure joy as they play the aggressive roles. Ask them to decide after each skit if the response was passive, aggressive, or assertive. Point out that the assertive manner is going to win them the most satisfaction and self-respect in the long run. Discussion will be lively and there may not be enough time to thoroughly discuss all of the skits. You may want to save a set of the skits for the final session review.

Questions they should be able to answer: What is the difference in passive, aggressive, and assertive responses? Have you had personal experiences similar to the various roles in the skit situations? How do you typically respond to such circumstances?

Villains and Victims Skits

Skit # 1

Julie: Look at those ugly shoes!

Keisha: Where did you get them—the dollar store?

Monica: None of your business.

Keisha: Really, you look like a homeless kid.

Monica: They look better than your shoes.

Julie: Keisha, are you going to let her talk to you like that?

Keisha: Well, I don't really want to touch her. I might get AIDS.

Monica: Like your mama.

Keisha: You're going to eat dirt right now.

Skit # 2

Julie: Look at that ugly coat!

Keisha: Where did you get it—Goodwill?

Monica: It's just a coat. It does what it's supposed to do—keep me warm.

Julie: Like you don't care that it looks like dog poop.

Monica: I really don't. Coats don't matter to me.

Keisha: So, where did you get the cheap-looking tee shirt?

Monica: Hey, I didn't know school had turned into a fashion shoot. I just opened my closet, picked out my clothes, and got ready for school. And I feel just fine about what I'm wearing.

Julie: Come on, Keisha. Let's get out of here. Her poverty might be contagious.

Keisha: Yeah. What a loser.

Skit # 3

Julie: Look at those awful jeans!

Keisha: They look so cheap.

Julie: I think we should do a makeover on you.

Keisha: That might be impossible.

Monica: (starting to cry) Why don't you leave me alone?

Julie: Why don't you dress better? You make this school look like a ghetto.

Monica: I can't help it.

Keisha: Hey, Julie. Remember. She's nothing but trailer park trash.

Julie: Oh, yeah. We can forget about her looking any better. Let's go.

Skit # 4

Michelle: You are about to lose your boyfriend.

Emma: Why?

Michelle: Shania is over there, and you know what that means.

Emma: Well, let's go stop her.

Michelle: Get away from Emma's boyfriend.

Shania: What is the problem?

Emma: We know how you are. You'll be making out with a guy two minutes after you meet him.

Shania: That's not true, but I'll leave.

Michelle: Go far away, like maybe you-know-where.

Emma: Yeah, that's where you belong.

Shania: Whatever. (walks away, head down)

Skit # 5

Michelle: Have you noticed how Shania has been hanging around Jared? I think she's making a move on him.

Emma: That sneaky slut! She is always stealing somebody's boyfriend.

Michelle: I think we should go over there and tell her what we think.

Emma: Yeah. Let's go.

Michelle: Shania, you are nothing but a slut. Everyone hates the way you steal other girls' boyfriends.

Shania: What are you talking about? And who are you to call me a slut?

Michelle: We've seen you putting your hands on Jared. You know he's Emma's boyfriend. Why don't you bug off?

Shania: I haven't done anything. We're just friends.

Emma: Yeah, like who is going to believe you? Everyone knows what you did with Leah's boyfriend last summer.

Shania: Look, Emma, maybe its Michelle you should be yelling at. She's been flirting with Jared ever since you started going out. She's a liar and a back-stabber.

Michelle: You aren't getting away with that, Shania. (slaps her face)

Skit # 6

Michelle: Look over there at Shania, flirting with your boyfriend.

Emma: She sure has a lot of nerve.

Michelle: Let's go tell her off.

Emma: Okay.

Michelle: Shania, we see you chasing after Jared. You're such a slut.

Shania: I wasn't chasing Jared. We were talking about our group project.

Emma: It didn't look like you were just talking.

Shania: I know he's your boyfriend. I'm surprised you think I'd go for him.

Emma: So you weren't flirting?

Shania: No, I wasn't. I've always considered you and me friends. I'd like for it to stay that way.

Michelle: You aren't going to buy that, are you, Emma?

Emma: Well, I think I believe Shania. Let's just let it go.

Skit # 7

Allison: Are you going to Lauren's sleepover birthday party this Friday?

Dayzha: I didn't know anything about it.

Allison: You mean you weren't invited?

Dayzha: No, I guess not. We're not best friends or anything.

Allison: I think you should post something bad about her on Facebook.

Dayzha: No, that's going overboard. It's okay that you get to go to the party and I don't.

Allison: What's okay about that?

Dayzha: Hey, everyone can't go to every party. I'm all right with it.

Allison: I think you might be jealous.

Dayzha: Not really. I'm just not going to get worked up over something that I don't care much about.

Skit # 8

Dayzha: Let's go to the mall after school today.

Allison: Okay, as long as you don't invite Lauren.

Dayzha: What have you got against Lauren?

Allison: She talks about everybody behind their back. You wouldn't invite her if you knew what she said about you.

Dayzha: What did she say?

Allison: She said she didn't like you and that's why she didn't invite you to her party.

Dayzha: Well, she can just burn in you-know-where. Let's call her up right now and tell her.

Skit # 9

Allison: I heard something bad about Lauren.

Dayzha: What?

Allison: I heard that she sent a nude picture of herself to James from her cell phone.

Dayzha: Are you kidding?

Allison: No. Why don't we see if we can find that picture and send it to a bunch of people, maybe even her parents?

Dayzha: Well, I don't know. That seems wrong.

Allison: And you think it was right of her to send that picture to James? And you shouldn't forget that she didn't invite you to her party.

Dayzha: Well, okay. I guess we could do it.

Skit # 10

Yasmine: What are we going to do about lunch now that there aren't enough seats at our table? Since Leah has moved back from Florida, we can't all sit together.

Kelsie: Well, it's not my problem. I get there early, so I'll always get a seat.

Gina: Yeah, whoever is last will just have to sit alone.

Kelsie: Hopefully, it will be Olivia. She's getting on my nerves.

Yasmine: That doesn't sound like a very fair way to handle this situation.

Gina: Who made you peacemaker? Just don't worry about it.

Kelsie: Yeah, Yasmine. You're starting to get on my nerves, too.

Yasmine: Well, okay. I'll just forget about it.

Skit # 11

Yasmine: What are we going to do about lunch today? Now that Leah has moved back to our school, we don't have enough seats at our lunch table.

Kelsie: Yeah, there are eight seats at the round table and nine of us.

Gina: We could leave Olivia out. She's not much fun.

Yasmine: I heard her parents just got a divorce. Maybe she's got a right to be in a bad mood.

Kelsie: Yeah, but we don't have to be around her and her bad mood. I like to laugh and have fun at lunch.

Gina: Yeah, me, too. If Olivia tries to sit here, I think we should just tell her it's saved.

Yasmine: I don't feel good about leaving Olivia or anyone else stranded. Maybe a couple of us could break away and sit somewhere else, taking turns each day sitting at the big table.

Gina: Well, I'm not crazy about the idea.

Yasmine: But think how you would feel if you were the one left out.

Kelsie: Yeah, that would be bad. I guess we could do that. It would be fair.

Yasmine: I think we'd all feel better if we at least gave it a try.

Skit # 12

Yasmine: Now that Leah has moved back to our school, the lunch table situation has changed.

Kelsie: Yeah, you're right. How can we all sit together?

Gina: We can't. Do the math. Nine people, eight seats.

Yasmine: Maybe we could work out a deal where a few of us took turns sitting elsewhere each day.

Kelsie: No way am I giving up my seat to do that.

Gina: Me, neither. Yasmine, you can start another table if you want to. A table for losers. Take Olivia with you. She's not much fun.

Yasmine: That was mean.

Gina: Well, you're just trying to mess up our fun at lunch time. So just go away. Nobody likes you anyway.

Yasmine: You guys are the losers. I guess I won't be seeing you at lunch. Or anywhere else, if I can help it.

Session 3 Topic: Making Decisions

Session 3 Supplies: For leader—Whiteboard, Markers, Copy of FAIR Game cut into small (1" × 3") pieces, 10 large (at least 11" × 14") sheets of construction paper, Basket

Session 3 Content:

Start with a discussion of consequences. Ask the students to generate various behaviors and the resulting consequences they have faced for various situations in life, both at home and at school. They may describe negative home behaviors such as not cleaning their rooms, talking back to parents, and fighting with siblings. The consequences list will probably include being grounded, having cell phones or other electronics confiscated, being lectured, and maybe even being spanked. Negative school behaviors may include talking too much, being off task, arguing with teachers, and not completing work. Consequences may include dropping off the Honor Roll, having parents receive a phone call from teachers, suffering through silent lunch, staying for detention, and being suspended. Then ask them to list negative behaviors that can occur with friends. They will generate many examples: talking about a friend behind her back, turning others against someone, telling secrets, criticizing clothes, stealing boyfriends, leaving someone out. Consequences for these relationship problems may include ostracism, cyber-bullying, rumors, and even physical fights.

Then it's time for the FAIR Game. Set the ten sheets of construction paper one beside another to form a line. Put the small strips of paper with the behavior choices on them in the basket. Then decide who is going first and ask that student to draw a strip of paper from the basket. The student must read aloud the statement and take the appropriate step(s). For example: Mr. Hahn selected Jen as "Most Improved Student," but Monique whined and called her a teacher's pet. Go back 1 space. Another example: Kristen pushed Cynthia when she got the last ice cream at lunch. Go back 2 spaces. A more positive example: Erica messed up on the step team at the talent show. Some of the girls cursed her, but Mia stood up for her and told them to stop. Go forward 2 spaces. Drawing a free space means that the student moves forward one step without having to do anything: it's a stroke of good luck. If the student draws one which states she must go back a space and she hasn't made it onto the construction paper yet, then she just remains behind the starting line until her next turn when hopefully she'll be able to advance. If the basket is empty before anyone has reached the tenth step or finish line, then recycle them. They'll want to play on through even if it means hearing the statements twice. They will have great fun but also recognize that negative choices can set them back.

Questions they should be able to answer: When have you chosen a negative behavior and faced consequences for it, at home and at school and with friends? How did playing the game make you more aware of how your behavior affects both you and others? Have you experienced situations similar to those presented during the game? If so, how did those incidents work out?

FAIR Game

Cynthia was saving a seat for Taylor at lunch, but Taylor decided to sit with someone else. Cynthia threw a hamburger at her. Go back 2 spaces.	Mia and Sarah usually work together in social studies, but the teacher made Mia work with another girl. Mia was rude and wouldn't talk. Go back 1 space.
Jaleen and Kristen just realized they like the same guy. Jaleen posted a note on Facebook calling Kristen a slut. Go back 2 spaces.	Abby is planning to go to the mall with some friends. Fran asks to go, too. Abby tells her they've changed their minds but they go anyway. Go back 1 space.
Erica messed up on the step team in the talent show. Some of the girls cursed her, but Mia stood up for her and got them to stop. Go forward 2 spaces.	Taylor made an A on her science project. A girl on another team pressured her into letting her use it in her science class. Go back 1 space.
There was a rumor going around that Monique was pregnant. Tonya helped squelch the rumor by telling people it wasn't true. Go forward 2 spaces.	Mr. Hahn selected Jen as "Most Improved Student." Monique whined and called Jen the teacher's pet. Go back 1 space.
Kristen pushed Cynthia when she got the last ice cream at lunch. Go back 2 spaces.	When Monique bumped into Mia in the hall, she quickly apologized. Go forward 1 space.
Kristen knew that Jaleen was thinking about running away, so she talked her into visiting the counselor. Go forward 2 spaces.	Taylor helped Jaleen solve math equations during study hall instead of going outside for free time. Go forward 1 space.

Sarah told Fran that her boyfriend was ugly and that she should break up. Fran did, and then Sarah started going out with him. Go back 2 spaces.	Grace heard that Olivia was going to jump her for no reason. She went straight to Olivia, got in her face, and called her the b-word. Go back 2 spaces.
Erica said to Jen, "Your mama is nothing but a slut." Jen kept her cool and said, "You know that's ridiculous," and walked away. Go forward 2 spaces.	Olivia saw a $10 bill hanging out of Mia's purse. She could've easily taken it, but she chose to tell Mia instead. Go forward 2 spaces.
Jaleen knows Grace has been cutting herself, but she promised not to tell. She wants to tell the counselor, but is unsure about telling Grace's secret. Go forward 1 space.	Jen thinks Abby bosses her around too much, so she tells her she wants to be friends but feels frustrated when she tells her what to do. Go forward 2 spaces.
Abby tells Grace she should stop hanging around Jen. Grace doesn't listen to Abby and decides she can be friends with both. Go forward 2 spaces.	Fran calmed down Sarah and Tonya when they were arguing by getting them to cool off and then take turns really listening to each other. Go forward 2 steps.
Sarah told Tonya that she'd brought her mom's prescription medicine to school and was going to take it during gym class. Tonya didn't tell anyone, and Sarah was rushed to the hospital in serious condition. Go back 2 spaces.	Fran started a rumor that Taylor was racist when she would not let her copy her test answers. Go back 2 spaces.

1 free space	1 free space
1 free space	1 free space
1 free space	1 free space
1 free space	1 free space
1 free space	1 free space
1 free space	1 free space
1 free space	1 free space
1 free space	1 free space

Session 4 Topic: Recognizing Worth

Session 4 Supplies: For students—Copies of Interest Assessment, Pencils; For leader—Seashells (or rocks or apples)

Session 4 Content:

The focus of this session is respecting the uniqueness of each individual but also recognizing things they have in common. Start your discussion by asking them to name one-of-a-kind things (snowflakes, signatures, fingerprints, DNA, etc.) Use any items that look very similar for the uniqueness activity—seashells, rocks or even apples would do. Hand each of them a seashell and have them examine its shape, shade, markings, etc. Then take them all up in a bag and scatter them on the floor, telling them to find their own seashell. Almost without fail, they will be able to find the correct ones. Ask a few to explain briefly how they were able to identify their seashells.

Then shift discussion to how unique the group members are in appearance, personality, abilities, likes and dislikes. And though they share some things with others in the group- same gender, same grade, same lunchtime, same books, same wish that summer were here—they, like the seashells, are one-of-a-kind. There are several points to make:

- You can do things no one else can, using your own style and your own approach (examples: design a house, paint a picture, write an essay, compose a song).
- You may feel free to express yourself through clothes, hair, writing, talking. It's all right to be different!
- Use your creativity and imagination to solve conflicts. Sometimes there is a perfect answer to a problem that only you can think of.
- You can learn to respect yourself, value your performance, and trust your perceptions.

Next, suggest that knowing and appreciating their unique abilities can be enhanced by exploring interests. Distribute the Interest Assessment forms. Ask them to check the appropriate items—those that appeal to them. When they have finished, mention each item briefly and ask group members to raise hands to indicate what they checked. They will be able to see who else has something in common with them. Hopefully they will discover that mutual interests exist with others whom they may have experienced relationship difficulties with in the past. Note that, though they may share some interests with others, each Interest Assessment is unique when total responses are considered.

Questions they should be able to answer: How easy was it for you to select your seashell from the pile on the floor? How are you different from others in the group? How are you alike? How easy was it to see yourself as a person of value? What are your interests? Do you have an interest that no one else selected? What interests do you have in common with others in the group?

INTEREST ASSESSMENT

Mark the following items that you like to do or think you are good at doing:

_____Singing

_____Drawing

_____Working with plants

_____Cooking meals

_____Working in a group

_____Being a leader

_____Working with your hands

_____Designing things

_____Working independently

_____Convincing people to see things your way

_____Giving a speech

_____Following directions

_____Taking care of children

_____Learning a foreign language

_____Working without a lot of rules

_____Paying attention to details

_____Doing school projects

_____Working with animals

_____Working outside

_____Working on the computer

_____Building things

_____Reading aloud

_____Doing math

_____Writing

_____Organizing things

_____Acting in a play

_____Creating things

_____Greeting people

_____Cleaning house

_____Making jewelry

_____Playing sports

_____Painting the house

_____Directing others

_____Following orders

_____Working in an office

_____Selling things

_____Teaching others

_____Dancing

_____Helping sick people

_____Leading exercises

Session 5 Topic: Handling Anger

Session 5 Supplies: For students—Copies of When I Am 23 worksheet, Pencils; For leader—Anger Relief Tension Tamers, Whiteboard, Markers

Session 5 Content:

Start the session by having group members complete the When I am 23 worksheet. This particular activity will probably be taken more seriously if completed individually rather than jointly. After they have had time to finish, suggest they take turns reading the statements and the multiple choice answers. Ask for volunteers to share how they answered each one. Explain that the more favorable answers (the ones anyone would be more likely to choose) require practical planning and good decision-making. They need to hear that their lives can take unfortunate paths if they make choices based on anger or whim, with no eye to the future. For example, a person who frequently becomes angry at her workplace is more apt to quit her job, thus making it difficult to amass the money needed to live independently. A girl who chooses a relationship partner without valuing herself may be more likely to end up as a victim of dating abuse. An even more serious situation would be the person who loses control of her anger, makes a rash decision, and ends up imprisoned.

Discuss the often troubling emotion of anger. Explain that anger is a natural feeling which will pop up quite often in their lives, and they must find suitable ways to cope with it. Ask them for examples of when anger has led them to make poor decisions. You will probably hear such actions as cursing a best friend over a minor disagreement, dumping a good boyfriend due to jealousy, and sending a mean text message. Then ask them to generate ideas for cooling off anger. Allow them to take turns writing them on the whiteboard. Be sure that they include counting to fifty (ten is too short), squeezing stress balls, writing in a secret journal, taking a walk, listening to music, drawing or painting, playing sports, and simply talking it out with a good listener.

Then lead them in Anger Relief Tension Tamers, which are similar to activities for relieving stress.

1. Begin with deep breathing exercises. Ask students to sit up properly in their chairs and take a deep breath through the nose with mouth shut. Hold for three seconds and then open mouth, and with lips pursed, exhale loudly. Do this four times.
2. Then try muscle relaxation exercises that affect the parts of your body that become tense during anger. Start by tensing the muscles in your forehead, as you would in making a frown. (That's easy enough to do when you're angry.) Hold it a few seconds. Then relax it so that it is smooth. Tell them to notice how different tenseness and relaxation feel. Then proceed to the eyes, closing them very tightly. Then relax your eyes, but keep them closed, as if you were taking a nap. Again, tell the students to notice the difference in how tenseness and relaxation feel. Continue by moving to the teeth (clenching them and then releasing). Then try the shoulders (hunching them and then relaxing). Move to the arms, which you do one at a time, holding them out straight and making a fist, then relaxing. Do the same with legs, pointing toes and then relaxing.
3. Another Tension Tamer involves using a repetitive mantra that expresses positive thoughts. Encourage them to create two to three short sentences to repeat silently when stressful situations arise. Ask them to try this aloud at first, even though they may think it's silly. Some examples of positive self-talk statements to use when angry are: I can keep my cool. I can handle this. I'm going to be okay. This isn't worth getting mad about.

4. Next, tell group members about the benefits of mental imagery. Assure them that their imaginations can distract them from their anger, taking them to a calming place even in the midst of chaos. If they need examples, suggest a beautiful forest scene, a silent snowfall on a moonlit night, or the steady wash of waves upon the shore.
5. If you're feeling brave, try silent meditation. Ask the students to sit in the lotus position on the floor if they are dressed appropriately. Otherwise just suggest they sit up straight in their chairs. Ask them to close their eyes, with you keeping yours open to ensure no one bothers them. Tell them to clear their minds of problems and worries. Suggest they listen to their breathing. Then keep silent for three minutes. Five is better, but you'll be lucky to keep them quiet for three minutes. This is a school, after all. That obnoxious intercom might come on, or maybe you'll just hear a few giggles among the group members. Suggest that they try this particular exercise at home where hopefully there is more peace and quiet.

After practicing the anger reduction techniques, introduce the topic of forgiveness. Some may associate the term only in a religious context; you may need to explain that you are speaking of forgiveness in a broader sense. Emphasize that everyone makes mistakes, and that forgiveness is a vital part of most long-term relationships. Clarify that forgiveness can help a person shrug off burdensome anger and move on. Prolonged anger takes a toll on a person, heightening stress and harming both physical and psychological health (MayoClinic.com, 2009). Being able to let go of some of that anger can be a freeing experience; forgiving may help you more than it does the person being forgiven. Ask group members if they can recall a situation in which they offered forgiveness. You may need to give them a couple of examples, such as allowing a friend who has wronged them back into the group or deciding to let go of an old grudge against someone. Ask how they felt before, during, and after the forgiving episode.

In addition, they should not only consider offering forgiveness but seeking it when they have done something wrong. There is relief to be found in apologizing as well. Ask them to recall situations in which they offered apologies and to note whether they were meaningful ones or shallow ones. Also ask if the apologies were accepted or rebuffed. See if they will share how they felt before, during, and after the apology. The girls should walk away from this session with a new awareness of the presence of anger in their lives and its potential for harm to them. They should also view the concept of forgiveness in a new light.

Questions they should be able to answer: How difficult was it for you to imagine yourself at age 23? What are some methods you use to cool off your anger? What are some Anger Relief Tension Tamers that you are willing to try? Which do you think will be most effective for you? Before this session, had you ever thought about the benefits of forgiving someone? Were you able to share a time when you offered forgiveness? Were you able to share a time when you offered an apology?

When I am 23

1. I will go places by
    a. Driving my new car.
    b. Catching a city bus.
    c. Calling a friend for a ride.
    d. Driving a beat-up junk car that works only sometimes.
2. I will wear clothes from
    a. Upscale stores at the mall.
    b. Discount stores.
    c. Yard sales.
    d. Crisis Assistance Clothing Closet.
3. I will have a job
    a. With my own private office.
    b. In a fast-food restaurant.
    c. In a factory that is noisy and crowded.
    d. That is only temporary and then I don't know what I'll do to pay bills.
4. I will go out to eat once a week at
    a. An expensive Italian restaurant.
    b. A fast-food restaurant.
    c. My mother's house.
    d. A soup kitchen.

5. I will celebrate Mother's Day by

    a. Going to visit my mother and being thankful that I have delayed having children.

    b. Receiving handmade cards and hugs from my four children ranging in age from ten months to seven years old.

    c. Patting my pregnant tummy as I prepare to have my first child.

    d. Being jealous of other people's children because I have developed a sexually transmitted disease that has made me infertile.

6. I will be sleeping

    a. In my own apartment or house.

    b. At my mother's house.

    c. At a homeless shelter.

    d. In a crack house.

7. I will be sleeping with

    a. My husband.

    b. My teddy bear.

    c. My 57th lover.

    d. An IV stuck in my arm in a hospital bed, dying from AIDS.

8. Other ideas about being 23: ______________________________

____

____

____

____

Session 6 Topic: Examining Friendship/Review

Session 6 Supplies: For students—Copies of Relationship Dilemmas; For leader—Whiteboard, Markers, Leader's complete folder (for review)

Session 6 Content:

Begin this session by asking group members to generate positive qualities of friendship, expressing it in one-word descriptions. Allow them to take turns writing a word on the board. Expect such answers as trustworthiness, honesty, helpfulness, loyalty, dependability, and fun. Then ask them to name friendship destroyers: gossiping, lying, cheating, excluding, ignoring, blaming, cursing, fighting, and spreading rumors.

Then read and discuss the Relationship Dilemmas. Ask group members to describe how they would handle the situations, sharing the words they would use if faced with the dilemmas. Allow for alternative answers. One example involves a girl noticing that a certain friend spends time with her only when no one else is around, and she is considering confronting her about it. Someone may suggest she approach her in a very straightforward manner; another may suggest she just let the friendship drift away and seek a new friend who may appreciate her more. Expect a variety of strongly voiced opinions.

To review, briefly identify topics and activities of each session. Ask what they can remember from the sessions, and which ones they found most helpful or meaningful. You may want to include a set of the Villains and Victims Skits from the second session if you were unable to complete them all at that time. At the end, thank them for participation and remind them that you will continue to assist them as needed throughout the year. Dismiss them with a wish for more harmonious relationships!

Questions they should be able to answer: What are positive and negative qualities of friend relationships? Which of the Relationship Dilemmas had the biggest impact on you? How were the situations similar to some you have experienced? Could you recall what each session was about? What did you learn about others during these group sessions? What did you learn about yourself?

Relationship Dilemmas

1. Myra and Annalisa both claim to be best friends, but Annalisa has noticed that Myra hangs around her only when there is no one else around. Annalisa is thinking of confronting her about it.

2. Bianca has noticed many times that Shakira has bad breath. Some of the kids are making fun of her behind her back. Bianca hates for them to do that because Shakira is a really nice person.

3. Emma is suspicious that her friends Jill and Kayla may be taking steroids to enhance their track ability. She knows that this is dangerous as well as illegal. She knows she should do something.

4. Lenora is friends with Victoria and Melissa. Lenora is running for Vice-President of Student Council. Victoria and Melissa found an old picture of her from sixth grade in which she looked very ugly, and they sent it via text to everyone they know. Lenora doesn't know who played this mean trick, and she called up Victoria crying. Now Victoria feels guilty about it and wants to confess.

5. Claire and Nikita have been spending the night with each other nearly every Friday night for the whole seventh grade. Claire is tired of it but doesn't want to let Nikita down.

6. Hillary told Keri that she liked Luke, a very popular guy, but made her promise not to tell him. Later they got mad over a small thing, and Keri decided to tell Luke that Hillary liked him. He laughed and said he couldn't stand Hillary, which Keri promptly told her. She saw the anger and hurt in Hillary's face and now regrets what she did.

7. Liz had wanted to hang around with the "in" kids like Serena who sat at the first table in the cafeteria. One day she was sitting at the second table with her friends when Serena invited her over. She picked up her tray and moved, leaving her old friends behind. After a few minutes at the first table, she got the feeling Serena was making fun of her.

8. Simone and Cassidy didn't think their friend Ella would ever get a boyfriend because she was overweight, so they made up a boy on Facebook who started an online relationship with Ella. They had a lot of fun doing this and could hardly keep their faces straight when Ella talked about it. Cassidy started thinking they should quit, but Simone refused.

Teacher Post-Group Assessment of Behavior

Teacher name ____

Name of student ____

In the last 6 weeks, I have observed/witnessed/heard that this student took part in the following number of negative relational behaviors:
1 = Not at all, 2 = A small amount, 3 = Average amount, 4 = More than average, 5 = Very much

1. Talking negatively about a peer

   1.................2.................3.................4.................5

2. Huddling with peers while pointing or staring at another girl

   1.................2.................3.................4.................5

3. Teasing or taunting a peer

   1.................2.................3.................4.................5

4. Yelling at a peer

   1.................2.................3.................4.................5

5. Attempting to force a peer to sit elsewhere at lunch

   1.................2.................3.................4.................5

6. Starting a harmful rumor about someone

   1.................2.................3.................4.................5

7. Giving a peer the silent treatment

   1.................2.................3.................4.................5

8. Communicating negative comments through texting or social media

   1.................2.................3.................4.................5

Evaluation for Friends and Important Relationships (FAIR) Group

Rate yourself by circling the number which corresponds with how you evaluate each statement.
1 = Not at all, 2 = A small amount, 3 = Average amount, 4 = More than average, 5 = Very much

1. I felt comfortable discussing relational aggression issues in the group.

   1.................2.................3.................4.................5

2. I recognized the difference in aggressive, passive, and assertive interactions.

   1.................2.................3.................4.................5

3. I recognized that there are consequences for decisions that I make.

   1.................2.................3.................4.................5

4. I learned about the uniqueness and the commonalities I shared with others in the group.

   1.................2.................3.................4.................5

5. I practiced the anger management techniques I learned in the group.

   1.................2.................3.................4.................5

6. I learned about the benefits of offering forgiveness and apologies.

   1.................2.................3.................4.................5

7. I was able to share my opinion about various facets of the relationship dilemmas.

   1.................2.................3.................4.................5

8. I grew closer to members during the course of the group.

   1.................2.................3.................4.................5

Suggestions for making the group better: ____

____

References

Crick, N. & Grotpeter, J. (1995). Relational aggression, gender, and social-psychological adjustment. *Child Development, 66*(3), 710–722. (ERIC Journal No. EJ503787)

Facecrooks Home Page. (2010, November 14). *Cyberbullying statistics*. Retrieved August 27, 2011, from http://facecrooks.com/Cyberbullying-internal/Cyberbullying-Statistics.html

Lenhart, A. (2007, June 27). The gender gap: Pew Internet & American life project. *Pew Research Center's Internet & American Life Project*. Retrieved April 16, 2011, from http://www.pewinternet.org/Reports/2007/Cyberbullying/1-Findings/02-The-Gender-Gap.aspx

MayoClinic.com. (2009, November 21). *Forgiveness: Letting go of grudges and bitterness.* Retrieved April 30, 2011, from http://www.mayoclinic.com/health/forgiveness/MH00131

Simmons, R. (2002). *Odd girl out: The hidden culture of aggression in girls*. New York: Harcourt, Inc.

Chapter 10

Self-Esteem: Making Our Way

Making Our Way Group Outline

I. Introductory Information, Sentence Completion Activity

  A. Outline, Schedule, Parent Permission, Rules

  B. Sentence Completion Activity

II. Uniqueness

  A. Seashell Activity

  B. Interest Assessment

III. Acceptance and Problem Solving/Goal Setting

  A. Things You Can/Cannot Change Activity

  B. Problem Solving/Goal Setting Strategies

IV. Friendship Traits and Assertiveness

  A. Traits of Friends

  B. Definitions of Aggressive, Passive, and Assertive Responses

  C. Skits of Refusing Requests

V. More Friendship Issues, Positive Thinking

  A. Can This Friendship Be Rescued? Discussion

  B. Positive Thinking Poster Activity

VI. Review, Collage

  Review of Prior Sessions

  Collage Activity

American School Counselor Association (ASCA) Standards

Career Development

Standard A: Students will acquire the skills to investigate the world of work in relation to knowledge of self and to make informed career decisions.

C:A1 Develop Career Awareness

C:A1.3 Develop an awareness of personal abilities, skills, interests, and motivations

Personal/Social Development

Standard A: Students will acquire the knowledge, attitudes, and interpersonal skills to help them understand and respect self and others.

PS:A1 Acquire Self-knowledge

PS:A1.1 Develop positive attitudes toward self as a unique and worthy person

PS:A1.3 Learn the goal-setting process

PS:A1.5 Identify and express feelings

PS:A1.10 Identify personal strengths and assets

PS:A2 Acquire Interpersonal Skills

PS:A2.3 Recognize, accept, respect, and appreciate individual differences

PS:A2.6 Use effective communication skills

PS:A2.8 Learn how to make and keep friends

Standard B: Students will make decisions, set goals and take necessary action to achieve goals.

PS:B1 Self-knowledge Application

PS:B1.1 Use a decision-making and problem-solving model

PS:B1.4 Develop effective coping skills for dealing with problems

Rationale for Making Our Way Self-Esteem Group

Though the word "self-esteem" has fallen out of favor somewhat in school settings, there are still many adolescents who need counseling assistance in this area. Students who demonstrate excessive shyness, isolation from others, and anxiety in social situations are likely to suffer from low self-esteem. Too often they resign themselves to a life of rejection, teasing, loneliness, and depression

What leads to low self-esteem? Adolescence is a land mine for many students, a prolonged period of time in which it is especially troubling to be viewed as different or inferior in some way. Students diagnosed with autism, ADD, and learning disabilities often exhibit behaviors that peg them as different. However, students who are viewed by others as too fat, too skinny, too short, too tall, underdeveloped, or too developed—it can be anything—can become targets of bullies. After years of being victimized, they find themselves incapable of taking responsibility for their own happiness. They blame others, having long ago lost their motivation to attempt to reach their full potential. Or they suffer in silence, stifling their personal goals out of fear of failure. It can become an unending cycle, in which the victims feel worse and worse about themselves and the world around them (Pickhardt, 2010). In a study of wellness factors, it was found that low self-esteem was connected to poor health and depression in adolescents (Myers, Willse, & Villalba, 2011).

Providing a group to address these concerns may help adolescents cope during this difficult passage. In one study of a social skills group composed of adolescents diagnosed with Asperger Syndrome, the successful implementation of targeted skills did not reach hoped-for levels. However, the students formed friendships that endured beyond the length of the group, which presented a tremendous self-esteem boost for these often rejected children (Interactive Autism network community, 2011). Frequently students with low self-esteem issues are channeled into friendship or social skills groups. Or they show up in relational aggression groups, usually as the victim of such though sometimes as the aggressor. Sometimes they end up in anger management groups. I have provided a group that touches on all those issues, with the unifying factor being the presence of low self-esteem.

My group includes sessions on uniqueness, acceptance, goal-setting, and friendship problems. Group members build relationships together through interactive activities such as performing in simple skits, responding to scenarios, and making a collage. And, hopefully, at the end, they have gained a new friend or two.

What Makes It Work:

1. Students feel a sense of belonging to something at last. No scary audition, no intimidating tryouts—they have gained membership.
2. Students bond with others in a safe environment. They know they will not be bullied or put down here.
3. They have the opportunity to examine themselves and appreciate their own value.
4. Hopefully, students gain acceptance of themselves and can focus on other important parts of life.

Challenges:

1. Even naming this group is a challenge. Try something like "Mission: Possible" or "In Search of Me." I like "Making Our Way" because it implies moving forward, but at one's own pace.
2. The general slide from popularity of the term "self-esteem" has perhaps hurt the willingness of many counselors to provide this type of group. But anyone who works with children in elementary and middle school will be quick to tell you that there are many students with very low self-esteem that needs to be elevated somehow!
3. Some students in the group will sense that they are all "losers." The very nature of this group does often indicate a predominance of social misfits. You may want to confront this straight on but delicately. Emphasize the need for them to reach a place where they can learn to accept themselves yet make small changes to improve their lot.
4. The highly deficient social skills of some students are difficult to eradicate once they have reached middle school.

Making Our Way Group Sessions

Session 1 Topic: Introductory Information, Sentence Completion Activity

Session 1 Supplies: For students—Copies of outline, schedule, and parent permission form; For leader—Copy of Sentence Completion Statements cut into strips, Basket

Session 1 Content:

Begin with the customary explanation of the outline, schedule, parent permission, and group rules. Emphasize that the focus of the group is for students to see themselves as valuable and worthy of respect, which will result in self-acceptance and also a broader acceptance of others.

Then start the Sentence Completion Statements activity. Pass the basket and have each one draw a strip, one at a time, to keep them from concentrating on forming their own comments instead of listening well. Remember to tell them that they can pass and draw another. Some of the statements may seem too personal, especially since group bonding will not have occurred yet.

Questions they should be able to answer: What are the topics that will be covered in group? How does the schedule work? What are the group rules? When is the parent permission form due? How easy was it for you to complete the sentences you drew? What did you learn about others in the group in this introductory session?

Sentence Completion Statements

When I must read in front of the class, I feel ______________________________.

Sometimes I feel like people dislike me when I ______________________________.

I wish I could ______________________________.

I feel ______________ when my parents brag about me.

When someone tells me that I am too shy, I ______________________________.

When I make a good grade, I feel ______________________________.

The best thing that happened to me last year was ______________________________.

The best thing that has happened so far this year was ______________________________.

The quality I look for most in friendship is ______________________________.

I feel ______________________ when I am called on by the teacher.

I sometimes dream that I am ______________________________.

Whenever I do something stupid, I ____.

One of the most embarrassing things that ever happened to me was ____________________.

My report card usually makes me feel ____.

When someone seems interested in me in a boyfriend/girlfriend way, I __________________.

I flip out when ____.

If I were given three wishes, one of them would be for _____________________________.

If I could change one thing about my personality, it would be _______________________.

When I get caught doing something wrong, I _____________________________________.

My parents usually describe me as ____.

I would like to be described as ____.

I only tell my secrets to ____.

I like to think that one day I'll be able to ____.

Session 2 Topic: Uniqueness

Session 2 Supplies: For students—Copies of Interest Assessment, Pencils; For leader—Seashells (or rocks or apples)

Session 2 Content:

The focus of this session is the uniqueness of each individual. Start your discussion by asking them to name one-of-a-kind things (snowflakes, signatures, fingerprints, DNA, etc.) Use any items that look very similar for the uniqueness activity—seashells, rocks, or apples. Hand each of them a seashell and have them examine its shape, shade, markings, etc. Then take them all up in a bag and scatter them on the floor, telling them to find their own seashell. Each person can usually find the one that belongs to him or her. Ask several of them to briefly explain how they were able to do this.

Then shift discussion to how unique they are as individuals (appearance, personality, abilities, likes and dislikes, etc.). And though they share some things with others—same grade, same lunchtime, same books, same wish that summer were here—they, too, are one-of-a-kind. There are several points to make:

- You can do things no one else can, using your own style and your own approach (examples: design a house, paint a picture, write an essay, compose a song).
- You are free to express your individuality through clothes, hair, writing, talking.
- Allow yourself to use your imagination and be creative. Why shouldn't your ideas be as good as those of anyone else?
- At times you may want to try accepting being different instead of trying to assimilate.
- You can learn to respect yourself, value your performance, and trust your perceptions. Put yourself in the #1 spot!

Then distribute the Interest Assessment sheets and pencils. Have them check the appropriate items—those that appeal to them. Ask them to choose their interests with future careers in mind. Perhaps several will share what job prospects they have in mind for when they grow up. Afterwards, mention each item briefly and ask how many checked it so that they can see who might have something in common with them. Note that, though they may share some interests with others, each Interest Assessment is unique when total responses are considered.

Questions they should be able to answer: How are you different from others in the group? How are you alike? How easy was it to see yourself as a person of value? What are your interests? Were you able to connect the interests with possible careers? Did you have an interest that no one else checked? What interests did you have in common with others in the group?

Interest Assessment

Mark the following items that you like to do or think you are good at doing:

_____Singing

_____Drawing

_____Working with plants

_____Cooking meals

_____Working in a group

_____Being a leader

_____Working with your hands

_____Designing things

_____Working independently

_____Convincing people to see things your way

_____Giving a speech

_____Following directions

_____Taking care of children

_____Learning a foreign language

_____Working without a lot of rules

_____Paying attention to details

_____Doing school projects

_____Working with animals

_____Working outside

_____Working on the computer

_____Building things

_____Reading aloud

_____Doing math

_____Writing

_____Organizing things

_____Acting in a play

_____Creating things

_____Greeting people

_____Cleaning house

_____Making jewelry

_____Playing sports

_____Painting the house

_____Directing others

_____Following orders

_____Working in an office

_____Selling things

_____Teaching others

_____Dancing

_____Helping sick people

_____Leading exercises

Session 3 Topic: Acceptance and Problem Solving/Goal Setting

Session 3 Supplies: For students—Copies of Things You Can/Cannot Change and Problem Solving/ Goal Setting Strategies, Pencils; For leader—Whiteboard, Markers

Session 3 Content:

First, explain the importance of realizing that there are some things in life that can be altered and others that cannot be changed, no matter how hard they try. See if group members can come up with some examples of such. Then give them copies of the Things You Can/Cannot Change worksheet. Ask them to complete them independently and then go over the answers together. You will have some laughter as they reveal differences in opinion.

Then hand out the Problem Solving/Goal Setting Strategies form and pencils. You may also want to write on the whiteboard the step-by-step process of problem solving:

1. State the specific problem or concern and what goal you want to reach.
2. Brainstorm strategies to address the problem or reach the goal.
3. Evaluate strategies and narrow to 2 or 3 to try.
4. Set a time for a trial period. (Suggest 3 weeks so that they can report back to the group at the final session.)
5. Evaluate how well the problem was solved or goal was reached. (to be completed later)
6. Revamp plan/goal if needed. (to be completed later)

Encourage them to set realistic plans and goals. If someone feels his problem is that he is unpopular and his goal is to be elected president of a club, then you may want to suggest he try setting a goal of obtaining a lesser position such as treasurer or chair of a committee within the club. Then ask if several students will share their problem solving plan with the group. Open up the group to the idea of helping each other choose strategies for reaching goals.

Questions they should be able to answer: What were some of the differences in opinion about whether or not things could be changed? How easy was it for you to generate strategies in the goal setting activity? Were you willing to share your problem solving plan?

Things You Can/Cannot Change

Read the following statements. If it is something you can change, put a Y for yes in the blank. If it is something you cannot change, put an N for no in the blank.

_____ 1. You made an F in science on your last report card.

_____ 2. Your uncle died last summer.

_____ 3. You hate giving a report in front of the class.

_____ 4. You have only one good friend.

_____ 5. Your mom shouts at you when you don't help with dinner.

_____ 6. You live on Eastway Drive.

_____ 7. You are failing math.

_____ 8. You do not know how to bake a cake.

_____ 9. You have brown eyes.

_____10. Other people say that you are shy.

_____11. Your favorite color is blue.

_____12. You feel unpopular.

_____13. You are African American.

_____14. You are the oldest child in your family.

_____15. Your mom's car was totaled when a garbage truck backed into it.

_____16. You are overweight.

_____17. You want to live in a 5-bedroom Italian villa.

_____18. Your boyfriend/girlfriend dumped you for someone else.

_____19. You hate eating green beans.

_____20. You are lucky when playing cards.

Problem Solving/Goal Setting Strategies

1. State the specific problem or concern and what goal you want to reach:

    ____

    ____

2. Brainstorm solutions to address the problem or reach the goal:

    ____

    ____

    ____

    ____

    ____

3. Evaluate strategies and narrow to 2 or 3 to try:

    (1) ______________________________________

    (2) ______________________________________

    (3) ______________________________________

4. Set a time for a trial:________________________

5. Evaluate how well the problem was solved or goal was reached:

    ____

    ____

6. Revamp plan/goal if needed:

    ____

    ____

Session 4 Topic: Friendship Traits and Assertiveness

Session 4 Supplies: For leader—Copies of Refusing Requests skits, Whiteboard, Markers

Session 4 Content:

Start this session by asking them to generate positive and negative traits of friendship. Call upon group members to write these traits on the whiteboard, since nearly everyone loves to write on the board, but some students may be too inhibited to do so in the regular classroom. Expect to see such positives as honest, kind, loyal, trustworthy, and fun. Negative terms associated with friendship (or more specifically, when friendship problems have arisen) may include two-faced, dishonest, insincere, bossy, and irresponsible. Anyone who has ever had a friend has also found some dissatisfaction with the relationship, but most people learn to accept imperfections and consider friendship an endeavor worth maintaining. Students with low self-esteem may struggle more when they have been hurt by peers and find it difficult to bounce back.

A discussion of passive, aggressive, and assertive communication will help students recognize how they currently respond to peers. Present the following definitions of passive, aggressive, and assertive:

- Passive—being a pushover, being too fearful to express your own opinion or seek your rights, accommodating others just to keep the peace.
- Aggressive—being too demanding or intimidating, expressing your opinion in an overwhelming fashion which does not consider the feelings of others.
- Assertive—expressing your feelings honestly and standing up for your rights without hurting others.

A little assertiveness can go a long way in helping make better connections with peers. Yes, learning to be assertive takes effort, but it can be most beneficial.

Distribute parts in the Refusing Requests Skits. Note that all of these scenarios implement proper assertive responses. Let the students suggest different responses, including passive and aggressive ones. These skits cover such issues as loaning money and sharing homework, very familiar issues for most students. You will find that they enjoy the skits, as even shy students cannot find enough chances for dramatic acting at this age.

Questions they should be able to answer: What do you consider negative and positive traits of friendship? What are the differences in passive, aggressive, and assertive behaviors? Which of the three types of behaviors do you use most frequently in responding to others? How easy is it for you to refuse requests?

Refusing Requests Skits

1. Christina keeps borrowing clothes from Lindsay. She has at least two of her shirts, a sweater, and a pair of jeans that she has not returned to her. Lindsay doesn't want to keep loaning clothes to Christina, but she doesn't want to lose her friendship.

   Christina: Wow, Lindsay! I like your jacket. I bet it would look good on me. Can I borrow it?

   Lindsay: I don't think so. You still haven't returned those clothes I let you wear last week.

   Christina: Oh, I'll get them to you. I think they're in the dirty clothes pile.

   Lindsay: I asked you for them a few days ago and you said the same thing.

   Christina: Well, I always give them back to you at some point. So, let me try on that little jacket.

   Lindsay: No, I can't lend you any more clothes.

   Christina: I thought you were my friend.

   Lindsay: I am your friend, but I just can't let you borrow my clothes any more.

   Christina: You are acting mean.

   Lindsay: I'm not being mean. I am just not going to let you borrow anything now.

2. Trey didn't watch television last night because he worked on his social studies questions for over two hours. Ryan asks him during homeroom if he can look over his answers since he didn't do his homework. The last time Trey let him do that, Ryan copied every answer and Trey was worried about getting into trouble.

   Ryan: Hi, Trey. What about showing me your social studies homework?

   Trey: Not this time.

   Ryan: What do you mean by that?

   Trey: Just two days ago you copied all my math homework.

   Ryan: So? I have soccer practice every day and I don't have time to do homework.

   Trey: If you play a sport, you still have to find time to study just like everyone else.

   Ryan: So, who made you my mother?

Trey: Look, Ryan. I had to give up watching the football game on television last night because of my homework. It's not fair for you to just copy mine.

Ryan: I thought friends helped each other.

Trey: They do, but they also don't take advantage of each another. And we could both get in trouble if you copy my work. Sorry, but I'm not sharing this homework.

Ryan: Whatever.

Trey: See you later.

3. Ben has a habit of borrowing money from everybody. Most people are sick of it but give in so there won't be harsh feelings. James has decided to do something about it.

Ben: Hey, has anybody got a dollar I can borrow?

James: Are you borrowing money again?

Ben: Yeah. Looks like I am. What have you got?

James: Ben, I am not loaning you money anymore.

Ben: Why not? I'll pay you back.

James: No, you won't.

Ben: Yes, I will.

James: What about the five bucks I loaned you on the field trip last week? And the lunch money you needed yesterday? And what about all the pencils and paper I've given you since school started?

Ben: What's your problem, man?

James: It's like this: I've decided that I am not going to loan you any money until you pay me all that you owe me first.

Ben: I said I'd pay you back.

James: When you do, things will be different.

Ben: What kind of friend are you?

James: One who is tired of losing money. I just can't help you out anymore.

Session 5 Topic: More Friendship Issues, Positive Thinking

Session 5 Supplies: For students—Copies of Can This Friendship Be Rescued? and Positive Thinking Poster Activity, Construction paper (or printer paper), Pencils, Markers; For leader—Whiteboard, Marker

Session 5 Content:

Begin the session by reminding group members of last week's topic of using assertive responses when needing to refuse requests from peers. Then hand them copies of the Can This Friendship Be Rescued? sheet. Read and discuss each scenario. One example involves a friend who talks incessantly about her own troubles and does not give you a minute to discuss anything else. Someone may suggest stopping the other person mid-sentence with a statement such as, "Whoa! Let's just focus on one of your problems at a time and then I want to tell you about one of mine." Or "I feel overwhelmed by all that you just told me. Why don't we just talk about your parents' divorce today?" Still another response: "Some days I feel like your own personal counselor, and I'm just a kid with problems of my own." Expect them to have varying opinions, but remind them to seek an assertive response in handling the scenarios.

Then hand out the Positive Thinking Poster Activity sheets and read the statements, one by one. Ask group members to circle three favorites, and then require them to rank those three. Give them supplies for making a small poster to illustrate their chosen statement. Encourage color and illustrations. Urge them to post their pictures in their bedroom or on a closet door or bathroom mirror. Also, reinforce uniqueness by pointing out how everyone's poster looks different, even if several have chosen the same statement. If there is time and you have plenty of paper, let them illustrate their second and third choices as well.

Questions they should be able to answer: How easy was it to respond in the assertive mode to the friendship scenarios? Did you find the responses of others acceptable for your own use? Which Positive Thinking Poster Activity statements did you select as your favorite? Which were your second and third choices?

Can This Friendship Be Rescued?

1. Brittney tells you whom she likes as a boyfriend and makes you promise not to tell. At a sleepover truth-telling game, you feel like you have to tell Brittney's secret to all the girls there. Brittney is so mad she refuses to speak to you, and you feel hurt and angry also.

2. Tony was a fun friend at first, but now it seems that he doesn't want you to have any other friends. If you hang out with anyone else, he pouts and acts like you've deserted him. You like Tony, but you'd sure like to have a few other friends, too.

3. Latonya tells you that Meredith is always making up lies. You nod your head, but then go tell Meredith that Latonya has been talking about her behind her back. When Meredith begs to know what Latonya said, you feel like you have to tell her because she's your friend. Then Meredith tells you she always liked you better anyway and that Latonya is a loser. You agree, but you feel that it's only fair for Latonya to know what Meredith is saying.

4. Kasey has her share of problems—divorcing parents, a mean brother, severe allergies, and constant run-ins with teachers at school. Whenever you are on the phone, she wants to go on and on about her problems. At first they seemed important and you didn't mind listening, but now it's like the same story over and over. You hardly ever have a chance to talk about the things on your mind.

5. Stephen tells you that he likes Amanda and wants to ask her out. You've had your eye on Amanda all year but have been too shy to act. Since you have some classes with Amanda, Stephen asks you to talk with her and see if she would be interested in seeing him. You feel confused.

Positive Thinking Poster Activity

Read the statements below. Circle 3 that appeal to you. Then make a poster of your favorite point and post it where you will see it daily.

1. If life kicks you in the tail, let it kick you forward.
2. Drop the three L's – Lack, Loss, and Limitation—from your vocabulary.
3. Stop minimizing yourself.
4. Never let any mistake cause you to stop believing in yourself.
5. You can if you think you can.
6. When life gives you lemons, make lemonade.
7. You can be greater than anything that can happen to you.
8. If at first you don't succeed, try, try again.
9. Skip "if only" and concentrate on "next time."
10. The tests of life are not to break you but to make you.
11. Always keep hope going for you.
12. Bloom where you are planted.

Session 6 Topic: Review, Collage

Session 6 Supplies: For students—Magazine pictures (pre-cut to save time), Construction paper, Glue, Scissors; For leader—Leader's complete folder (for review), Problem Solving/Goal Setting Strategies sheets (from before)

Session 6 Content:

Set out materials group members need for making collages. Ask them to select pictures that they feel represent their interests and talents. While students are working, review the past five sessions, asking what they remember about each. When they have finished the collages, ask them to share their pictures and explain their choices.

Then hand out the Problem Solving/Goal Setting Strategies sheets from before and ask them to complete numbers 5 & 6, evaluating how well the problem was solved or goal was reached. If they have been unable to reach their goal, ask if they are willing for group members to suggest other strategies. Or they may decide to revamp the goal. Remind them that only a few weeks have passed and that perseverance is needed to reach most goals in life. Encourage them to reevaluate their personal goals every month or so and to celebrate even small points of progress. In closing, encourage them to check in with you periodically to let you know how they are progressing with their goals and to allow you to assist them with any problems that may come up.

Questions they should be able to answer: What do you remember about each session? What did you share with others when talking about your collage? Were you able to meet the goal you wrote several weeks ago? If not, what is your current goal and plan? How do you feel about your relationship with others in the group?

Evaluation for Making Our Way Self-Esteem Group

Rate yourself by circling the number which corresponds with how you evaluate each statement.
1 = Not at all, 2 = A small amount, 3 = Average amount, 4 = More than average, 5 = Very much

1. I felt comfortable discussing issues related to self-esteem in the group.

   1.................2.................3.................4.................5

2. I recognized and appreciated my uniqueness.

   1.................2.................3.................4.................5

3. I learned to set realistic goals.

   1.................2.................3.................4.................5

4. I learned to refuse requests from peers in an assertive manner.

   1.................2.................3.................4.................5

5. I was able to state my opinion on how to handle difficult friendship scenarios.

   1.................2.................3.................4.................5

6. I was able to choose a positive thinking poster which appealed to me.

   1.................2.................3.................4.................5

7. I was able to express many facets of myself through a collage.

   1.................2.................3.................4.................5

8. I grew closer to members during the course of the group.

   1.................2.................3.................4.................5

Suggestions for making the group better: ____

____

References

Interactive Autism network community. (2011, February 15). *IAN Research findings: Social skills groups.* Retrieved April 3, 2011, from http://www.iancommunity.org/cs/ian_research_reports/treatment_series_social_skills_groups

Myers, J., Willse, J., & Villalba, J. (2011, Winter). Promoting self-esteem in adolescents: The influence of wellness factors. *Journal of Counseling & Development 89*(1), 28–36.

Pickhardt, C. (2010, September 6). Adolescence and self-esteem. *Psychology Today: Health, help, happiness + Find a Therapist.* Retrieved April 17, 2011, from http://www.psychologytoday.com/blog/surviving-your-childs-adolescence/201009/adolescence-and-self-esteem

Chapter 11

Standing Up To Stress

Standing Up To Stress Group Outline

I. Introductory Information, Stress Definition, Stress Scale
  A. Outline, Schedule, Parent Permission, Rules
  B. Discussion of Stress Definitions, Posters, and Stress Level Chart

II. Physical/Mental Effects of Stress, Rating Stressors
  A. List of Effects, Stress-Producing Events Activity
  B. Stress Reduction Exercise: Deep Breathing

III. School Stress
  A. Time Management, Test Anxiety
  B. Stress Reduction Exercise: Muscle Relaxation

IV. Family Stress
  A. Family Scenarios
  B. 10 Rules for Getting Along With Parents
  C. Stress Reduction Exercise: Guided Imagery

V. Friendship/Relationship Stress
  A. Friendship Dos and Don'ts
  B. Positive Self-Talk
  C. Stress Reduction Exercise: Repetitive Mantras

VI. Review/ Stress Reducers
  A. Review of Previous Sessions/Stress Reducers
  B. Stress Reduction Exercise: Silent Meditation

American School Counselor Association (ASCA) Standards

Academic Development

Standard A: Students will acquire the attitudes, knowledge, and skills that contribute to effective learning in school and across the life span.

A:A1 Approve Academic Self-concept

A:A1.5 Identify attitudes and behaviors which lead to successful learning

A:A2 Acquire Skills for Improving Learning

A:A2.1 Apply time management and task management skills

Personal/Social Development

Standard A: Students will acquire the knowledge, attitudes, and interpersonal skills to help them understand and respect self and others.

PS:A1 Acquire Self-knowledge

PS:A1.5 Identify and express feelings

PS:A2 Acquire Interpersonal Skills

PS:A2.3 Recognize, respect, accept and appreciate individual differences

Standard B: Students will make decisions, set goals, and take necessary action to achieve goals.

PS:B1 Self-knowledge Application

PS:B1.4 Develop effective coping skills for dealing with problems

Standard C: Students will understand safety and survival skills.

PS:C1 Acquire Personal Safety Skills

PS:C1.10 Learn techniques for managing stress and conflict

Rationale for Standing Up To Stress Group

The stresses facing teens are many. School stresses include competition for grades, demands of teachers, commitment to extracurricular activities, and relationships with friends. Peer pressure to try drugs, engage in sexual activity, and take other risks are common. Bodies are growing at a galloping rate, bringing hormonal changes. Relationships with family are often strained at a time when the support of parents can be vital (Lifespan, 2010). Parents are not always aware of how much stress their children are facing. The American Psychological Association conducted a study in 2009 which indicated that 45% of teenagers felt more worried in 2009, even though only 28% of parents estimated their child was more stressed than before (Coping with stress, 2011).

The physical effects of stress are alarming. Stress can cause various aches and pains such as headaches and backaches. Stress is associated with having lower immunity to colds and viruses. Problems with digestion, difficulty with sleeping, and flare-ups with skin conditions are all health issues which are worsened by stress (Helpguide, 2011). Cardiovascular health—yes, even in teens—can be compromised by excessive stress. Stress that grows out of control can lead teens to anxiety, depression, and drug and alcohol abuse (Guide to stress, 2009).

A stress relief support group offers adolescents an opportunity to become more aware of their stressors and learn techniques to combat them. My group offers sessions on stress as it relates to school, family, and friends. Students can measure their test anxiety, react to family scenarios, and discuss friendship dos and don'ts. Each session begins with students rating their current stress level between one and ten on a chart. Each session ends by practicing a stress reduction skill, such as deep breathing, muscle relaxation, imagery, and silent meditation.

What Makes It Work:

1. The concept of being over-stressed is widely experienced by both youth and adults.
2. Most people recognize the detrimental effects of stress on their physical and mental health.
3. At each meeting students are asked to identify their stress level on a chart, and some may find it relieving just to have the opportunity to express this to others.
4. At the close of each session, group members are taught a useful exercise to reduce stress. They have an opportunity to practice deep breathing, muscle relaxation, guided imagery (not too long), repetitive mantra, and silent meditation (again, not too long!).
5. Hopefully students gain lifelong skills to combat stress.

Challenges:

1. Sometimes the very act of missing class can be stressful for students, causing you to wonder if you're doing more harm than good in some cases.
2. Some parents may have a hard time accepting that kids this age suffer from stress.
3. It is often difficult for kids this age to give up their inhibitions for such exercises as imagery, muscle relaxation, or deep breathing. They can act silly and start giggling over nothing.
4. Some Health/PE classes offer stress reduction tips and exercises, so you might be duplicating efforts.
5. Remember that, when they rate their stress each week on the chart, they will waste star stickers if you do not dole them out in small numbers.

Standing Up To Stress Group Sessions

Session 1 Topic: Introductory Info, Stress Definition, Stress Scale

Session 1 Supplies: For students—Copies of outline, schedule, and parent permission form, Star stickers; For leader—Stress Posters, Stress Level Chart

Session 1 Content:

Begin with the usual explanation of the outline, schedule, parent permission, and group rules. It may be important to reassure group members that teachers are allowing them to make up the work they miss while in group.

Merriam-Webster defines stress as "constraining force or influence, as a physical, chemical, or emotional factor that causes bodily or mental tension and may be a factor in disease causation" (Stress — Definition, 2011). Some refer to stress as simply the absence of peace and harmony. Ask them if they have heard other definitions, perhaps in their health classes. Talk about the difference in external stress (example: someone bullying you) and internal stress (example: worrying about failing a test).

Discuss the Stress Posters, which cover such topics as forgetfulness, perfectionism, and pressure to succeed. Ask group members to name descriptive words or feelings that they associate with each poster. Their list may include: overwhelmed, angry, afraid, tense, depressed, dissatisfied, uncomfortable, and out of control. Encourage them to volunteer personal examples that relate to some of the posters.

Show them the Stress Level Chart. Pass around the star stickers and ask each to indicate his current stress level, with one being "no measurable stress" and ten being "very high stress." Explain to them that this will be the first thing they do at each group session, while they are waiting for everyone to arrive.

Questions they should be able to answer: What are the topics that will be covered in group? How does the schedule work? What are the group rules? When is the parent permission form due? How would you define stress? How well do the Stress Posters relate to your experiences? What is your stress level today? What did you learn about others in the group in this introductory session?

I forget deadlines, appointments, and personal possessions.

Things must be perfect.

I am irritable, short-tempered, and disappointed in the people around me.

I have trouble

falling asleep.

I feel under pressure to succeed at all times. I must not fail.

I am unable to laugh at a joke about myself.

Table 11.1

Name of Student	*Stress Level*									
	1	*2*	*3*	*4*	*5*	*6*	*7*	*8*	*9*	*10*

Session 2 Topic: Physical/Mental Effects of Stress, Rating Stressors

Session 2 Supplies: For students—Star stickers; For leader—Stress Level Chart, Whiteboard, Marker, Stress-Producing Events cut into strips, Basket

Session 2 Content:
Start this session and all the rest by having group members indicate their current stress level on the Stress Level Chart. Allow them to elaborate.

Ask group members to generate what they think are some of the physical and mental effects of stress. Write them on the board, or allow the students to do so. Group members may require help coming up with ideas. Select from below to complete the lists:

- Physical—sweating palms, rapid heartbeat, feeling nervous, upset stomach, problems with sleeping, problems with eating, headache, backache.
- Emotional/ Mental—getting upset easily, feeling depressed, feeling out of control, crying, forgetting things, anger out of proportion.

Then note what behaviors elevated stress may lead to: getting into trouble, blowing up in anger, avoiding situations, arguing, saying or doing hurtful things, taking unwise risks. Help them see how unmanaged stress mimics untamed anger, creating more havoc in their lives.

Next, pass the basket with the Stress-Producing Events cut into strips and ask each student to pull one. Then ask the student to rate it from one to ten. These are common upsetting experiences for their age group: missing the bus, going to a grandparent's funeral, being dumped by a boyfriend or girlfriend, shooting a tie-breaker basket, moving to a new school, and taking a test. Encourage expression of alternate opinions. Promote tolerance, pointing out that what bothers one person in an extreme manner may not bother another person at all.

Close with deep breathing exercises. Ask students to sit up properly in their chairs and take a deep breath through the nose with mouth shut. Hold for three seconds and then open mouth, and with lips pursed, exhale loudly. Do this four times.

Questions they should be able to answer: What are some physical and mental effects of stress? What are some behaviors associated with elevated stress? What were some of the differences in opinion during the Stress-Producing Events activity? What were your feelings while participating in the deep breathing exercises?

Stress-Producing Events

Missing the bus

Having a relative in the military

Shooting a tie-breaker basket

Taking a test

Moving to a new school

Hearing that your parents are getting a divorce

Trying out to make a team

Going to a grandparent's funeral

Giving a report in front of the class

Being dumped by a boyfriend or girlfriend

Having too much homework due the next day

Flying in an airplane

Trying to do a pull-up on the bar

Apologizing to a friend

Going to the dentist

Eating a strange food

Buying a gift for your best friend

Explaining a bad grade to your parents

Coming back to school after being sick for a week

Going out with a new boyfriend or girlfriend

Trying a new dance when a lot of people are watching you

Getting caught telling a lie to someone

Session 3 Topic: School Stress

Session 3 Supplies: For students—Star stickers, Copies of Time Management Tips and Sample Test Anxiety Questionnaire; For leader—Stress Level Chart

Session 3 Content:

After completing the Stress Level Chart, let them talk about all the things at school that stress them. Tests, homework, teachers, team tryouts, rules! You will have trouble getting them to stop talking. This may venture over into issues with friends. Tell them to save that for another session if they can.

Then explain that many find reduced school stress through practicing study skills such as time management and organization. Hand out copies of the Time Management Tips. Allow them to use funny voices or accents as they read them, one by one.

Then hand out the Sample Test Anxiety Questionnaire from *Test Anxiety & What You Can Do About It* by Dr. Joseph Casbarro (2005, p. 164). Again, go over each statement, one by one. Discuss ways to reduce test anxiety:

- Try to get a good night's sleep before a big test.
- Don't skip any meals (especially breakfast) on the day of a test.
- Get to class early so that you have time to sharpen your pencil and look over your notes for a few minutes.
- Take a few deep breaths before beginning.
- Skim over the test to see how long it is and what type of questions it is made of.
- Check the clock occasionally.
- Do not spend too much time working on any one question. Move on.
- Tell yourself you can do it!

Close with muscle relaxation exercises. Start by tensing the muscles in your forehead, making wrinkles. Hold it a few seconds. Then relax it so that it is smooth. Tell them to notice how different tenseness and relaxation feel. Then proceed to the eyes, closing them very tightly. Then relax your eyes, but keep them closed, as if you were taking a nap. Again, tell the students to notice the difference in how tenseness and relaxation feel. Continue by moving to the nose (wrinkling it), the mouth (smiling forcedly), the teeth (clenching them), and the shoulders (hunching them). Move to the arms, which you do one at a time, holding them out straight and making a fist, then relaxing. Do the same with legs, pointing toes and then relaxing. Leave out other body parts. They'll act too goofy.

Questions they should be able to answer: What are some things at school that stress you? What time management tips can you put into practice right away? What do you think about your test anxiety level? What are some tips to reduce test anxiety that you are willing to try? How did you feel during the muscle relaxation exercise?

Time Management Tips

1. MAKE LISTS! Always write down your homework each day in an assignment book. Place a star beside assignments that are due the next day.

2. PLAN AHEAD when you have projects due. You may have more time this week than next week. So get started NOW!

3. Take advantage of CLASS TIME to do homework if your teacher allows it. If you have questions about the homework, this is a great time to ask.

4. Have a set STUDY TIME each day and stick to it! Schoolwork should be your #1 priority.

5. Once you have started an assignment, try to FINISH it before starting another one. This helps keep you organized.

6. PACK your book bag the night before. Remember lunch money, gym clothes, signed forms, school supplies, and your HOMEWORK.

7. LIMIT yourself to 30 minutes of telephone talking or texting. Combine your phone time with a simple chore like folding laundry or walking the dog.

8. Keep paper and pen handy in your pocket or purse so that you can JOT NOTES or make lists of things you need to do.

9. READ whenever you go somewhere in the car (if you do not get carsick). This is valuable time that many students forget to use!

10. Watch out for the giant time-robber: TELEVISION. Limit yourself to one program a day. If you have sports practice or a meeting, consider that your television time for the day. Try one day a week as a "T.V.-Free" day.

11. When you have a chore to do, DON'T ARGUE about it. This wastes time. Just do it!

12. Take a few minutes of time just for FUN! Then you won't mind the work that must be done.

Sample Test Anxiety Questionnaire

	Never	*Sometimes*	*Always*
I become nervous several days before I have to take an important test.	☐	☐	☐
I cannot sleep the night before a test.	☐	☐	☐
I cannot eat the morning of an important test.	☐	☐	☐
My palms sweat, my stomach has butterflies, or I have other similar symptoms when the test is being handed out or distributed.	☐	☐	☐
I cannot focus or concentrate when I first open the test booklet.	☐	☐	☐
I have to read and re-read the directions many times.	☐	☐	☐
I feel light-headed or like I'm going to pass out during the test.	☐	☐	☐
I cannot concentrate or focus during the test.	☐	☐	☐
My mind goes blank during the test.	☐	☐	☐
Negative thoughts enter my mind during the test.	☐	☐	☐
I change my answers many times.	☐	☐	☐
I constantly worry about what time it is and how much time I have left.	☐	☐	☐
During the test, I feel like I'm going to have a panic attack.	☐	☐	☐
After the test, I am totally exhausted.	☐	☐	☐
After the test, I usually think I have failed.	☐	☐	☐

Session 4 Topic: Family Stress

Session 4 Supplies: For students—Star stickers, Copies of Family Scenarios and 10 Rules for Getting Along With Your Parents; For leader—Stress Level Chart

Session 4 Content:

Start with the Stress Level Chart. Note how many of the students are rating something highly stressful which involves their families. Then ask them to generate causes of family stress. Pushy mothers, protective fathers, stepparent issues, parents arguing, impossible siblings, and so on. A reminder of confidentiality may be in order if students venture into serious problems such as drug-abusing family members, terminally ill parents, chronic fighting, and financial need. You may decide to direct a student to speak with you privately after class.

Hand out copies of Family Scenarios. Ask someone to read each one and encourage group members to suggest various solutions to the problems. The situations include such topics as babysitting younger siblings, parental expectations for academics, and arguments between parents.

Then hand out copies of 10 Rules for Getting Along With Your Parents, taking turns reading them. One example is that the wise teenager does not try to win every argument but gives in sometimes when it is not something vitally important to him or her. Remind group members that they must learn to take responsibility for their own role in troubling family relations.

Close with a guided imagery exercise. Ask them to close their eyes. Tell them you'll keep your eyes open to ensure that no one messes with their stuff. Read this slowly, with short pauses between sentences:

> You are at the beach, just coming over the sand dune and walking toward the ocean. The sand is deep and hot and a little hard to walk through, but as you keep moving, you reach the smoother, flatter sand. A few more steps and then you touch the damp cool sand, where you can squish your toes. Finally you reach the water and you're ankle deep in the surf. The ocean spray feels so good that you decide to take a long walk down the beach toward the pier in the distance. You notice that no one else is around, just you and nature. You feel the sun warming your back, but you're not worried about harmful rays because you have put on sunscreen. You kick at the water, enjoying the splash it makes. You smell the salty air and you feel the perfect breeze ruffling your hair and cooling you off. You hear the cry of seagulls above the roar of the waves. You see some dolphins diving in the distant surf. You keep walking, aiming for the pier that's not so far away now. You plod along, enjoying the never-ending motion of the waves, coming toward shore and then receding, over and over. After awhile, you see someone in the distance walking toward you, but you're not worried. You feel totally safe and are enjoying your wonderful walk along the shore. You keep walking, the combination of sun and breeze keeping your body at a comfortable temperature. You see a pretty seashell and stop to pick it up. You keep walking, walking, and realize the person you saw earlier is moving much closer. You squint at the person in the bright sunlight and then realize it's a friend from your stress reduction group. So, OPEN your eyes now and greet the person next to you, saying, "Oh, it's you. I'm so happy to see you." (They love this.)

Questions they should be able to answer: What are some causes of family stress for you? Have you experienced any of the situations covered in the Family Scenarios? What are some tips from 10 Rules for Getting Along with Parents that you intend to try? How did you feel during the guided imagery exercise?

Family Scenarios

What are some possible solutions to these problems?

1. Your mother has started working late and she expects you to take care of your eight-year-old sister until she arrives home at 6:30 pm. You were hoping to try out for the school play, but it will involve daily practice until 5 pm if you are lucky enough to win a part. Your best friend is also trying out and has promised you a ride home after practice.

2. Your brother insists that football games on television overrule everything else. Your dad tends to agree with him. You only watch two or three programs a week, and every week a football game occurs during one of them. You feel that it is unfair for your brother to get his way since he sees five or six games every week, and you ask to watch so few things.

3. Your sister gets to stay up later than you, but you share a room. She'll leave her cell phone on after you've gone to bed and thinks nothing of taking calls while you're trying to sleep. Whenever you tell your mother about it, she acts like you are being unreasonable and says for you to work it out together.

4. Your dad has promised to quit smoking many times but has failed over and over again. Your mother puts him down every time he messes up, and then he accuses her of doing the same thing regarding losing weight. They end up having this same argument several times a week. Your younger brother just puts on headphones and ignores them, but it bothers you.

5. You are pretty sure that your older sister has started using drugs. You want to talk to her about your concerns but you think she'll call you a baby. You've thought about telling your parents, but you're afraid that will make her sneak even more.

6. You made the Honor Roll all last year but this year you are having trouble with a few classes. Your parents ground you for a whole month every time you make Cs. Your friends can make Cs and aren't punished. You are starting to feel very frustrated.

10 Rules for Getting Along With Your Parents

1. Remember, there are times when you are no bargain to live with either! It's tough to be a teenager, but it is also hard to be a parent of one. So when things get rough between you and your parents, look in the mirror and recognize that you do have faults.

2. You can't always get what you want. There are other people in the world besides you. Be sure to back off now and then to see the whole picture. Your family probably wants what is best for you. And they may be right.

3. Let others have their way sometime. The wise teenager doesn't try to win every argument. If you show your parents that you are willing to give in at times, they will be more likely to cooperate when it's some big deal that you really care about.

4. Show some empathy (seeing the world through another's eyes). Think about the Golden Rule and treat others as you would like to be treated.

5. Make a vow to say "thank you" to parents at least once a day. Saying "thanks" is an important key to building respect for one another. They will feel appreciated.

6. At least once a week do something nice for family members. Any little thing will do, as long as they were not expecting it and it will make life a little easier for them.

7. Do not do anything to betray their trust or make them question your honesty. When your family loses faith in you, you have lost more than you want to lose. It's a long slow process to regain their trust.

8. Ask your parents' advice now and then on something big enough to make them feel important.

9. Learn to talk using "I feel" language instead of accusing them or putting them down. Also take time to really listen.

10. Learn how to handle anger appropriately. Seek time to cool off if necessary. Be willing to compromise. When you need to apologize, be willing to say "I'm sorry. I was wrong."

Session 5 Topic: Friendship/Relationship Stress

Session 5 Supplies: For students–Star stickers, Copies of Friendship Dos and Don'ts and Self-Talk: Good and Bad worksheet, Pencils; For leader—Stress Level Chart

Session 5 Content:

Begin with the Stress Level Chart, as usual. A lot of stress in adolescence comes from dealing with friends and relationships. Ask group members to give you some examples of friends bringing on stress and write these on the board. They will make comments about friends talking about them behind their backs or treating them disrespectfully, a best friend moving away, feeling left out, not having a boyfriend or girlfriend, and peers starting unkind rumors. Describe such issues as jealousy, competition, untrustworthiness, and the "sometimes" friend (one who seems to want to be with you only when there is no one else available). They will talk on and on. Distribute the Friendship Dos and Don'ts sheet and go over each point. One important point is to respect a friend's privacy, not revealing their secrets.

Then hand them the Self-Talk: Good and Bad worksheet and ask them to indicate positive and negative answers. One example of negative self-talk is when a student says, "I sound ridiculous when I talk to someone I have a crush on." An example of positive self-talk is when someone states, "I get along well with most people but not everybody." When they have finished, go over the worksheet aloud. Ask if they have ever said these statements or similar ones to themselves.

Close with a repetitive mantra that expresses positive thoughts. Encourage them to choose two to three short sentences to repeat silently when stressful situations arise. They may want to try it aloud first, but be prepared for some laughter instead of seriousness. Some examples of positive self-talk statements are:

I am going to be okay.

I can deal with this.

I'm doing my best.

I can handle this.

I'm proud of who I am.

I can get through this.

It's going to be all right.

Questions they should be able to answer: What are some examples of stressful encounters with friends? Did you recognize yourself in any of the "dos and don'ts"? How can positive self-talk help you? How did you feel during the repetitive mantra exercise? What words did you choose to repeat?

Friendship Dos and Don'ts

DOS	DON'TS
1 Listen as much as you talk.	1. Talk about friends behind their backs.
2. Appreciate your own uniqueness.	2. Restrict your friends to only you.
3. Forgive friends for some mistakes	3. Demand your friends to agree with you.
4. Be willing to make the first move.	4. Isolate yourself from others.
5. Reach out to new people.	5. Rule out misfits and outcasts as friends.
6. Respect the other person's privacy.	6. Reveal your friends' secrets.
7. Refuse to spread gossip.	7. Appoint yourself as a messenger.
8. Seek help for big problems.	8. Give too much advice.
9. Be assertive in relationships.	9. Be passive or aggressive.
10. Stand up for what you think is right.	10. Be a doormat.

Self-Talk: Good and Bad

Put a + in the blank if it is good self-talk. Put a – in the blank if it is bad self-talk.

_____ 1. I can't do this.

_____ 2. I'm a zero at doing math.

_____ 3. I get along well with most people but not everybody.

_____ 4. I feel good about the way I did my book report.

_____ 5. I think I have the worst hair in the seventh grade.

_____ 6. The answer I'm thinking of is probably wrong.

_____ 7. Everything I said at lunch today was stupid.

_____ 8. I can never be as good an athlete as that student.

_____ 9. I am sure I can get this right.

_____10. I never get called on—why raise my hand?

_____11. I look all right in my new jeans.

_____12. I sound ridiculous when I talk to someone I have a crush on.

Session 6 Topic: Review/Stress Reducers

Session 6 Supplies: For students—Star stickers, Copies of Stress Reducers; For leader—Stress Level Chart, Leader's complete folder (for review)

Session 6 Content:

After doing the Stress Level Chart, review previous sessions. Ask how much they remember about each session.

Then give students the Stress Reducers list. Go over each one, elaborating various points. One important item addresses the benefit of finding a good listener to hear them out when they feel stressed. Yes, pets are nice and sometimes actually act as if they are listening but you really need an empathetic human being. The value of physical exertion in helping people feel better cannot be overemphasized. The final point speaks to knowing when you are truly overwhelmed and seeking help for it. In this event, talking to an adult is in order.

Close with silent meditation. Ask the students to sit in the lotus position on the floor if they are dressed appropriately. Otherwise just suggest they sit up straight in their chairs. Ask them to close their eyes, with you keeping yours open to ensure no one bothers them. Tell them to clear their minds of problems and worries. Suggest they listen to their breathing. Then keep silent for three minutes. Five is better, but you'll be lucky to keep them quiet for three minutes without some giggles or an intercom interruption or a fire drill. Remind them this particular exercise will work better at home! In closing, state your availability to see them on an individual basis as needed throughout the school year.

Questions they should be able to answer: What do you remember about each session? Which of the Stress Reducers do you think will work for you? How did you feel during the silent meditation exercise? How well can you identify your stress level of the day now? What do you think of the stress management exercises you have experienced in the group?

Stress Reducers

1. **TAKE CARE OF YOURSELF.**

   Eat healthy meals. Go to bed at a reasonable hour. Use an umbrella when it's raining, wear a jacket when it's cold.

2. **TRY PHYSICAL ACTIVITY.**

   Get plenty of exercise. Walk the dog. Run laps around the house. Play sports.

3. **SHARE YOUR STRESS.**

   Talk to a good listener when you're feeling overwhelmed. Venting can reduce your frustration.

4. **CHECK OFF YOUR TASKS.**

   Mark things off your list as you do them and you will feel a sense of accomplishment.

5. **ALLOW YOURSELF TO CRY.**

   Sometimes you just need to, and it will bring you relief.

6. **MAKE TIME FOR FUN.**

   Everyone should have some fun every day! Sometimes it may be minor fun instead of major fun, but it still counts.

7. **LEARN TO RELAX.**

   Try to find a small piece of time in your day when you do absolutely nothing. Take a few deep breaths, stretch your muscles, and think positive thoughts.

8. **CREATE A QUIET SCENE.**

   No matter how chaotic your world is, in your mind you can go anywhere—a quiet forest stream, a peaceful seaside cottage, or a sunny backyard deck.

9. **MAKE YOURSELF GET INVOLVED.**

   Get out of your room! Say "yes" when a friend asks you to go somewhere. Join a club. Volunteer at a nursing home or rake leaves for a neighbor.

10. **KNOW YOUR LIMITS.**

    When you feel you cannot stand another minute, let someone know that you are overwhelmed. Get the help you need.

Evaluation for Standing Up To Stress Group

Rate yourself by circling the number which corresponds with how you evaluate each statement.
1 = Not at all, 2 = A small amount, 3 = Average amount, 4 = More than average, 5 = Very much

1. I felt comfortable discussing issues related to stress in the group.

   1.................2.................3.................4.................5

2. I was able to recognize the physical and emotional components of stress.

   1.................2.................3.................4.................5

3. I was able to rate how stressful certain things were to me.

   1.................2.................3.................4.................5

4. I learned ways to combat school stress through time management and test anxiety tips.

   1.................2.................3.................4.................5

5. I was able to state my opinion on how to handle difficult family scenarios.

   1.................2.................3.................4.................5

6. I was able to distinguish between friendship dos and don'ts.

   1.................2.................3.................4.................5

7. I was able to practice stress reduction techniques.

   1.................2.................3.................4.................5

8. I grew closer to members during the course of the group.

   1.................2.................3.................4.................5

Suggestions for making the group better: ____

____

References

Casbarro, J. (2005). *Test anxiety & what you can do about it*. Port Chester, NY: Dude Publishing.

Coping with stress. (2011). *Stress statistics*. Retrieved April 3, 2011, from http://www.ourstressfullives.com/stress-statistics.html

Guide to stress management — tips, techniques, and resources. (2009). *Effects of stress on teens*. Retrieved April 4, 2011, from http://www.guidetostressmanagement.com/effects-of-stress/effects-of-stress-on-teens.html

Helpguide.org. (2011). *Understanding stress: Signs, symptoms, causes, and effects*. Retrieved April 4, 2011, from http://www.helpguide.org/mental/stress_signs.htm

Lifespan. (2010). *Helping teens cope with stress*. Retrieved April 3, 2011, from http://www.lifespan.org/services/childhealth/parenting/teen-stress.htm

Stress — Definition. (2011). *Dictionary and Thesaurus-Merriam-Webster online*. Retrieved May 15, 2011, from http://www.merriam-webster.com/dictionary/stress

Chapter 12

Study Skills: Going for the Gold Star[1]

Going for the Gold Star Group Outline

I. Introductory Information, Academic Goal Setting
   A. Outline, Schedule, Parent Permission, Rules
   B. Setting Academic Goals
II. Time Management
   A. Scheduling Other Students: Scenarios
   B. Scheduling Yourself: Your 24 Hours Activity
III. Organization
   A. Demonstration of Organizing Materials
   B. Blank Calendar
   C. Going Through Backpacks
   D. Study Skills Tips
IV. Memorization Skills
   A. Memorization Tips
   B. Wildflowers Activity
V. Test Taking
   A. Test Taking Tips
   B. Sample Test
VI. Test Anxiety, Review
   A. Test Anxiety Questionnaire
   B. Academic Progress Report, Review of Prior Sessions

1 Parts of this chapter first appeared in *Counseling Today*, February 2011. Reprinted with permission from American Counseling Association.

American School Counselor Association (ASCA) Standards

Academic Development

Standard A: Students will acquire the attitudes, knowledge and skills that contribute to effective learning in school and across the life span.

A:A1 Improve Academic Self-concept

A:A1.2 Display a positive interest in learning

A:A1.5 Identify attitudes and behaviors that lead to successful learning

A:A2 Acquire Skills for Improving Learning

A:A2.1 Apply time-management and task-management skills

A:A2.2 Demonstrate how effort and persistence positively affect learning

Standard B: Students will complete school with the academic preparation essential to choose from a wide range of substantial post-secondary options, including college.

A:B1 Improve Learning

A:B1.3 Apply the study skills necessary for academic success at each level

A:B2 Plan to Achieve Goals

A:B2.1 Establish challenging academic goals in elementary, middle/jr. high and high school

Standard C: Students will understand the relationship of academics to the world of work and to life at home and in the community.

A:C1 Relate School to Life Experiences

A:C1.1 Demonstrate the ability to balance school, studies, extracurricular activities, leisure time, and family life

Personal/Social Development

Standard A: Students will acquire the knowledge, attitudes and interpersonal skills to help them understand and respect self and others.

PS:A1 Acquire Self-knowledge

PS:A1.3 Learn the goal-setting process

PS:A1.5 Identify and express feelings

Rationale for Going for the Gold Star Study Skills Group

Why do students fail? Lack of motivation, poor attendance, attention disorder, behavior problems, and absence of future goals—all of these can be factors (Focus adolescent services, 2008). Sometimes the student just needs to be redirected from spending too much time with the television, telephone, and computer. Students who spend three or more hours each day watching television are 82% more likely to experience school failure and become dropouts than those who watch less than an hour per day (Khamsi, 2007).

Why do we worry so much about it? Failing grades do not bode well for most career plans. Students who are not achieving at their best level are shutting down opportunities. Besides the obvious loss of not reaching their potential, students who fail a lot of tests and courses are likely to fail the whole grade. And students with retentions are more likely to drop out. It is reported that approximately 6.2 million students between sixteen and twenty-four dropped out in the United States in 2007 (CNN, 2009).

By the time students reach middle school, active studying must take place for most to achieve at their full capability. Up to this time, some have managed to make fairly good grades without truly applying themselves. Suddenly school requires higher level thinking and more intensive effort, and many are caught off guard. They do not know how to begin to study—how to prioritize, organize, and utilize critical thinking skills. A study skills group provides students an opportunity to acquire needed expertise in an enjoyable manner. Students in my group are actively engaged while they learn about the important study concepts of goal setting, time management, organization, memorization, and test taking.

What Makes It Work:

1. Many students are desperate to improve their grades, and this sounds to them like an easy way to do so. But in order to keep my sanity with the high numbers who may sign up, I recommend that the group be limited to students experiencing Ds or Fs on their report cards.
2. Parents love the idea that someone is teaching their kids to study!
3. Teachers and administrators usually like these groups more than any others because there is a direct tie to academics (though, of course, they would prefer them to meet after school).
4. Hopefully, students learn some concrete ways to improve their grades through studying time management, organization, memorization tips, and test taking info.

Challenges:

1. Recruiting students for study skills groups often results in overwhelming numbers of students wanting such help. If you try to run as many as five of these groups simultaneously, I can vouch that the task will require a large chunk of your schedule and you will probably not be able to manage any other groups during that six weeks.
2. Many students who sign up *want* better grades but are unwilling to put forth the effort or do the work.
3. Some of the students who join exhibit misbehavior, which may be both a result of and a cause of their academic difficulties. Thus you may need rigid rules to keep control of the sessions.

4. It is harder to make this group fun than some of the others. You may have a few students in each group who decide they don't want to be in it after two or three sessions. It's a little disheartening (and NEVER happens in Divorce group!), but at least then you'll be able to give more concentrated help to those remaining.
5. The students in these groups are missing class, and they are the ones who can least afford to do so. This can be a hard sell with some teachers. You could offer one study skills group after school, alongside your full school day schedule, to appease them. Then they will see that you are *trying* to do this after school, but invariably there will be only five to seven students who join this group and fifty in your school day groups. Help your teachers understand that if you offer groups ONLY before and after school, you will miss large numbers of students who desperately need your group services but cannot participate because of transportation problems.

Going for the Gold Star Group Sessions

Session 1 Topic: Introductory Information, Academic Goal Setting

Session 1 Supplies: For students—Copies of outline, schedule, and parent permission form, Index cards, Pencils

Session 1 Content:

At the first session, explain the outline, schedule, and parent permission form. Go over group rules. With this group it may be particularly helpful to point out at each session that they must be sure to make up work they have missed while in group. It would also be wise to praise them for wanting to improve academics, as this demonstrates a positive attitude toward learning. Assure them that joining the group indicates they are already one step closer to better grades!

Distribute the index cards and pencils and ask the students to list their current grade averages in all subjects. Then ask them to set goals for the next grading period, writing them beside their current grades. Hopefully, a few students will be willing to share this information with the others. Ask them for specifics regarding their academic difficulties. Try to help them determine if it is a matter of not studying enough, not knowing how to study, lack of motivation because of prior frustration, difficulty concentrating, lack of interest in the material, or some other reason.

Questions they should be able to answer: What are the topics that will be covered in group? How does the schedule work? What are the group rules? When is the parent permission form due? How realistic are your academic goals? What do you think are the chief reasons that your grades are suffering? What did you learn about others in the group in this introductory session?

Session 2 Topic: Time Management

Session 2 Supplies: For students—Copies of Your 24 Hours worksheets, Pencils; For leader—Scheduling Scenarios, Whiteboard, Marker

Session 2 Content:

This session covers effective time management. The first activity works best as a class discussion. Refer to your Scheduling Scenarios, starting out with "Jeremy." You should write quickly on the whiteboard his tasks and assignments and then ask students to suggest times for him to do each one. Let them disagree, but remind them that they must fit all activities into the day's schedule. What would take one student thirty minutes might take another a full hour. Note that many students have a designated bedtime that they must abide by, which eliminates the ability to keep putting off something until later. Remind them of other events that must take place every evening: eating dinner, walking the dog, taking a shower. Then try a couple of the other sample scenarios. If this session is held late in the day and they have had time to assemble their own homework assignments, it is helpful to personalize this session by writing their lists on the board and discussing valid time frames for completion of their work.

Next, hand them the Your 24 Hours pie chart worksheet. Be sure to note that the "school" piece has already been marked, and suggest that they designate a "sleep" piece of about the same size as the "school" one before filling in the other portions. Help any who seem to not understand the size of an hour piece. Do the actual one first, and then do the ideal. Insist that the ideal one must show time for homework, or else they are wasting their time in a study skills group.

Questions they should be able to answer: How easy was it for you to determine schedules for "Jeremy" and the others? How can you apply scheduling to yourself? How realistic was your pie chart? How did your actual schedule jive with your ideal one?

Scheduling Scenarios

1. Jeremy has the following assignments due tomorrow: (1) Read 20 pages in novel for English, (2) Do 10 word problems in math, and (3) Study for a social studies map test. He arrives home at 4:30. He has soccer practice at the Y from 6:30–7:30. His usual bedtime is 9:30. How should he spend his time today?

2. Rodney has the following assignments due tomorrow: (1) Read 10 pages for his reading journal and get parent to sign, and (2) Study for math test on decimals. It is Thursday afternoon at 3:45 and he has just arrived home. Tomorrow he goes to his dad's house for the weekend, but only if he has completed his weekly chores by 6:00 Friday evening. His chores include vacuuming the house and changing the cat litter box, and he hasn't done either yet. His room must also be straightened up before he leaves on Friday. His room is a disaster area at this point because he has not picked up anything all week. His usual bedtime is 9:00. What should he do?

3. Lynn has the following assignments due tomorrow: (1) Read 4 pages in science book and answer 8 questions at the end of the section, (2) Do 12 equations for math, (3) Study for weekly spelling test, (4) and Bring back signed permission form for field trip. Every day she has basketball practice after school until 5:30. Her favorite hour-long television program is tonight. During sixth period her best friend told her she must call her tonight to talk over a problem she is having with a boy. She doesn't have a usual bedtime—sometimes it is as early as 9:30 and sometimes it is 11:30. It is now 3:20 and school is dismissing. How should she spend her day?

4. Meredith has the following assignments due tomorrow: (1) Write a rough draft paragraph about her family, (2) Do 20 multiplication problems for math, and (3) Read 5 pages in social studies book and answer the 6 questions at the end of the section. In addition, she has a science project due on Friday which is finished except for spray painting it. Also, on Friday she knows that she always has a spelling test with 20 words, and she thinks the words are hard this week. It is now 4:00 Wednesday and she has just arrived home. On Wednesday nights she has Girl Scouts from 7:00–8:00. Her grandmother is sick in the hospital and she may go with her mom to see her. Her usual bedtime is 10:00. How should she spend her time today?

Your 24 Hours

Divide the pie charts into fractions showing how much time you think you actually spend and should ideally spend on such activities as: sleep, eating, sports, homework, television, video games, computer, telephone, chores, and other. (School is already marked.)

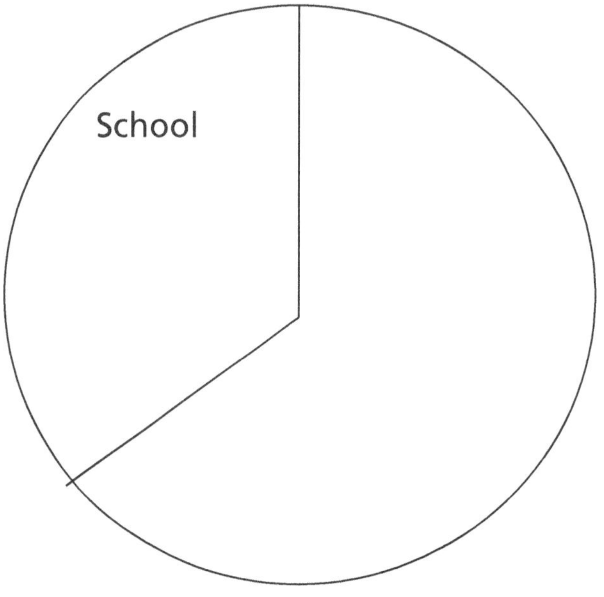

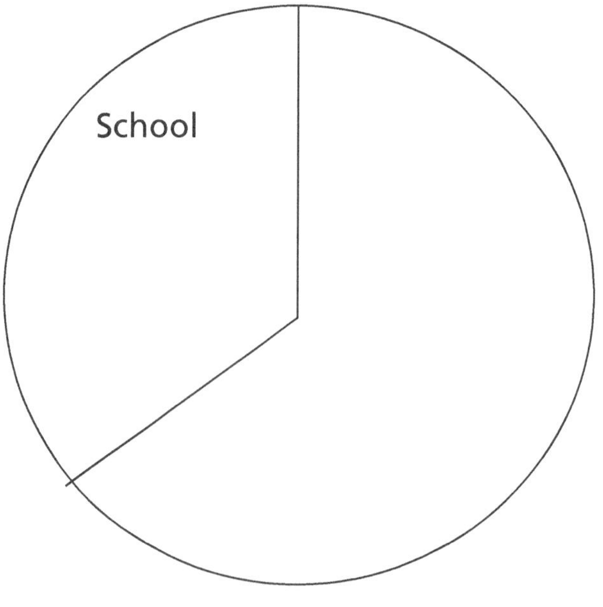

Session 3 Topic: Organization

Session 3 Supplies: For students—Copies of blank calendar page, and Yes, You Can Study; Pencils; For leader—Folders in bright colors (if possible, enough to give one to each student), a locker organizer, several binders of various styles—especially those with accordion-style dividers or separate sections and pockets, sticky notes of various sizes (if possible, enough to give them some), calendars and date books of various sizes, desk organizers, etc.

Session 3 Content:

If convenient, try to schedule this session during the last period of the day and suggest that the students bring their book bags. Link this session to the last one by stating they'll be able to manage their time better and find things more quickly if they are organized.

Collect an assortment of the supplies mentioned above and demonstrate the usefulness of each item. Ask the students for their own ideas or those of their teachers about helpful organization practices.

Then give them copies of the blank calendar page and pencils, completing this task during group. Ask them to fill in the dates for the current month (or the next month if you are near the end of the month), and then write in items beyond the ordinary daily grind, such as when book reports and projects are due. Remind them to add soccer games and practices, music lessons, and other community events if they are not daily activities. They may prefer using a more sophisticated form of calendar such as the one on their phones or other technological devices, but sometimes it is more practical to have one they can paste in their notebooks or on their closet door at home.

Ask those who brought book bags to empty them in various corners of the floor or on the table. Tell them to throw away trash (candy wrappers, broken pencils, crumpled paper). Those who did not bring book bags can assist those who did by making suggestions for ways to better organize.

Give each a bright folder and urge the students to use it as an "all-purpose" folder, in which they will deposit all their homework upon completion that night. They should plan to bring it to all classes, turning in all homework each day, and it should go home empty to be refilled for the next day. It is also a good place to put permission forms or tests requiring parent signatures.

Next, hand them a copy of Yes, You Can Study sheet. Ask them to take turns reading from various points or positions in the room. Some will choose to sit under the table, some will try spinning in a circle, and usually one will do a headstand. Tell them that they may find it easier to study and remember info if they can connect what they were doing at the time (standing on the front porch or perching in a tree) to the facts. Build suspense: tell them they'll learn a lot more about memorization at the next session.

Questions they should be able to answer: Which organizational supplies do you think would help you most? How busy does your calendar look? How disorganized is your book bag? Which of the Yes, You Can Study tips will you put into practice immediately?

Month

Sun	Mon	Tue	Wed	Thu	Fri	Sat

Yes, You Can Study

1. Plan to take a 10-minute BREAK for every hour of studying. Research shows that most students need a break after 45–50 minutes of studying.

2. Always WRITE down homework assignments. Don't trust your memory. Have you noticed that adults make lists all the time?

3. Ask for the PHONE NUMBERS of one or two responsible classmates in each class so you can check on assignments and ask for help after you get home

4. OVERESTIMATE THE TIME it will take you to prepare for major tests and projects. Don't wait until the day before to begin.

5. Have a SET study time each day, flexing as needed with your extracurricular activities.

6. If you do not need 2 hours for your homework, spend part of that time REVIEWING class notes and skimming chapters that the teacher has gone over in class.

7. Try to study the SAME SUBJECT at the SAME TIME each day. This creates a habit of doing that subject at that time and it will seem easier for you.

8. CHECK over the work you are about to turn in. You will catch the careless errors instead of letting the teacher do so.

9. Write down all your grades in a SPECIAL PLACE as you receive them so that you know where you stand in each class. Don't be caught by surprise!

10. Use TRICKS to help you. Example: HOMES = Great Lakes (Huron, Ontario, Michigan, Erie, Superior). Make up your own!

11. Set goals that are RIGHT for you. Don't aim for the A/B Honor Roll until you have begun to move Fs to Ds to Cs.

12. Don't make EXCUSES for poor grades. Take control! Even if you don't reach the Honor Roll, you can make improvements. No one should settle for an F!

Session 4 Topic: Memorization Tips

Session 4 Supplies: For students—Copies of Memorization Tips and Wildflowers, Pencils

Session 4 Content:

A great session, this one! Hand out the half-sheet of Memorization Tips. Ask the students to read them, one by one, stopping for your input. The first point is to try to visualize at what location on the page was the information that they are trying to recall. Was it at the top, the bottom, or in the middle? Talk about using graphs or visual maps, such as "thinking maps" to help them organize and remember information. When you reach the one about putting the info into a song, start humming the "Alphabet" song and ask them if they can identify it. After someone does, then remind them that it is also the tune to "Twinkle, Twinkle, Little Star," a nursery school song they all learned very young. How clever for someone to put the ABC's into a tune all kindergartners would recognize!

When you discuss mnemonics, give this example: "My Very Educated Mother Just Sent Us Nothing"—the order of the planets. (Yes, I remembered that Pluto has been demoted and left it off.) Another example: "HOMES" – the acronym for the Great Lakes (Huron, Ontario, Michigan, Erie, and Superior). A clever acronym—who wouldn't like to have HOMES on those giant Great Lakes? Then show them how to make up their own. To memorize the Great Lakes, they could use one like this: **H**e **S**wims **E**very **O**ther **M**onday. Note that it is best to tie the sentence to the topic you are trying to remember: swimming and lakes.

After reading over the tips, hand them a copy of the Wildflowers sheet. Read these unfamiliar names to them and inform them that they will be able to memorize all ten without looking at the page. Suggest they jot down notes on their page if that will help them. Demonstrate how to make a story out of them: "One day I was walking in the Canada Lily woods and smelled something stinking like Skunk Cabbage but it was only Jack-in-the-Pulpit who was smoking his Indian Pipe and talking junk about seeing Queen Anne's Lace…". Or they could make it into a rap or song. Another method: break the ten names down into three small groups or categories, such as one section of "people"—Queen Anne's Lace, Lady's Slipper, Jack-in-the-Pulpit, Evening Primrose; one section of "animals"—Skunk Cabbage, Oxeye Daisy, Birdsfoot Trefoil; and one section of "places"—Canada Lily, Indian Pipe, Great Laurel (as in Great Lakes). The majority will be able to call out at least eight of the ten, and everyone will be surprised that it is so easy to memorize something as strange as these wildflower names! Some will want to go again and again until they name all ten.

Questions they should be able to answer: Which of the Memorization Tips are you planning to adopt? Can you think of an acronym that would help you learn something? How well did you do on the Wildflowers exercise?

Memorization Tips

1. Try to visualize the information on the page—remember how it looked, where it was on the page (bottom, top, middle).
2. Study different facts in different places (under the table, on the deck, in your closet, in the kitchen). During a test try to remember where you learned certain facts and it might jog your recall.
3. Make up songs and stories using the info.
4. Use graphics or mapping.
5. Break a long list into a short list.
6. Write a word or fact over and over again.
7. Use mnemonics. Example: My Very Educated Mother Just Sent Us Nothing (order of planets).

Memorization Tips

1. Try to visualize the information on the page—remember how it looked, where it was on the page (bottom, top, middle).
2. Study different facts in different places (under the table, on the deck, in your closet, in the kitchen). During a test try to remember where you learned certain facts and it might jog your recall.
3. Make up songs and stories using the info.
4. Use graphics or mapping.
5. Break a long list into a short list.
6. Write a word or fact over and over again.
7. Use mnemonics. Example: My Very Educated Mother Just Sent Us Nothing (order of planets).

Wildflowers

Use any way you can to memorize all ten wildflowers. You may choose to tell a story, sing a song, organize by categories, use mnemonics, alphabetize, etc. Feel free to write on this page if it helps you organize your thoughts.

Skunk Cabbage

Jack-in-the-Pulpit

Evening Primrose

Queen Anne's Lace

Indian Pipe

Oxeye Daisy

Lady's Slipper

Canada Lily

Birdsfoot Trefoil

Great Laurel

Session 5 Topic: Test Taking

Session 5 Supplies: For students—Copies of Test Taking Tips and Sample Multiple Choice Quiz, Pencils

Session 5 Content:

This session involves taking a quiz, and not an easy one, though I did modify it to make it less difficult for my students. Mr. Dennis Congos, Academic Advisor and Learning Skills Specialist at the University of Central Florida, developed a thorough list of Test Taking Tips and the Sample Multiple Choice Quiz from which I obtained questions (Congos, n.d.). To begin, distribute the Test Taking Tips and ask group members to read them one by one. It may help if you give some examples along the way.

Then distribute copies of the Sample Multiple Choice Quiz. Depending on the level of your students, you could have them complete this independently at first. After all, that is what they are accustomed to doing when they take tests. But since the students who have signed up for this group have difficulty making acceptable grades, it is probably best to complete the test together and go over each answer, one by one. Let them know that there will be words they do not know but they should still be able to figure out the answers to the questions by referring to the Test Taking Tips. Do not define any unknown words for them until after the answer is given. As you go over the test, ask students to raise their hands to indicate who picked a, b, c, or d. Give them the correct answer, and then ask which tip(s) from the Test Taking Tips information they used to select the right answer. Ask them to write the number of the tip(s) used beside each question on the test so that they can identify how the answer was reached if they look back over it later. It is important to stress that the best scores on tests come from students who have actually taken the time and effort to study, and that this information is for when they have "forgotten" to study or do not otherwise have any idea what the answer is. You may want to suggest they give this test to their parents for fun. Answers are 1) d, 2) a, 3) d, 4) c, 5) c, 6) b, 7) a, 8) b, 9) d, 10) b, 11) d, 12) a.

Questions they should be able to answer: How well did you do on the Sample Multiple Choice Quiz? What was it like to take a test with such unfamiliar subject matter? How well were you able to identify the tip(s) from the Test Taking Tips list that matched each question?

Test Taking Tips

The following tips should be used when taking multiple choice exams when guessing or trying to decide between similar answers. Of course, the #1 test taking tip is to BE PREPARED BY KNOWING THE MATERIAL.

When you are not certain of the correct answer…

1. Choose the most logical answer.
2. Choose the longest answer when the others are much shorter.
3. Choose the answer with a middle value whenever other answers are higher or lower.
4. Do not choose an answer that is very similar to one or two other answers.
5. Choose the answer that agrees grammatically. (examples: an, a; singular, plural)
6. Count the number of blanks with fill-in-the-answer type tests. (think "hangman")
7. Do not choose answers with absolutes in them. (examples: all, never, none, always)
8. Choose among familiar answers. Avoid totally unknown options.
9. Choose the answer most like key words in the question.

Sample Multiple Choice Quiz

1. A salve made of jipsen seed is put on an inflamed area of the skin because jipsen
   a. has a toxic effect.
   b. heals every kind of wound.
   c. has no effect on inflamed areas.
   d. is soothing.
2. The government department responsible for education and welfare on the national level is
   a. the U.S. Dept. of Health, Education, and Welfare.
   b. the U.S. Dept. of Foreign Services.
   c. the U.S. Supreme Court.
   d. the U.S. Dept. of Agriculture.
3. Fantasy and make-believe are pastimes which are
   a. experienced only by the very young.
   b. always indicative of psychological instability.
   c. never demonstrated by intelligent adults.
   d. sometimes beneficial when moderate in dimension.
4. Which of the following is an example of an instrument that measures the level of expressed self-esteem?
   a. the Strong-Campbell Vocational Interest Blank.
   b. the Kidder Personal Preference Inventory
   c. the Tennessee Self-Concept Scale
   d. the Vassey Adult Intelligence Scale.
5. The Roman philosopher Tuscus believed that
   a. the fall of Rome was bound to happen.
   b. nothing could be done to save the Roman Empire.
   c. man, properly aware of the impending fall, could prevent it.
   d. the direction of decay and decline in Rome was irreversible.
6. The bill of the woodpecker robin is
   a. blunted and short.
   b. sharp and long.
   c. almost nonexistent.

   d. curved and small.

7. The most reticent animal you are likely to find in a zoo is an
   a. elephant.
   b. gorilla.
   c. giraffe.
   d. lemur.

8. The economic policy practiced by both Britain and France during the seventeenth century, which restricted trade by the colonies to the mother country, was _____________.
   a. feudalism.
   b. mercantilism.
   c. socialism.
   d. capitalism.

9. Bendaline's opera "The Three Bells" focuses on
   a. marital discord.
   b. spouse problems.
   c. divorce.
   d. conflict between an old man and his wife.

10. The atmospheric temperature at which cats feel best is
    a. 40 degrees F.
    b. 65 degrees F.
    c. 90 degrees F.
    d. 98.6 degrees F.

11. A noted French biologist was
    a. Williams.
    b. Sagendorf.
    c. Polanski.
    d. La Seur.

12. Which of the following statements related to Emily Dickinson is correct?
    a. For a part of her life, Emily Dickinson was a recluse.
    b. Emily Dickinson always wrote poetry about melancholia.
    c. Emily Dickinson never exhibited any talent for poetry other than free verse style.
    d. Emily Dickinson always dealt with the most trivial themes of existence in her poetry.

Session 6 Topic: Test Anxiety, Review

Session 6 Supplies: For students—Copies of Sample Test Anxiety Questionnaire, Pencils; For leader—Index cards (from before), Leader's complete folder (for review), Tape recorder and blank tape (or other recording device)

Session 6 Content:

The last session is still packed with information. Start by asking them to complete the "Sample Test Anxiety Questionnaire" from *Test Anxiety & What You Can Do About It*, by Dr. Joseph Casbarro (2005, p. 164). Be sure to go over each question, and privately note if there are students in the group who are seriously anxious. I determine this by the frequency of the "always" answer and also by noting how they scored on numbers four, seven, and thirteen, which refer to physical concerns. You may need to set up an individual counseling session or two for those students. Give the following general information about relieving test anxiety to all:

- Try to get a good night's sleep before a big test.
- Don't skip any meals (especially breakfast) on the day of a test.
- Get to class early so that you have time to sharpen your pencil and look over your notes for a few minutes.
- Take a few deep breaths before beginning.
- Skim over the test to see how long it is and what type of questions it is composed of.
- Check the clock occasionally but not constantly.
- Do not spend too much time working on any one question. Move on.
- Tell yourself you can do it!

Then return the index cards that they completed at the first session. Ask them to update their grades. Encourage some to share their progress.

After a quick review of previous sessions, turn on the tape recorder (or other recording device). Ask them to take turns stating three things they are doing now or plan to do to aid their studying. Let them use silly voices or accents if they choose. Play them back and be prepared for laughter. Never overlook an educable moment: point out that if they have recording capabilities at home, they can read their whole science chapter or notes into the recorder. Then they can play it back during a long bath or while they're getting ready for school on the day of the test.

Last of all, you should indicate your willingness to see them individually throughout the year if they need continued help with study skills. Encourage them to keep updating their index cards each time report cards or progress notes are issued.

Questions they should be able to answer: What do you think about your test anxiety level? What are some tips to reduce test anxiety that you are willing to put into practice? How well were you able to meet your academic goals? What do you remember from each of the sessions? Which three things did you choose to put into effect to aid your studying?

Sample Test Anxiety Questionnaire

	Never	*Sometimes*	*Always*
I become nervous several days before I have to take an important test.	☐	☐	☐
I cannot sleep the night before a test.	☐	☐	☐
I cannot eat the morning of an important test.	☐	☐	☐
My palms sweat, my stomach has butterflies, or I have other similar symptoms when the test is being handed out or distributed.	☐	☐	☐
I cannot focus or concentrate when I first open the test booklet.	☐	☐	☐
I have to read and re-read the directions many times.	☐	☐	☐
I feel light-headed or like I'm going to pass out during the test.	☐	☐	☐
I cannot concentrate or focus during the test.	☐	☐	☐
My mind goes blank during the test.	☐	☐	☐
Negative thoughts enter my mind during the test.	☐	☐	☐
I change my answers many times.	☐	☐	☐
I constantly worry about what time it is and how much time I have left.	☐	☐	☐
During the test, I feel like I'm going to have a panic attack.	☐	☐	☐
After the test, I am totally exhausted.	☐	☐	☐
After the test, I usually think I have failed.	☐	☐	☐

Evaluation of Going for the Gold Star Study Skills Group

Rate yourself by circling the number which corresponds with how you evaluate each statement.
1 = Not at all, 2 = A small amount, 3 = Average amount, 4 = More than average, 5 = Very much

1. I felt comfortable discussing study skills in the group.

   1.................2.................3.................4.................5

2. I was able to set realistic academic goals.

   1.................2.................3.................4.................5

3. I learned helpful time management tips.

   1.................2.................3.................4.................5

4. I learned how to set a realistic daily schedule.

   1.................2.................3.................4.................5

5. I learned how to become better organized.

   1.................2.................3.................4.................5

6. I learned useful memorization tips.

   1.................2.................3.................4.................5

7. I put into practice specific test taking techniques for multiple-choice tests.

   1.................2.................3.................4.................5

8. I grew closer to members during the course of the group.

   1.................2.................3.................4.................5

Suggestions for making the group better: ____

____

References

Casbarro, J. (2005). *Test anxiety & what you can do about it.* Port Chester, NY: Dude Publishing.

Congos, D. (n.d.). *Test taking strategies for multiple choice tests.* University of Central Florida. Retrieved May 19, 2011, from http://www.sarc.sdes.ucf.edu/documents/learning_skills/test_taking/MC-STRATE.pdf

CNN.com. (2009, May 5). *'High school dropout crisis' continues in U.S., study says.* Retrieved May 1, 2011, from http://www.cnn.com/2009/US/05/05/dropout.rate.study/index.html

Focus adolescent services. (2008). *If your teen begins to fail in school.* (2008). Retrieved April 5, 2011, from http://www.focusas.com/School.html

Khamsi, R. (2007, May 8). Too much TV may result in academic failure. *New Scientist Life.* Retrieved April 5, 2011, from http://www.newscientist.com/article/dn11803-too-much-tv-may-result-in-academic-failure.html

Chapter 13

Underachievers: Boys Improving Grades (BIG)

Boys Improving Grades Group Outline

I. Introductory Information, Goal Setting, Self-Rating
   A. Outline, Schedule, and Rules
   B. Academic Goal-Setting
   C. Self-Rating Activity
   D. Points System Explanation
II. Self-Examination
   A. Comparison of Student and Teacher Ratings
   B. Things About Me Activity
   C. Quality World Ranking Collage Activity
III. Recognizing the Power of Choices
   A. Choices and Consequences
   B. Boys to Men Game
IV. Guest Speaker—College Student
V. Computer Lab Activity—Comparing Colleges
VI. Goal Checking/Review
   A. Academic Progress Check, Points System Awards
   B. Self-Rating Activity
   C. When I Am 23 Activity
   D. Review of Prior Sessions

American School Counselor Association (ASCA) Standards

Academic Development

Standard A: Students will acquire the attitudes, knowledge, and skills that contribute to effective learning in school and across the life span.

A:A1 Improve Academic Self-concept

A:A1.2 Display a positive interest in learning

A:A1.5 Identify attitudes and behaviors that lead to successful learning

A:A2 Acquire Skills for Improving Learning

A:A2.2 Demonstrate how effort and persistence positively affect learning

A:A3 Achieve School Success

A:A3.1 Take responsibility for their actions

Standard B: Students will complete school with the academic preparation essential to choose from a wide range of substantial post-secondary options, including college.

A:B1 Improve Learning

A:B1.1 Demonstrate the motivation to achieve individual potential

A:B2 Plan to Achieve Goals

A:B2.1 Establish challenging academic goals in elementary, middle/jr high and high school

A:B2.2 Use assessment results in educational planning

A:B2.6 Understand the relationship between classroom performance and success in school

A:B2.7 Identify post-secondary options consistent with interests, achievement, aptitude, and abilities

Standard C: Students will understand the relationship of academics to the world of work and to life at home and in the community

A:C1 Relate School to Life Experiences

A:C1.1 Demonstrate the ability to balance school, studies, extracurricular activities, leisure time, and family life

A:C1.6 Understand how school success and academic achievement enhance future career and vocational opportunities

Career Development

Standard A: Students will acquire the skills to investigate the world of work in relation to knowledge of self and to make informed career decisions.

C:A1 Develop Career Awareness

C:A1.3 Develop an awareness of personal abilities, skills, interests, and motivations

Personal/Social Development

Standard A: Students will acquire the knowledge, attitudes, and interpersonal skills to help them understand and respect self and others.

PS:A1 Acquire Self-knowledge

PS:A1.2 Identify values, attitudes and beliefs

PS:A1.3 Learn the goal-setting process

PS:A1.5 Identify and express feelings

PS:A2 Acquire Interpersonal Skills

PS:A2.3 Recognize, accept, respect, and appreciate individual differences

Rationale for Boys Improving Grades (BIG) Group

Boys seem to be getting a bad rap these days. More and more they are associated with underachieving. Fewer are graduating from high school ranked in the upper percentiles, and fewer are going to college—with a rate of 4 women to 3 men. Not only are their grades poorer, males are more likely to be retained. They are more apt to be diagnosed with learning disabilities and more likely to face suspensions for misbehavior. The long-term ramifications of this are considerable: less marriageable partners for women leads to more single motherhood and more fatherlessness for children (Wintery Knight, 2010).

Girls are taking more Advanced Placement classes in high school and are winning the valedictory spot much more frequently than boys. More alarming, graduation figures indicate that 65% of boys wear the cap and gown; 72% of females do so (Henley, 2009). Students who are unmotivated academically are more apt to act out in school. Boys are suspended at double the rate of girls, and they are three times more likely to face expulsion (Whitmire, 2010).

In my own school I study the mid-year failure list, which consists of students failing one, two, three, or four classes. One year boys outnumbered girls at an astounding rate: 33 boys, 4 girls. I was particularly interested in students I considered to be underachievers, those who had standardized testing scores which indicated they were capable of grade level work but were failing their actual subjects. I found ten boys on the failure list who had passing levels on state-mandated Reading and Math tests, and those became the focus of my first Boys Improving Grades group.

This group differs from a study skills group in that these students do not need lessons on organization, time management, memorization, and test taking. What they need help with is motivation to succeed, with no time to waste! I include sessions for them to explore who they are—their interests, priorities, and values—and thus help them realize their potential. I attempt to stir up interest in education by exposing them to an online website of college information for my state and by inviting a college student speaker. I require them to complete pre- and post-tests to clarify their status. I also ask teachers to perform similar pre- and post-tests and then I share them with the students. In the end when you assemble all of your data, you hope to show quantifiable progress in each student. (In my first run of the group, I was able to demonstrate measurable progress in eight of the ten boys. One moved away early in the course of the group, and one unfortunately showed absolutely no improvement.) With its measurable academic focus, this group packs a punch.

What Makes It Work:

1. Students with acceptable standardized test scores paired with low classroom performance are often bored but will be very interested in anything that removes them from the classroom.
2. Parents are on their last nerve with their underachieving children. They are in favor of anything that might motivate them. (I have included a sample letter.)
3. Teachers are also frustrated with these students and want someone to help turn them around. Teachers don't mind them missing class since they usually don't do their class work anyway.
4. These boys are capable of making up the class work they miss without becoming too far behind. Of course, that doesn't mean they'll bother to do it.
5. Somewhere along the way these students stopped meeting expectations. A miracle is not needed to boost their grades. Because they are capable, there is a strong possibility of your efforts actually working and their grades rising. It may take only someone noticing them and guiding them back to the path of academic success.
6. The best time to start this six-week group in most schools will be a few weeks after a formal report card has occurred so that another report card will occur by the end session, making comparisons more readily observed. If not, then you may need to pull the students together again after the group has ended to schedule a check on how well they reached their academic goals.

Challenges:

1. Again, it may be hard to get the students to make up the work.
2. Students like these are often very stubborn and not interested in changing their ways.
3. Because they are easily bored, one must keep an invigorating pace.
4. A group of all boys tends to be more unruly than a mixed group or a group of girls.
5. It would be disheartening but definitely possible to end up with data showing little or no appreciable upward movement.
6. It takes time (a valuable commodity) for teachers to conduct the Pre-group and Post-group forms, and some may resent spending extra effort on these students. You may need to emphasize that this data is important in assessing the effectiveness of the group.

February 3, 2011

Dear Parent/Guardian of ____:

I am starting a six-week group for boys who have strong academic capability but are not working up to their potential. These students were failing two or more subjects on the January report card, yet they scored at Level 3 or 4 on the End-of-Grade tests last May. The group is called BIG (Boys Improving Grades). Students in the group will meet at a different period each week so that each class is missed only once. Students are expected to make up any work missed while in group.

Students who are not motivated to achieve are often frustrating to both their parents and their teachers. The goal of the group is to help them realize how they are limiting their futures and direct them away from such self-destructive behavior. We will work on realistic goal setting for improving grades. Besides test scores, I will be monitoring the turning in of homework, participation in class work, and completion of projects. I am hoping that this intensive focus will drive them to take responsibility for their work.

If you would like for your child to participate in the group, please sign the form below and return it to me by Thursday, February 10. If you have questions, you may call me at 704-455-4700 or email me at debra.efird@cabarrus.k12.nc.us.

Sincerely,

Debra Efird
School Counselor

++

I give permission for my child ____
to participate in the BIG (Boys Improving Grades) group. I understand that my child will miss one class per week and is required to make up work from those classes.

____ ________________

Parent/Guardian signature Date

Boys Improving Grades (BIG) Group Sessions

Session 1 Topic: Introductory Information, Goal Setting, Self-Rating

Session 1 Supplies: For students—Copies of outline, schedule, and Student Rating Pre-Group Scale forms, Index cards (with current grades previously marked by leader), Pencils

Session 1 Content:

Begin by explaining the general purpose of the group, which is demonstrated by the name, Boys Improving Grades. They will like the acronym BIG. (Since this group has been hand-selected based on test score data, parent permission letters have already been returned.) Go over basic information such as the outline, schedule, and group rules.

Distribute to each an index card on which you have previously written their most recent report card grades for each of their subjects. Hand out pencils—these are not students who will come to group prepared. Ask them to set academic goals and write them on the card beside each subject. Remind them to be realistic, as this bunch may throw down all As, even though current grades include Ds and Fs. There may be a little bit of cockiness since they've been praised over time for having passing or even excellent standardized test scores. Explain to them that, because of their ingrained study habits (or lack of them), it is unlikely that they will pull off the A Honor Roll at the next report card. Then take up the cards, as you'll be monitoring their grades and returning them at the last session.

Next, hand out the Student Rating Pre-Group Scale forms, which address turning in homework, completing class work, completing projects, and passing tests. Each student should receive a separate form for each subject. You may want to ignore electives and address only four main subjects: English, Math, Science, and Social Studies. Otherwise, you and they are handling a lot of paper. The student rates himself on his work level from 1 to 5, indicating either Never, Rarely, Sometimes, Frequently, or Always. Encourage them to be honest: after all, they wouldn't have poor grades if they were doing all the right things. Usually they don't mind admitting their omissions; some even boast about it. Your work is cut out for you! Take up all the forms, telling the boys they will rate themselves again at the last session. Once you've collected them, inform them that their teachers will also be rating them on the completion of homework, class work, projects, and test scores. You'll be able to tell by their faces if they've been honest.

Adding a competitive angle will help inspire them. Develop a points system in which you award one or two points for catching group members exhibiting behaviors that lead to improved grades. As you go through the week, do a spot check on each student at least once to see if he is engaging in grade-enhancing acts. For example, if one has completed his assignment agenda that day—indicating all his homework—award him a point. Other opportunities to win points could come from making a C or above on a test, participating in class by asking questions, turning in a project on time, and asking for extra credit work. Checking on some of these activities will involve you taking time to consult with teachers. Keep your checks on the students random and frequent and as equitable as possible, which means you may have to visit some students multiple times to "catch" them doing well.

Questions they should be able to answer: What are the topics that will be covered in group? How does the schedule work? What are the group rules? How difficult was it for you to complete the self-assessment? How do you think you will do on the points system? What did you learn about each other in the introductory session?

Student Rating

Pre-Group Scale

Student Name ______________________________

Teacher Name ______________________________

Subject ______________________________

Date ____________________

Please rate yourself on your work in the above subject by indicating the following:

1 = Never, 2 = Rarely, 3 = Sometimes, 4 = Frequently, 5 = Always

Turn in homework 1..............2..............3..............4..............5

Turn in class work 1..............2..............3..............4..............5

Complete projects 1..............2..............3..............4..............5

Pass tests 1..............2..............3..............4..............5

Session 2 Topic: Self-Examination

Session 2 Supplies: For students—Copies of Things About Me worksheet, Pencils, Pictures for collage (pre-cut, categorized, and organized into envelopes) and long strips (6"× 18") of construction paper, Glue; For leader—Copies of Student and Teacher Rating Pre-Group Scales

Session 2 Content:

Begin the session by distributing the Teacher Rating Pre-Group Scale forms, which the teachers have already completed, along with the Student Rating Pre-Group Scale forms which the students finished last week. Have the students compare the assessment of their teachers regarding turning in homework, turning in class work, completing projects, and passing tests with their own self-assessments. They will surely find some wild discrepancies! Then take up all the forms for safekeeping.

Give the students copies of the Things About Me worksheet, in which they indicate whether statements are true or false for them. This activity is a compilation of simple statements such as "I have a dog" and "I usually like group work at school." The purpose of this activity is simply to establish similarities in the students which may help them bond. You may choose to have the boys take turns reading aloud each statement and taking a tally right then and there, or you may have them read and complete them independently with plans to share the tallies with them at the next session.

Next, it is time for the Quality World Ranking Collage activity, which is collage-making with a twist. William Glasser, a noted counseling theorist, made the term "quality world" a part of his choice theory work (Ridgway, 2007). The concept involves people placing in their world the people and things that please them, a point that you will want to explain to group members. Prior to the group session, you may need to make certain assumptions about what these students would find important in their quality world and search magazines and sales catalogs for such pictures. In my group I include these eight categories: televisions, phones, beds (indicating sleep), food, sports, friends, families, and school. Select enough pictures in each category for each boy to have one. Put all the "food" pictures in an envelope, all the "sports" pictures in another, and so on. At the meeting, distribute to each boy a picture from each envelope. (You could set the pictures in separate piles on the table and ask the students to choose their own, but I prefer the express way. My handing them out also eliminates mild arguments about who grabbed the best pictures.) Ask the boys to rank the categories in their quality world in order of importance and then glue them to the long strip of construction paper from top to bottom in that order. You will see a wide range of priorities, with school usually coming in dead last. Encourage each boy to share his collage and expand upon why he chose items in that particular order. Televisions and phones tend to rank at the top, showing that materialism is of high importance, though friends and sports also show up near the top. Remind them to respect individual differences in the rankings.

At the close of the meeting, remind them that you will continue to make unannounced check-ins during the week for the points system competition.

Questions they should be able to answer: Were there any surprises about the way your teachers rated you? Do you think that you have much in common with others in the group? How difficult was it for you to prioritize various aspects of your life in the collage activity? How did your collage priorities compare to your peers? Were you able to gain any points in the last week?

Teacher Rating

Pre-Group Scale

Student Name ____

Teacher Name ____

Subject ____

Date ____________________

Please rate the student by indicating the following:

1 = Never, 2 = Rarely, 3 = Sometimes, 4 = Frequently, 5 = Always

Turns in homework 1..............2..............3..............4..............5

Turns in class work 1..............2..............3..............4..............5

Completes projects 1..............2..............3..............4..............5

Passes tests 1..............2..............3..............4..............5

Things About Me

Mark T for True, F for False beside the following statements:

_________ 1. Most days I bring my lunch to school.

_________ 2. I am from a divorced or separated home.

_________ 3. I usually like group work at school.

_________ 4. I am an only child.

_________ 5. I am the oldest child in my family.

_________ 6. I enjoy snow days.

_________ 7. I have a dog.

_________ 8. I like PE class.

_________ 9. I usually make good grades on projects for school.

_________10. I play video games at least 4 times per week.

Special Question: Most people think I am ______________________________.

Session 3 Topic: Choices and Consequences

Session 3 Supplies: For leader—Copy of Boys to Men Game, cut into small (1" × 3") pieces; 10 large (at least 11" × 14") sheets of construction paper, Basket

Session 3 Content:

Begin the session by asking group members how they would've answered the question about what they wanted to be when they grew up back when they were kindergartners. Then ask how they'd answer that question now. Do not accept the "I don't know" answer. Require them to name a few things they might consider doing as their life's work. Ask what education and training may be required for those jobs.

Then switch gears and ask students to list consequences of not doing school work. They should come up with dropping out of school, disappointing their parents, not being accepted into college, not getting a good job, not making much money, and so on. They may even assume the worst: heavy drug use, life in prison, death from gang involvement. Point out the disconnection between what they want as a career and the paths they are currently taking.

Then play the Boys to Men Game, named such in hopes they will see the positive steps they need to take to become more mature. If weather permits, games are always more fun outdoors. Place ten large sheets of construction paper in a line, curving it if you like. Have each one line up behind the first sheet, draw a slip of paper from the basket, and read it aloud. Then he should proceed to position himself on the "game board" accordingly, moving forward or backward one or two steps as directed. If they draw a "Go back" before they even get started, make them stay behind the first sheet until they earn a step forward. One example involves Kevin turning in his project one day late, forfeiting twenty points. Still, he is allowed to go forward one space. Why is this considered a forward move instead of backward? Because at least he did choose to turn in the project, instead of just blowing it off. Another example involves Stan daydreaming about being a basketball star during his English test and consequently failing the test. He must go back two spaces. Play on out until at least half of them have reached the finish line. You may run out of slips, but just put them back into the basket. It won't hurt them to hear them twice.

Questions they should be able to answer: What are a couple of jobs or careers you'd like to do as your life's work? Have your ideas changed since kindergarten? What are some actions you can take that will detract from your life goals? What are actions you can take to help reach your life goals? What are negative behaviors you can change in your daily life at school? Were you able to gain any points in the last week?

Boys to Men Game

Joe turned in his project on time, even though he wasn't pleased with it. Go forward 1 space.	Mr. King picked Ricardo as "Student of the Month" for improving grades. Go forward 2 spaces.
Stan reached a new level playing video games but blew off his math homework. Go back 2 spaces.	Jamal texted his girlfriend for four hours and studied for his science test at the same time. Go forward 1 space.
Davis helped Jared with his math homework. Go forward 2 spaces.	Kevin turned in his project one day late, which cost him 20 points. Go forward 1 space.
Alex started on his project but didn't like the way it looked so he stopped working and didn't turn it in. Go back 2 spaces.	Brad visited his brother at college for the weekend and decided he wants to apply there. Go forward 2 spaces.
Sergio chose to sleep during class when he saw there was a substitute teacher. Go back 2 spaces.	Shaquille made fun of Davis for making the Honor Roll, even though he made it himself last year. Go back 1 space.
Ray told jokes to his lab partner and didn't do the science experiment. Go back 2 spaces.	Edgar made the wrestling team, but he had to go to math tutoring in the mornings to keep up with class. Go forward 2 spaces.
Jared made 4 B's on his report card but failed P.E. because he refused to dress out. Go back 1 space.	Tyler chose to bring weed to class because he thought school was boring. Go back 2 spaces.

Ricardo checked out a harder book than usual at the library. Go forward 1 space.	Maurice lied to his parents, telling them he had no homework. Go back 2 spaces.
Felipe felt unchallenged in his social studies class so he decided to do nothing. Go back 2 spaces.	Hayden stayed after school to help the teacher set up a science lab and . received some needed extra credit. Go forward 2 spaces.
Joe argued with the teacher about his test grade to the point he used profanity and had to go to ISS. Go back 2 spaces.	Stan daydreamed about being a big basketball star during his English test and ended up failing. Go back 2 spaces.
Sergio brought up 3 grades from F's to D's. He'd hoped for C's. Go forward 2 spaces.	Jamal got a "100" homework grade, even though it was mostly incorrect. Go forward 2 spaces.
Edgar stayed up past midnight watching a movie and then pretended he was too sick to go to school. Go back 2 spaces.	Tyler copied a paper straight off the Internet but the teacher caught it and alerted his parents, plus he got an "F." Go back 2 spaces.
Davis made the football team, but his parents took him off when he didn't make the honor roll. Go back 1 space.	Jeremy managed to keep C's and above while playing basketball and volunteering at the animal shelter. Go forward 2 spaces.
Maurice reached his goal for making a B in English but his math grade actually went down from C to D. Go forward 1 space.	Shaquille went on a tour of a local college, visiting the gym, library, dorms, and classrooms. Go forward 2 spaces.

1 free space	1 free space
1 free space	1 free space
1 free space	1 free space
1 free space	1 free space
1 free space	1 free space
1 free space	1 free space
1 free space	1 free space
1 free space	1 free space

Session 4 Topic: Guest Speaker

Session 4 Supplies: For leader—Questions for College Speaker (cut into strips), Basket

Session 4 Content:

Arrange to have a male college student come speak to the group. These boys need to hear that college is not all work—it's also a lot of fun. Of course, caution should be used and the speaker should be prewarned that tales of wildness such as drinking escapades are taboo. Allow the college student to describe the basic structure of classes, dorm life, sports events, and so on. Encourage him to share what sort of student he was when he was their age. Permit the boys to ask their own questions. To ensure certain points are mentioned, you will probably want to pass the basket containing the questions you have pre-selected, with each boy taking turns pulling a strip to ask a question.

At the end of the session, remind the group members to continue trying to gain points for such academic-enhancing activities as writing homework in their agendas, asking teachers for help, and turning in projects on time.

Questions they should be able to answer: What are some aspects of college life that sound interesting to you? What does it take to be a successful college student? What are the benefits of going to college? Do you have a college in mind that you'd like to attend? Were you able to gain any points in the last week?

Questions for College Speaker

1. Do you have much free time?
2. Do you live in a dorm?
3. What if you don't like your roommate?
4. Where besides the dorm do you meet friends?
5. Do you have time to play sports? What are some of the sports available?
6. Is it easy to meet people with whom to form romantic relationships?
7. Do you have to study every day?
8. How often do you have tests?
9. What was your biggest fear about going to college?
10. What have you found to be disappointing?
11. What has been your best discovery?
12. What if you don't know what you want to be?
13. Describe a typical day.
14. Describe a typical weekend.

Session 5 Topic: Exploring Colleges

Session 5 Supplies: None (other than having arranged computer lab access)

Session 5 Content:

In this session students will meet in a computer lab to explore college information. The leader needs to use a reputable college search site or have students specify individual universities in which they are interested. (I use information from the College Foundation of North Carolina [CFNC.org, 2011] at http://www.cfnc.org/index.jsp, which gives details on over a hundred colleges in the state of North Carolina. However, I also allow them to search individual websites for out-of-state colleges of their choice.) Point out the various types of information available at their fingertips—especially student life, financial considerations, and admissions requirements. Give them brief explanations of high school credits, GPA (grade point average), standardized tests (SAT and ACT), and other information necessary for them to understand the admissions process. Advise them to take career interest inventories on their own to help them match their interests with certain jobs. The overall goal of this session is to spark interest in attending college in these students with so much potential (that they are currently wasting). We want them to see that doors will be closed to them if they do not change their ways very soon!

Questions they should be able to answer: What are the basic admissions requirements for a particular college in which you are interested? What is the approximate cost of attending that college? What are some appealing aspects of student life at that college? What other colleges might you consider? Were you able to gain any points in the last week?

Session 6 Topic: Goal Checking/Review

Session 6 Supplies: For students—Copies of Student Rating Post-Group Scale forms, Copies of the When I Am 23 worksheet, Index cards (from before), Pencils; For leader—Leader's complete folder (for review), Bag of candy

Session 6 Content:

Start the final session by returning the index cards with their earlier report card grades and goals. In most schools, some formal assessment of grades (either report cards or progress reports) should have taken place during the run of your group. Give the students pencils and ask them to write their newest grades on the cards, or pre-record them yourself if you have access to the information. Ask for volunteers to share which grades they have brought up. Compliment any rise, even if it was merely an F moving to a D. As I have indicated previously, I do not end my groups with parties; however, to acknowledge improvements in grades, I have occasionally been known to reward students with small pieces of candy. Each improved grade equals a piece of candy. The boys like comparing their loot at the end. Then ask the students to set goals again, marking them on the card. Remind them that sometimes maintaining rather than improving a grade is an adequate goal.

After taking up the index cards, announce winners of the points system. Again, candy works as a simple reward if you don't have any sporty baseball caps or tee shirts at your disposal. You can choose to celebrate only the student who achieved the most points, or you could honor the top three or so.

Then distribute the Student Rating Post-Group Scale forms. Have them evaluate themselves without the benefit of seeing what they wrote on the Pre-Group assessment. After they have completed the forms, hand out the Pre-Group forms and ask them to compare. Collect all the forms so that you can study the results. You will need to request teacher input for the Teacher Rating Post-Group Scale Forms, and then plan to pull the students together again in a few weeks to go over the results.

It's time for one final fun activity. Distribute copies of the When I Am 23 worksheet. Ask them to take turns reading aloud the statements and allow time for each to mark answers as they go. An example: When I am 23, I will eat out once a week at: (a) An expensive Italian restaurant, (b) A fast-food restaurant, (c) My mother's house, (d) A soup kitchen. Be sure that they see the positives and negatives in the answer choices. They will laugh a little and, of course, usually choose the high-dollar, high-success selections. Ask them how they will afford these options. Point out the connection of working hard to reach success, and how they shortchange their futures by making poor choices.

Close the group by referring back to the main goals and activities of former sessions. Remind them that you will call them together again one more time after you have obtained and reviewed the documentation from teachers. Encourage them to come to you individually as needed throughout the rest of the school year.

Questions they should be able to answer: What grades did you improve? Were there any that went down? How did you do on the points system? Which academic activities did you choose to gain points? When comparing the Pre-Group to the Post-Group forms, what did you find? What will your life be like at age twenty-three? What do you need to do now to reach a satisfactory level of success?

Student Rating

Post-Group Scale

Student Name ______________________________

Teacher Name ______________________________

Subject ______________________________

Date ______________________

Please rate yourself on your work in the above subject by indicating the following:

1 = Never, 2 = Rarely, 3 = Sometimes, 4 = Frequently, 5 = Always

Turn in homework	1..............2..............3..............4..............5
Turn in class work	1..............2..............3..............4..............5
Complete projects	1..............2..............3..............4..............5
Pass tests	1..............2..............3..............4..............5

When I Am 23

1. I will go places by
   a. Driving my new car.
   b. Catching a city bus.
   c. Calling a friend for a ride.
   d. Driving a beat-up clunker that works only sometimes.

2. I will wear clothes from
   a. Upscale stores at the mall.
   b. Discount stores.
   c. Yard sales.
   d. Crisis Assistance Clothing Closet.

3. I will have a job
   a. With my own private office or company vehicle.
   b. In a fast-food restaurant.
   c. In a factory that is noisy and crowded.
   d. That is only temporary and then I don't know what I'll do to pay bills.

4. I will go out to eat once a week at
   a. An expensive Italian restaurant.
   b. A fast-food restaurant.
   c. My mother's house.
   d. A soup kitchen.

5. I will celebrate Father's Day by
   a. Being thankful I have delayed having children.
   b. Receiving handmade cards and hugs from my four children ranging in age from ten months to seven years old.
   c. Going to Lamaze class with my pregnant wife.
   d. Being jealous of other people's children because I have developed a sexually transmitted disease that has made me infertile.

6. I will be sleeping
   a. With my teddy bear.
   b. With my wife.
   c. With my 89th lover.
   d. In a hospital bed, dying of AIDS.

Other thoughts about being 23: ____

____

Teacher Rating

Post-Group Scale

Student Name ____

Teacher Name ____

Subject ____

Date ______________________________

Please rate the student by indicating the following:

1 = Never, 2 = Rarely, 3 = Sometimes, 4 = Frequently, 5 = Always

Turns in homework 1..............2..............3..............4..............5

Turns in class work 1..............2..............3..............4..............5

Completes projects 1..............2..............3..............4..............5

Passes tests 1..............2..............3..............4..............5

Evaluation of Boys Improving Grades (BIG) Group

Rate yourself by circling the number which corresponds with how you evaluate each statement.
1 = Not at all, 2 = A small amount, 3 = Average amount, 4 = More than average, 5 = Very much

1. I felt comfortable discussing my academic standing in the group.

   1.................2.................3.................4.................5

2. I was able to set realistic academic goals.

   1.................2.................3.................4.................5

3. My self-ratings compared closely to the teachers' ratings of me.

   1.................2.................3.................4.................5

4. I ranked items in my Quality World collage in order of importance to me.

   1.................2.................3.................4.................5

5. I learned about consequences for my choices.

   1.................2.................3.................4.................5

6. I learned about requirements of various colleges.

   1.................2.................3.................4.................5

7. I was able to gain some points in the Points System contest.

   1.................2.................3.................4.................5

8. I grew closer to members during the course of the group.

   1.................2.................3.................4.................5

Suggestions for making the group better: ____

____

References

CFNC.org. (2011). *Browse schools*. Retrieved May 22, 2011, from https://www1.cfnc.org/Plan/For_College/Explore_Postsecondary_Schools/Browse_by_Type_of_School/Browse_by_Type_of_School.aspx

Henley, K. (2009, June 14). No child left behind = All boys left behind. *Breaking news and opinion on the Huffington post*. Retrieved April 8, 2011, from http://www.huffingtonpost.com/kari-henley/no-child-left-behind-all_b_214937.html

Ridgway, I. (2007). *2321 Theory & practice: Lecture 5, reality therapy: William Glasser*. Retrieved August 27, 2011, from http://myauz.com/ianr/articles/lect5realitytherapyglasser.pdf

Whitmire, R. (2010). *Why boys fail: Saving our sons from an educational system that's leaving them behind*. New York: AMACOM.

Wintery Knight. (2010, November 21). *Are boys performing poorly in schools?* Retrieved April 8, 2011 from http://winteryknight.wordpress.com/2010/11/21/are-boys-performing-poorly-in-schools/

Chapter 14

Summary: Crossing the Finish Line

Now that you have traveled with me through a variety of group sessions you can pat yourself on the back. You have tackled a challenging course and come out a winner. You have affirmed the counselor's need to provide a smorgasbord of group options so that you can reach a large number of students in an efficient, effective manner. You have established personal relationships that you and the students will remember for a long time. But let's look ahead …

Times change. Schedules become increasingly demanding in schools with growing populations. You may feel that it is impossible to provide anything more than responsive crisis-based assistance to your students. Don't give in to this, please! If you have to reduce the number of groups or tweak the way you solicit members, then do so. But don't allow this important part of counseling to fall away. Start talking to your principal or boss about the need for an additional counseling position. Try to negotiate a reprieve from "duty" or other non-counseling demands on your time. Show your principal the numbers of students you have reached through groups. Remind people that if students can be excused from class for athletics, assemblies, and other non-academic activities, then they can be released for an occasional support group meeting.

As you gain confidence in providing group counseling, expand your creativity and try out your own ideas for sessions. Take pride in your work. Every counselor has so much to offer!

Index